Claim Success!

Claim Success!

Absolutely Everything You Need to Know to Get into Medical Billing and Practice Management to Create a Viable Career for Yourself

Kyle Farhat

Nancie Cummins, RMC

Claim Success! Absolutely Everything You Need to Know to Get into Medical Billing and Practice Management to Create a Viable Career for Yourself

Published by Wheatmark®
610 East Delano Street, Suite 104
Tucson, Arizona 85705 U.S.A.
www.wheatmark.com

International Standard Book Number: 978-1-58736-976-6
Library of Congress Control Number: 2007937591

ClaimTek Systems
3943 Irvine Blvd., #39
Irvine, CA 92602
800-224-7450

Contents

Introduction

Are you seeking an exciting new career to move your life forward? Are you concerned by the prospect of buying into a fast food franchise or retail store that costs $100,000 or more to get into but doesn't satisfy your career desires? Would you like to find a career you can be passionate about, one that brings you great satisfaction so that when you wake up in the morning, you are eager to greet your day? Do you want a job that pays you well for all the hard work you put into it? Do you want to make money for yourself or make money for someone else?

We have good news for you – medical billing may be the career you're looking for. Why? Because medical billing today is a serious, professional and respected business that involves a wide range of medical practice management tasks. People who do medical billing have a high degree of knowledge and skill, and work with serious, dedicated doctors, dentists, and other types of healthcare providers. Medical billing is a career you can learn and perform over a long period of time, all the while earning an excellent livelihood for yourself and your family.

Medical billing today is not some magical, easy profession that makes you rich in 30 days. It requires knowledge about a complex industry and a willingness to learn new things. You need business acumen, problem-solving ability, and patience. You also need a happy, pleasant personality that allows you to feel comfortable being around doctors, medical office personnel, and other healthcare providers who are typically intelligent and serious people. If you love the challenge of being an entrepreneur, are attracted to the medical field, and believe that working with doctors offers you the type of career you've been looking for, then we highly recommend that you read this book and learn how medical billing may be the right opportunity for your new career.

Let us tell you who we are and why we have written this book. First, we'll start with Kyle Farhat, senior author of this book.

Kyle

I have been involved in the medical billing and practice management field for more than 15 years. I have owned a medical billing company and a medical software company that designs and sells software for medical offices and billers. I know the inside story behind medical billing and am eager to share it with you. Through my company, *ClaimTek Systems*, I have worked with scores of people to help them start their own medical billing and practice management business. My company sells the most comprehensive and professional package of software, marketing support, and training you can find anywhere today.

ClaimTek has been in business since 1993. We are constantly updating our programs and software, as well as improving the business training and marketing support you receive when you buy our medical billing business opportunity package. And since 1995, we have been designing and programming our own advanced software, *MedOffice®*, to offer you the most advanced, state-of-the-art medical practice management software on the market. We are constantly expanding and enriching the features of our software to provide medical professionals with leading edge technology. We also pioneered the ability of people who work with us to resell numerous important ancillary services to doctors, such as Electronic Fund Transfer (EFT), Collection Services, Patient Well-care Services, document scanning services, and others so that you truly become a one-stop solution for nearly every medical practice management job that healthcare providers need to get done. Even as we write this book, we are readying ClaimTek to allow people who work with us to become resellers of Electronic Medical Records (EMR) software to doctors, truly the leading edge of healthcare that makes you a valuable resource to thousands of medical practices now eagerly seeking out EMR software.

The people who buy a medical billing business opportunity program from ClaimTek Systems come from all types of careers and professions – from accounting to nursing to retailing. Their background doesn't matter, because we train them extensively in the skills of medical practice management and marketing to doctors. Many of our clients have created highly successful, substantial income-generating medical billing businesses thanks to the extensive help, training, and support we provide them when they work closely with ClaimTek Systems.

I hope that after reading this book you will decide to work with ClaimTek Systems when you start your medical billing and practice management business. I am confident that you cannot – *and will not* – find a better business opportunity from another company that offers you the extent of industry and software training, business development, marketing materials, and technical backup you receive with a ClaimTek program. Even if you decide not to purchase our software and training from my company, you will learn and grow from this book. I have written it to instruct anyone who has a desire to learn about this career. I am happy to offer my significant expertise and to share my knowledge and skill with people interested in medical billing.

Nancie

I have owned a professional medical billing company for more than 15 years. I began my medical billing company, Cummins Professional Services, in 1991. It grew to provide billing and practice management services for as many as 30 doctors at a time. My billing company grew so large that I had several employees working for me. Some months, the income from my medial billing service has been in the five figures. I have done billing for many types of healthcare providers, from chiropractors to surgeons to physical therapists.

Through my business experience, I have learned all aspects of medical billing and practice management. I know the ins and outs of marketing to doctors and how to win contracts to take over their full practice management. I know about the requirements for billing claims to Medicare and commercial insurance companies. As the second author of this book, I have complemented Kyle's expertise with my years of experience in running a highly successful medical billing enterprise. I am also happy to help you look for accurate, clear information about this potential new career in your life.

The Myth versus the Reality of Starting a Medical Billing and Practice Management Business

Before launching into Chapter 1, let us address two important questions that people ask when they become interested in medical billing. Is this truly a viable business? Can I really make money at it?

Let us give you a forthright answer. In the early 1990s, there was extensive coverage in books and entrepreneurial magazines about medical billing as being a great business to get into – a business that promised an excellent future. One reason for this was that *electronic* medical billing was just beginning to take off. These were the early days of a new technology – "electronic data interchange (EDI)," whereby data could be quickly and easily transferred over modems and phone lines from one business or agent to another. The application of EDI was a perfect match for medical billing and electronic claims processing. It was enormously promising for the medical industry as well as for entrepreneurs.

As a result, numerous medical billing "business opportunity" companies popped up, advertising and selling electronic medical billing software. Unfortunately, some of these companies led people to believe that it was easy to get into electronic claims billing. Some vendors were more interested in selling their programs than in providing serious entrepreneurs with in-depth training and the degree of knowledge and support they needed to break into the business.

Many naïve people bought the software and went into medical billing thinking that all they had to do was show up at a doctor's doorstep to get the business. Many entrepreneurs failed because they simply did not understand the complexities of health insurance or medical practice management – and the companies from whom they bought their software did not train them well.

It is unfortunate, but some of these medical billing vendors not only took advantage of eager entrepreneurs, they also went to great lengths to denigrate their competitors, including ClaimTek. A few of them were unethical in attempting to eliminate competitors, by posting fraudulent complaints from consumers on various web sites or having "shills" pretend to have been customers of a medical billing company and then discrediting its reputation. This unscrupulous behavior was directed at my company several times, and I vigorously pursued all those who attempted to insult the high degree of professionalism that ClaimTek brought to the industry.

The strength of my company's reputation can be seen by the fact that ClaimTek has survived all these years – while nearly all other vendors have folded or were even forced out of business by government agencies. Some of the most scurrilous medical billing business opportunity vendors were investigated or prosecuted by their state's attorney general for fraudulent business practices. ClaimTek has remained in business, committed to selling a serious, honest, and professional business opportunity that provides professional software and training for those who sincerely seek to own a professional medical practice management business. We have consistently maintained the highest level rating from the Better Business Bureau for more than 12 years. Our clients are satisfied business owners, and many of them have created excellent incomes for themselves by starting a viable medical billing business.

ClaimTek has also invested years of time and money to develop the most extensive and sophisticated business entry package available to help people like you get into the medical billing field. Our team of support people works closely with every ClaimTek Systems buyer, showing each entrepreneur how to market to healthcare providers, how to win a billing and practice management contract, how to use our leading edge software, *MedOffice*, and how to do billing, claims filing, and every aspect of full medical practice management.

We go all out when it comes to teaching you how to market your business. We help you learn how to set up appointments with doctors to land your first contract. We provide you with thousands of professionally designed and printed brochures, fliers, and presentation materials to use in a sophisticated marketing campaign that has proven to work. Our customer support is available nearly 24/7 for questions and we do everything possible to help each entrepreneur succeed, providing you with professional business counseling and advice every step of the way.

Why does ClaimTek do this? The reason is, *medical billing is a serious, professional business that is here to stay and the proof of this is irrefutable.* There is a substantial opportunity for people to become professional medical billers and practice management consultants making very good incomes if they learn the business and approach this field seriously.

Medical billing is in demand because of the realities of our chaotic, complex American healthcare system that will not change. Despite occasional rumblings for a national healthcare system, our health insurance and medical systems are too ingrained in our society. We will always have a large segment of privatized, fee-for-service based healthcare, plus government-subsidized healthcare for seniors, retirees, and others (Medicare). This means that there will always be a need for insurance claims and medical billing.

One of the other realities that supports the growth of the professional medical billing industry is the fact that health insurance companies have become monsters, for lack of a better word. Today, doctors simply cannot deal with insurance companies on their own. Times have changed since the 1990s. Healthcare has become very expensive, and thus, insurance companies and Medicare have put the squeeze on doctors, paying them less for their claims and also making it harder for them to get paid.

Ask any doctor today and he or she will confirm that running a profitable medical office is far more challenging and complex than before. Most doctors don't have the training to run the business side of their medical practices. They don't know how to do billing correctly. Meanwhile, insurance companies play hardball with them, delaying or cutting down payments at every opportunity they can.

Insurance companies and Medicare also make it very difficult at times for doctors to file claims and receive reimbursements. They constantly change the rules and regulations on how to file claims and get reimbursements. This makes it nearly impossible for the average staff person in a doctor's office to keep up. For example, there are thousands and thousands of procedure codes and "modifiers" that must be used correctly when doctors submit claims. More and more claims are rejected or significantly underpaid because of errors in the coding or keyboarding of claims.

In general, doctors often don't realize how much money they lose because they code their claims wrong or do not take advantage of better coding that might allow them to charge more appropriately for the services they give their patients. You undoubtedly know of many doctors who will confirm this. They are tired of dealing with insurance companies which pay them less and less for their services.

Many doctors try to cope with this insurance chaos by training one of their in-house staff people to do billing and handle patient statements. The problem is, these people are most often considered clerical personnel, and they are seldom experts in billing. They usually don't have the interest or time to learn the ins and outs of medical billing or practice management.

And even when they are, they are pulled in many directions during their work day – helping patients, answering phones, running errands, making appointments and so on. Their ability to do billing and follow up on claims and patient payments is almost always severely restricted. If they do billing, their work is often insufficient because of the complexities of filing correct insurance claims.

It is well known that there is usually a constant turnover of personnel in most medical offices with departing staff who frequently leave the doctor's insurance billing and patient collections in shambles.

More and more doctors today are recognizing that it makes sense to outsource their medical billing and practice management to true professionals who have the expertise to get the job done right. They now see more and more of their colleagues using professional medical billing services and realize that they, too, might be better off using an outside expert to take over all their practice management functions.

This is the good news for anyone interested in medical billing and practice management, because it is getting easier and easier to demonstrate to a doctor who is currently using in-house staff why a professional always does a better job at billing. A professional biller can greatly reduce the waiting time to get paid while increasing a doctor's cash flow because of bigger reimbursements and on-time patient collections.

The future looks excellent for medical billing and practice management because this is effectively a recession-proof career. Given our decentralized and privatized American health insurance and medical system, we will always have medical claims that must be generated and submitted to insurance companies.

In fact, it's only going to get better because we have 60 million aging baby boomers. As the years go by, there is a guaranteed constant stream of medical claims as boomers increasingly visit doctors for the various health care problems associated with aging. The tip of the baby boomer generation is just beginning to tap into their Medicare benefits too, and that will also mean billions more Medicare claims to come, heaped on top of the more than one trillion claims already filed each year.

In short, the American healthcare system has truly gone beyond the ability of doctors to continue to deal with insurance and patient billing on their own. Numerous magazines published for doctors constantly run articles attempting to teach them how to do a better job at their billing. Month after month, you can read articles explaining to doctors why their coding is wrong, what to do about unpaid claims, how to appeal to insurers, how to select which insurance companies to work with, and so on.

This gap in doctors' knowledge about insurance and billing leaves a huge opportunity for serious entrepreneurs who are interested in starting their own professional billing and practice management business. If you can bring solutions to the multitude of billing problems that doctors have, you can literally write your own ticket to career success and substantial income generation.

If you're searching for a new career, there are many benefits to starting a medical billing and practice management business, especially compared with other types of entrepreneurial opportunities that are out there. First, it's a business you can enter for as little as a $10,000 or $15,000 investment. It has excellent income potential, and it offers you a high quality of life dealing with interesting people, with new things to learn every day and exciting challenges.

Compare medical billing with something like a fast food franchise where you must pay $100,000 or more to get into the business, plus pay royalties on all your revenues. What do you get from these types of business investments? You end up working long hours six or seven days a week, dealing with minimum wage employees, experiencing scheduling problems, all the while paying royalties to the mother company, just to make $50,000 to $70,000 per year or less.

In contrast, medical billing is a true professional service industry, where you work directly with educated health care providers in a fascinating and important line of work. It is a year-round business, not seasonal, so there is no risk of going months with reduced income. People go to doctors 12 months a year, and claims must be filed and patients billed each and every month, which means that you have income coming in constantly. And once you sign up a doctor as your client, as long as you are on top of the claims and creating positive cash flow, it's very likely that he or she will remain with you for years, constantly giving you repeat business without any further marketing costs to you.

If you constantly improve your knowledge and provide higher levels of service and greater profits, you can also earn more and more from each medical practice account you manage, by increasing your fees and by selling them more services, as you will learn about in this book.

If you are still wondering, "is there room for me in this business," the answer is definitely yes, but you need to understand that you are not getting into just *medical billing,* you are getting into the larger business called medical practice management. All the changes in American healthcare discussed in this chapter mean that the future is NOT in just filing claims for doctors. The *real* future lies in running a full service business helping doctors manage their entire practice!

Think of it this way: anyone can go out and buy TurboTax, but the existence of this software has not put accountants out of business. Companies still need professional accountants.

Medical billing is no different. Doctors can go out and buy their own billing software or they can hire an outside service to help them file medical claims, but they need far more support than just handling claims. The future is in becoming a total full service agency that offers doctors and other healthcare providers a complete range of services from soup to nuts that helps them run their practices profitably and independently. If you can provide consistency, expertise, knowledge, and commitment, you will have no trouble finding doctors who want your services.

What about competition? There are other medical practice management firms out there, but there are also increasing numbers of doctors. In addition, this is a growth industry and, as with all businesses, people always want choices. Wherever there is a fully open market, there is usually business for everyone to some degree. Just like when three grocery stores open up in your neighborhood, none go out of business. In a sense, if you build it, they will come, provided you have newer solutions, better service, and competitive pricing. And this book will help you learn to do all that.

Let us return for a moment also to the question of the best way for you to get into this business. We wrote this book to help you get an accurate idea of how the business works and what you need to do to enter it. We recommend that you read this entire book cover to cover. What you will learn from this book will give you a solid foundation, more than any other book you can find, about how to start a viable medical billing and practice management business.

As stated, I am the owner of ClaimTek Systems (which we consider the leading business opportunity in this field), and of course, I would love to have the pleasure to work with you and help you launch your business because I believe I can do it best. There are other medical billing business vendors out there who offer business opportunities, but we are convinced that you won't find another one with the level of professionalism and benefits you receive with a ClaimTek business package.

You can, of course, do it all yourself. You can buy any off-the-shelf medical billing software and possibly hire a technical and marketing consultant to help you start your business. But if this is your plan, ask yourself these questions: How are you going to be trained? How sophisticated is your software? How will you learn to use the software? Who will help you with the marketing? Who will help you prepare for interviews with doctors? How will you learn how much to charge?

You can take some courses at local community colleges in billing – but is that good enough? Education is always useful, and you may learn how to do billing, but in general, this type of training is not going to teach you to become the strong business person you need to be to get into this business. Schools simply don't teach you these things. If you have the time and energy, go ahead and do that. But don't expect to go to a community college training program and be in business. We can tell you that.

Ultimately, we believe you will benefit greatly by purchasing the type of turn-key operation that ClaimTek offers you. We give you far more than software and bits of odds and ends training. If you truly want to open a successful billing and practice management service, you are going to need to compete with others out there. You need to find a way to get into business in the sharpest, most professional way you can, where you immediately appear as a professional to potential clients.

Buying your own software and tech support is just not enough anymore. You need comprehensive medical practice management training as well as marketing training to succeed without wasting your time or your money. You also need to offer many services so you can capitalize on the fact that when you walk into a doctors' office, you can put your weight on the table and be a one-stop shop to doctors. You really can't survive selling "just claims" processing any more. You need to be able to offer sophisticated practice management, where you become an expert to your clients in advising them about many aspects of running their business and maximizing their income.

ClaimTek allows you to be completely prepared to handle this entire business. Even if you are new to this area and have no medical background whatsoever, we train you in every aspect of insurance, medical office procedures, billing and claims filing, coding, practice management, managed care, and even any medical specialty that you decide you want to focus on for your business. We teach you to become a knowledgeable professional, serving doctors and other healthcare providers with premium services and dedication to making their medical practices run smoothly and profitably.

When you buy our package, you also receive our leading edge software, *MedOffice.* This software is not a simple medical billing claims program; it is by far the most advanced full practice management system on the market. MedOffice is capable of handling billing for all classes and specialties of medicine – including podiatry, chiropractors, anesthesia, hospitals, Medicare, dental, ambulance, DME – and all other specialties that require special coding. MedOffice can be installed on your computer, or can be accessed via the Internet as a hosted application.

Most software does NOT give you the comprehensive features that we do. Given that you simply don't know which type of medical practice you may stumble onto, you need to be prepared to handle anything and everything if you want to grow your business and take on all types of medical practices. We give you this flexibility.

We also include dental billing software with most of our programs. In addition, we supply you with various ancillary software programs, such as coding software that helps your clients understand their coding issues, and billing cost analysis software to help doctors analyze how much they spend on in-house billing operations compared to hiring an outside service.

We also provide advanced and comprehensive marketing tools that prevent you from having to spend hours and hours and thousands of dollars to create them yourself. Think about the value of this alone. How much time would you need to devote to writing your own marketing materials – especially if you don't know the industry? We do all this for you, giving you thousands of pieces of professionally designed brochures, fliers, and letters to use. And when you are ready to send out your marketing materials, you can't be skimpy or shy, so we provide you with enough materials to conduct a significant professional campaign. All our marketing tools are professionally written, completely proofed with no errors, and printed in full color on high quality stock. All you do is print your company information, such as your business name and phone number, then mail them out according to specific instructions we provide you.

With ClaimTek Systems, you also receive the marketing materials you need to advertise and publicize numerous additional services you will offer, including Electronic Funds Transfer (EFT), Remote Backup Services (RBS), Collection Services, and Scanning and Medical Record Archival. These are all valuable services you can sell your clients that bring in extra income for yourself. If you had to invest time creating a brochure for each of these services, it would take you months, as well as being far more expensive to do it yourself.

In short, our professional marketing tools give you the edge you need. You'll win every time you compete against a slipshod billing company that sends out home-made brochures printed on lightweight paper. Our marketing materials deliver a powerful message on your behalf – that your medical practice management business is serious, stable, professional, and here to stay.

As mentioned earlier, ClaimTek even helps you learn how to set up your first appointments with prospective clients. We train you in what to say to doctors, what you need to know about billing a specific medical specialty, and how to land the contract. We prep you to the point where you can answer nearly any question professionally and knowledgeably.

Ultimately, ClaimTek gives you what matters most when you are seeking to start a new business. We provide a world of advantages compared to any other business opportunity you can find. Throughout this book, we will point out the specific benefits you will receive if you work with ClaimTek Systems.

We leave it to you to make up your own mind about how you get into medical practice management. However, we want you to know that we will work hard to get your business and help you succeed, and you won't regret for one minute working with ClaimTek!

What You Will Learn in This Book

With all that said about ClaimTek, we hope you are ready to dig in and learn all about how to start a medical billing and practice management business. In this book, we will teach you all the essentials and more, including:

- how medical billing has changed over the years into medical practice management, a very serious professional business that doctors need and seek out;
- how health insurance works and what all the types of insurance are;
- how "managed care" is changing the way doctors do business and how managed care groups such as PPOs have influenced claims filing and reimbursement;
- what coding is and how and why doctors need to learn how to use codes correctly because of the role coding plays in reimbursement;
- how to launch your company, including the nitty-gritty details of how to set up your office, register your business, purchase hardware and software, set up your paper filing systems, and many more important details you must know to operate the business;
- how to market successfully to doctors and other healthcare providers using seven different approaches, with substantial details about each approach that you won't find in any other book;
- how to set up appointments and meet with doctors, including what to say, what to wear, how to behave, and how to nail a contract;
- how to price your services with specific guidelines about whether to use a per claim method or percentage method for your fees, plus details on what percentages are appropriate;
- how to get started from the beginning once you actually have your first client, including 15 detailed steps that you need to do in setting up your software to file claims and record receivables;
- how to send out patient statements and create business practice reports for your doctors;
- how to sell additional products to your clients to augment your income and provide your clients with full-service practice management;
- *and much more.*

In the Appendix, we also provide you with further details about purchasing a ClaimTek Systems package and why our programs offer you the most bang for your investment dollar should you decide to get into this business.

We hope you will read this entire book and gain as much knowledge as you can about medical billing.

Please feel free to contact us at ClaimTek Systems at 800-224-7450 at any time with questions. We are here to help you and hope you will consider working with us.

Good luck and here's to your success!

Sincerely,
Kyle Farhat
Nancie Cummins

1 Everything You Want to Know about Medical Billing and Practice Management

What is medical billing and what exactly do medical billing services do? The answer to these questions is that medical billing services do many things. Especially in today's world where the practice of medicine has become very complex and healthcare providers of all kinds are increasingly forced to hire outside companies to manage their administrative functions. As a result, medical billers may end up doing one or more of the following tasks for their clients:

- Electronic and paper filing of insurance claims
- Patient billing and collections
- Collection of aged insurance claims
- Practice management including advising doctors about how to improve their business profitability
- Electronic funds transfer
- Conversion of paper records to optical (digital) records

All of these are aspects of a medical billing business that you may find yourself doing. We will be reviewing all of these in this book, but in this chapter, we will focus on just the basics of medical billing.

To begin with the simplest of definitions, the role of a medical billing service is to help healthcare providers file claims on behalf of their patients and receive reimbursement in order to get paid for their services. Note that when we say, "healthcare provider," we're including MD's of all types, as well as many other types of healthcare providers who have other medical degrees, such as chiropractors, physical therapists, dentists, psychologists, ambulance companies, suppliers of durable medical equipment

(DME), and medical laboratories. For simplicity in this book, we use the term "healthcare provider" as the basic word to include all the possible clients your medical billing service might have.

At the most fundamental level, medical billing services perform two essential activities for their clients:

- First, they take charge of filing insurance claims to the hundreds of private insurance companies and government-sponsored insurance programs (such as Medicare or Medicaid) in order to obtain reimbursement for the medical services that the provider has rendered to his or her patients; and
- Second, medical billing services record the receipt of money from insurers and patients and maintain the bookkeeping records for their doctor-clients.

Beyond those two basic functions, medical billing services may perform a wide range of other services. A second level beyond is known as "full practice management" and may include following up on denied and delayed claims, processing claims to secondary and tertiary insurance companies, handling the preparation and mailing of patient statements, and generating monthly management reports on billing activities for their clients.

There is also a third level of medical billing which is called advanced practice management. Here, you might help doctors determine which insurance plans are best to join based on the fee schedules each insurer offers, how to negotiate with insurers for better reimbursement rates, what type of medical services to emphasize in order to generate the greatest level of income, and how to improve cash flow by increasing their reimbursement ratio and speed. They may also offer several related ancillary services ranging from electronic funds transfer to collections, to software / hardware consulting, to electronic medical records, etc.

The distinction between these three levels of businesses is critical to your business. While some billing services perform just the lowest level, today, more and more billers handle a wider range of other activities and are increasingly performing either practice management or advanced practice management.

If you are interested in starting an independent medical billing service, you can choose to work at any level of service. Whichever level you choose depends on your background and skills, your goals, and your knowledge. This decision about the extent of your business will be discussed in detail many times in this book and we will help you make the decision. However, as we said in the introduction, the most successful medical billers today are veering towards full practice management, as this is where the future of the profession lies.

One reason for this is that there is far more money to be made when you do practice management. More importantly, though, is the fact that most doctors no longer want to hire a service that can only file claims. They want a company that truly knows the whole business and offers full practice management services. In short, if you are about to get into this business, you might as well think about jumping in and getting completely wet as a full practice management professional.

Why Has Medical Billing Become a Popular Business?

Medical billing services have been around for decades in one form or another. Medical billing services originated in the 1950s, especially because more and more Americans received health insurance plans from their employers and began seeing doctors regularly. In those days, people simply paid their doctors in cash (or bartered). But the expansion of health insurance to the masses in the 1950s and 1960s meant that doctors eventually had to resort to collecting money from insurance companies and sometimes invoicing their patients to get paid.

The 1960s witnessed a regular "cottage" industry of outside billing services that mushroomed to handle the bookkeeping for doctors and other healthcare providers. These billing services were sometimes run by CPAs who specialized in medical practice management but some of them were simply "moms at home" who did bookkeeping for a few doctors.

The medical billing profession began attracting more professional entrepreneurs in the 1990s for two reasons. First, the birth of small computers doing "electronic data interchange" (EDI) allowed billing to be done from anywhere, and second, the increasing complexity of healthcare drove doctors to seek help in managing their practice. Let's look at each of these forces.

The Computerization of Healthcare

Computers have been used in the healthcare field since the middle of the 20th century, just as in nearly all professions. But in the early days, large mainframe computers were mostly used in hospitals and large medical practices to expedite the handling of health insurance claims.

Using computers for doctor's billing took root with the development of the smaller personal computer in the late 1980s. The PC gave birth to many medical software companies which recognized the value of the PC to record patient data and handle medical claims preparation and filing. Personal computers were sold to doctors to automate their offices, replacing the manual typewriter.

The early days of medical software suffered from the lack of standard formatting for insurance claim filing. Some software used one format, other software used a different one. This meant that doctors could not send a "universal" claim form to all insurance companies because each insurer had their own data format.

A few medical software companies tried to resolve this problem by establishing themselves as routing stations (called "clearinghouses") where claims using many different formats could be translated and edited before being forwarded to an insurer. This was a good stopgap measure, but the development of a uniform data interchange standard took many more years and was not actually fully accomplished until recently.

The biggest boost to computerizing the healthcare industry occurred in the late 1970s when the U.S. government recognized that we were about to face an enormous problem because millions of Americans were getting ready to retire, and most likely would heavily use the federal health insurance program called Medicare. Note: The Medicare program originally took effect in 1966, under President Lyndon Johnson. At that time, the program was directed by an agency called the Health Care Financing Administration, known as HCFA (pronounced *Hick-fa)*. But in 2002, HCFA changed its name to the Centers for Medicare and Medicaid Services and is thus usually referred to as CMS (pronounced as individual letters, C.M.S.).

By 1980, HCFA was already processing several hundred million paper claims per year; as you can imagine, this was not just very expensive, it was enormously time-consuming to review hundreds of millions of paper claims.

In 1983, the agency began an aggressive campaign to encourage hospitals and physicians to file claims electronically rather than mailing paper claims. HCFA especially threw its weight behind a standardized set of diagnosis and procedure codes that doctors could use as shorthand on claim forms to indicate the patient's illness and the services performed. These codes replaced the hodge-podge coding system used by hundreds of insurance companies, which prevented electronic claims filing from taking off.

This standardization of codes became a driving force behind electronic billing. By the end of the 1980s, Medicare was receiving almost 500 million claims per year, 80% of which were from individual physicians, suppliers, and laboratories. Today, Medicare receives more than one billion claims per year.

Electronic claims were given the next big push when Congress issued a directive in September 1990 that required all physicians to file claims for any Medicare patient. Until this time, Medicare patients had to file their own claims, but now it would become the doctor's responsibility. In addition, HCFA declared that by the year 2000, they would give priority to electronic claims over paper. Their goal was to force healthcare providers to use computers, which offered Medicare many advantages and cost savings over paper claims.

As a result of these two directives, doctors suddenly found themselves inundated with thousands of patient claims, especially Medicare claims, that they had to file themselves. Among the hundreds of thousands of doctors, nearly all were unprepared for this. Most doctors did not have computerized offices and their staff lacked the expertise to file claims. Thousands of doctors eagerly began seeking the services of outside billing services. This was the key to what finally caused the revolution in medical billing, opening the door to many small and home-based businesses that recognized the opportunity to provide services to doctors.

In the 1990s, with more powerful PCs, some doctors began purchasing computers that allowed them to do their own claims filing. However, the majority of doctors still knew little about hardware and software, and recognized that they could not keep up with Medicare's rules and regulations. This general state of confusion was a big boost for those who came early into medical billing.

But Medicare was not the only driving force in the story of medical billing. Millions of Americans are not part of Medicare but have health insurance through thousands of private insurance companies, which generate billions of claims per year. All these claims have the same need for electronic filing so the insurance companies don't get overloaded with paper, just as with Medicare.

What Are Electronic Claims?

What exactly are electronic claims? How do they differ from paper claims?

As indicated above, before electronic claims, doctors and insurance companies used a variety of paper forms to communicate. Unfortunately, filing claims this way was a very tedious process requiring typing out information into little boxes on a paper form, and then mailing it to one of hundreds of insurance companies. Many insurance companies even had their own paper form and so a doctor's staff had to learn how to fill out each form correctly. As you might imagine, this frequently led to lots of errors and mistakes, causing a large percentage of claims to be rejected by the insurance company and returned to the doctors, who then had to redo the claim and file it again. As a result, doctors might sometimes wait months before being paid by an insurer.

Even when a doctor's office had a computer and billing software, it was common to key in the claims information into the computer and then print it out on paper and mail it. This process still did not ensure that the claims were error free, nor did it save much in the way of time.

Over time, the solution to this problem was clearly to make the entire process happen electronically. Rather than fill out a paper form when a patient visited a doctor, the goal became to use the computer throughout the entire process.

Essentially, the way electronic claims works is as follows. The medical billing person begins by typing in a patient's basic information (name, address, phone number, etc.) along with the date of service, place of service, and diagnosis and procedures codes. Next the medical billing software checks the claim to be sure there are no basic errors such as missing data. Once the claim is complete, the biller simply sends it electronically online or via modem to the insurance company or Medicare. (Actually, many billers still transmit their claims to an intermediary clearinghouse, as we will explain below.)

The advantages of electronic claims over paper claims are huge. First, paper claims are mailed via regular mail and then pass through many hands at the insurance office where they are sorted, microfilmed, and keyed into the insurer's computer system. In contrast, electronic claims are keyed just once and then sent from the doctor's office (or the billing company) directly to the insurance company in a matter of seconds.

Electronic claims thus save money in overhead costs in both preparation and processing time. If you consider the amount of time that a staff member in a doctor's office takes to fill out and file a paper claim compared to the amount of time it takes to type and file an electronic claim, it is clear that filing electronic claims saves doctors money. It is estimated that electronic filing might save between $5 to $12 per claim when you take into account the hourly salary and other benefits that a doctor pays the office staff person who handles the claims.

Another advantage of electronic claims is that they reduce the rejection rate because electronic claims have fewer errors. Some estimates indicate that nearly 1/3 of paper claims contain errors and are rejected by insurers. Errors may include simple typing mistakes or miscoding errors. Because the standardized HCFA claim form contains dozens of "fields" for data, it is easy to see how errors might occur frequently.

A final advantage of electronic claims is that they have shorter turnaround time even if they are rejected because software can provide early feedback about errors that allow you to correct the claim almost immediately. In contrast, paper claims can take weeks to correct, and worse, they often end up NEVER being reprocessed because the billing clerk at the doctor's office does not know what the mistake was or how to correct it. Some doctors have found entire desk drawers literally filled with rejected claims that were never resubmitted – amounting to tens of thousands of dollars in lost revenues.

In contrast, filing claims electronically cuts down on rejected claims in several ways. First, the software for electronic claims permanently stores a record for each patient, so the constant re-typing of a patient's information is minimized, reducing the chances of mistakes and missing data. Secondly, most medical billing software is programmed to perform error checking before sending out the claims. For example, the software can verify that all data fields are filled in, that the correct number of digits is used in each field (such as with an ID number), and that a numeric code is not used where an alphabetic code should be. Some medical billing software is intelligent enough to catch accidental mistakes involving transposed digits. These kinds of mistakes really do happen!

As indicated above, many medical billing software packages transmit their electronic claims to an independent clearinghouse company (which you can choose). Clearinghouses are a valuable intermediary in billing, because rather than sending claims to dozens of insurance companies one by one, you send them to just a single place, called a clearinghouse. The clearinghouse performs error checking on the claims to ensure correct processing.

For example, if you send a claim that has an accident diagnosis code, the clearinghouse will stop the claim if accident information is not submitted with it. Some clearinghouses notify the biller immediately via an electronic report if the claim has an error, so the biller can make a correction immediately rather than waiting weeks to receive it back by mail. The clearinghouse then forwards the claims to their respective insurance companies.

All these advantages add up to major benefits for healthcare providers.

Their cost savings is why Medicare and nearly all commercial insurance companies now *place a priority on electronic claims and process them more quickly.* Doctors are almost always reimbursed sooner because the claims are keyed more quickly, have fewer mistakes, and arrive earlier at the insurance companies.

While paper claims often take 30 to 60 days to get paid, even if they are clean (i.e., without errors), electronic claims may be paid in as little as 24 hours by commercial insurance companies. Most are paid within 5-14 days. Since the 1990s, Medicare's policy has also been that an error-free electronic claim will have a check cut within 14-19 days from submission into their system, and if it is not paid within this time frame, interest will be paid for the number of days the claim is late.

Fast payment of claims is critical for the cash flow of doctors. Since doctors may receive as much as 80 percent of their gross earnings from Medicare and commercial insurers reimbursements rather than from patients, it is a major advantage to have a fast turnaround between claims filing and payment. Doctors depend on cash flow to pay the salaries of their employees, their office rent, and other expenses. Doctors who wait 60 to 90 days or more to be reimbursed for services rendered will clearly suffer in the management of their medical practice.

You may think that if a doctor is already behind in payments and stays consistently behind, it doesn't matter that payments are late because the claims are always a few months behind. However, as they say, time is money. There is a cost of money that the doctor loses by having to wait two or three months to get paid.

Figure 3-8 in Chapter 3 contrasts the process and timing for paper claims vs. those for electronic claims, and we'll discuss this in greater detail in Chapter 3.

The Healthcare Nightmare No One Can Figure Out

As mentioned earlier, a major factor driving the growth of independent medical billing services is the increasing complexity of healthcare. While the United States has long had what is considered the best health care in the world, we also have the most complex system. Since the 1990s, the cost of healthcare has skyrocketed, increasing at an average rate of 10 to 14% *per year*, and the future promises to continue with such increasing costs.

The rise in costs is causing profound changes in healthcare, from the way consumers choose their doctors to the way medical providers practice medicine. We are no longer living in the 1950s when the good family doctor made house calls, nor are we living in the 1990s when doctors would not hesitate to perform test after test to find out what might be wrong with a patient.

Today, insurance companies and Medicare are trying to cut costs as much as possible. Doctors are being squeezed more and more to save money whenever they can. For each new patient, doctors must verify what insurance benefits that person has so they won't perform a service the person is not entitled to receive under insurance coverage. Even when the doctor decides on a treatment, they must often call to get pre-authorization approval before proceeding with that treatment.

When it comes to handling their billing, doctors are being asked to produce more and more paperwork to justify their fees. They must be more rigorous in specifying an exact diagnosis, requiring greater detail in diagnostic coding. For example, it is no longer enough for a doctor to select the generic code that indicates a patient has diabetes; the claim form must use a specific multi-digit code that tells the insurance company whether the patient has diabetes with renal manifestations or diabetes with ophthalmic manifestations. Many codes also require the use of an extra "modifier" digit that indicates further specificity about the procedures performed.

It is not an understatement to suggest that practicing medicine is almost not worth the trouble for many doctors. In fact, some doctors are now refusing to take insurance because they can't stand working with insurance companies. Instead, they require patients to pay them their total fees up front and they might agree to process claims for the patient, but the reimbursement will go to the patient, not to the doctor (except in the case of Medicare, where the doctor must file the claim on behalf of the patient in all cases.)

One additional result of the complexity of healthcare is that many insurance companies have created new types of insurance plans, including Health Maintenance Organizations (HMOs), Preferred Provider Organizations (PPOs), and other forms of "managed care" networks. We will discuss these types of arrangements in greater detail later, but suffice it to say that managed care insurance has greatly impacted the practice of medicine and claims processing because of things like contractor-required write-offs, patient co-payments, co-insurance, and deductibles that billers must understand.

This revolution in American healthcare is important for anyone interested in medical billing. As insurance claims become more complex, doctors are increasingly turning to professional "practice managers" – people who help them run the business side of their medical practice. This presents fantastic *opportunities* for medical billing professionals who are willing to learn the ins and outs of health insurance and reimbursement. If you are willing to do your homework to make this happen, you can be successful in today's healthcare world.

So Much Work, So Little Time – Who's Going to Do It?

Why can't the doctor's office staff handle all this? Isn't that what he or she is paying them for? The truth is that the complexity of running a medical practice and the mass of health insurance benefit rules go beyond the capabilities of most medical office personnel. Don't forget that the typical office secretary is not usually a highly trained person. He or she may have had just a few months of basic training, from books, with little on-the-job-practice. This person usually doesn't know the details of claims processing. Medium and large medical practices may have a skilled medical billing person, but that person may still have a difficult time keeping up with the rules and regulations of Medicare and commercial insurance coding and reimbursement. Additionally, employees can lack consistency in filing claims due to vacations, sick days, and busy patient loads.

It is far more common that small doctors' offices are staffed by people who do not have any skills or background in medical billing. They have little knowledge of coding, claims processing, insurance reimbursement regulations, or the ins and outs of managed care. Some of these employees also don't know how to use a computer very well, nor how to use sophisticated medical practice management software.

In addition, many doctors' offices have a constant turnover of personnel, creating lots of mistakes in their billing. It is easy to see that a low-paid clerical staff person has little motivation to file claims correctly or to follow up on unpaid and rejected claims. They are seldom "incentivized" to make sure claims are paid – they get their salary no matter what.

In the End, Doctors Need Your Services!

All these forces come together to create tremendous opportunity for you. Between the advantages of filing electronically (which many doctors are still not doing) and the increasing complexity of managing a medical practice against cost-cutting insurance companies, you have the chance of a lifetime.

Wow, can you see it? It's vibrant, it's a medical billing business, it's growing, and it's important.

In the next chapter, we'll get into the basics of health insurance and get you going on your way to learning how you can have a successful medical billing business.

2

Health Insurance 101 (and 102)

If you want to operate a successful medical billing practice, you need to have a solid understanding of health insurance. The health insurance industry is vast and complex (and usually the nasty opponent of doctors who want to get paid). It's also a confusing industry because there are hundreds of insurers and thousands of insurance plans.

Health insurance can be divided into federal / state government-sponsored health insurance plans versus private commercial health insurance plans. As a medical biller, you need to master the operation of both types of insurance plans, including all the types within each category, as well as the differences in primary, secondary, and tertiary plans. You also need to know about Medicare, Medigap, and Medicaid; deductibles, co-pays, and co-insurance; out of pocket limits, coordination of benefits; and more.

We have divided this chapter into four sections to make your study easier.

- Traditional private health insurance – including commercial insurance, self-insured plans, and the Blues.
- Managed care health insurance – such as HMOs, IPAs, PPOs, POSs, MSOs, etc..
- Public health insurance programs – Medicare, Medicaid, Tricare (CHAMPUS) and Worker's Comp.
- Dental insurance.

Unless you have a background working in a doctor's office or as a nurse, we encourage you to read this chapter closely to ensure that you really understand the issues of health insurance billing. We have tried to make this chapter as up-to-date and as comprehensive as possible so you can truly feel that you are on the way to understanding insurance claims. When you're done with this chapter, you will definitely have a solid grasp of the issues you will face as a medical biller. Please note that, despite the fact that this chapter is comprehensive, you must keep in mind that it is important to constantly stay up-to-date with the health insurance industry if you get into this business because rules and regulations change frequently. Each year, there are many types of new insurance plans and changes in health insurance payment rules, especially with Medicare.

Private Health Insurance Industry

You probably have some knowledge of the private health insurance industry because you are or have been a consumer of it. You undoubtedly have had your own health insurance policy, experienced having your health insurance claims paid, and received Explanation of Benefit (EOB) reports from your insurance company. But the question is, do you know what is going on behind the scenes with this type of health insurance? If not, this section provides you with the basics of private health insurance.

The largest segment of the private health insurance industry is the common fee-for-service plan offered by commercial insurance companies, of which there are hundreds. Fee-for-service plans insure millions of Americans who work for companies and businesses where the employer offers health insurance to employees. These plans are also available for purchase by individuals and small groups such as associations, unions, and such. Millions of Americans are insured under fee-for-service health insurance plans, and most such plans have certain common standards among them in terms of benefits, deductibles, patient co-payments and co-insurance, and so on.

Another form of private insurance is the self-insured plan, a type of coverage some employers use. In a self-insured plan, rather than paying premiums to an insurer, the employer sets aside money to pay employee claims. To handle the paperwork required, many employers hire what's called a "third party administrator" (TPA) to review claims and pay them. The administrator may be an insurance company or a professional management firm. Another variation of the self-insured plan is called the MPP, "minimum premium plan." These are plans in which the employer self-insures up to a certain dollar amount of claims, but then pays premiums to a commercial insurance company to assume the risk for claims beyond that amount.

In recent years, more and more private insurance companies have implemented "managed care" plans, which offer them greater control over medical reimbursement costs. There are several types of managed care plans, including Health Maintenance Organizations (HMOs), Preferred Provider Organizations (PPOs), Exclusive Provider Organizations (EPOs), and others. Many private health insurance companies and self-insured plans offer managed care plans in addition to their traditional health insurance policies.

A third type of private insurance is a plan offered by one of two companies, usually known as "the Blues," meaning Blue Cross or Blue Shield. Both these companies are not-for-profit insurers that offer many of the same types of plans obtainable from commercial for-profit health insurance companies.

Let's delve a bit deeper here to give you more details about these common private health insurance plans.

Commercial Fee-for-Service Plans

Private health insurance plans can be written as either *individual* or *group* plans. Don't be confused by the term "group." A group plan simply refers to the fact that the insurance is underwritten to cover a large group such as all employees of a company or all members of an association or other formal organization. Someone insured in a group plan may be covered as an individual or as a family. Similarly, the term "individual policy" does not mean that the policy only covers one person; instead, it refers to the fact that one person has purchased the insurance rather than an entire group. An individual policy itself can also cover either a single person or a family.

In general, people are better off being in a group health insurance plan because:

- The cost of a group plan is usually lower on a per person basis because the risk is spread out over many people.
- No individual member of a group plan may be canceled separately. The entire group must be canceled.
- When employees who are covered under a group plan leave their company or retire, or have a family change such as divorce, they can take advantage of the new federal rules including the Health Insurance Portability and Accountability Act (HIPAA) and the Consolidated Omnibus Budget Reconciliation Act (COBRA). These laws protect workers through such mechanisms as allowing them to convert their former group health insurance plan to an individual

plan after losing or leaving a job, as well as being entitled to health insurance despite having a pre-existing condition as long as they were previously insured.

Commercial insurance plans may be written in several ways. The most common policy is the "indemnity" plan, which means that the plan reimburses or indemnifies the patient for covered services up to a certain limit as specified in the policy. The healthcare provider must then recover any unpaid amount from the patient.

Most commercial plans are known as fee-for-service, in which the insurance company pays for each service that the healthcare provider has performed for the patient, as long as proper documentation is submitted with the claim. The insurer pays a fee according to what it considers to be "usual and customary" for each type of service. Insurance companies maintain "fee schedules" based on each type of procedure, where the doctor is located, and the usual and customary rate in that area. Physicians must agree to these fee schedules by not charging more than the insurance company allows.

If the healthcare provider is a member of that insurance company's network, he or she must accept the fee schedule amount (known as the *allowable amount*) and write off any amount above the fee that he or she would have charged the patient. However, keep in mind that most insurance policies do not pay 100% of the fee schedule; the patient usually must pay a *co-insurance amount* that ranges from 10% to 40% of the fee schedule amount, while the insurance company pays the complementary amount ranging from 60% to 90%.

If the provider is not part of the insurer's network, the patient must usually pay the entire difference directly to the provider after the insurer has paid its share, which is nevertheless still based on the fee schedule.

Fee-for-service plans usually do not pay for any healthcare until the subscriber has met his or her *deductible*. This is a pre-set amount in each plan that the person or family must pay in each calendar or policy year *before* any insurance kicks in. Deductibles may range from $500 to $2,000 for an individual, and $1,000 to $4,000 for a family. (The deductible for a family is generally two times the amount of the deductible for an individual.)

Commercial policies also place a limit on the total co-insurance amount that an individual or family must pay per year. This cap may range from $1,000 to $10,000 beyond the deductible. This is usually called the *out-of-pocket* limit. Once the subscriber has paid this amount, the insurer pays 100% of all further covered charges.

On the other hand, many commercial policies have an annual and lifetime cap, limiting the charges that the insurer is obligated to pay per year and during the life of the policy. For instance, many dental policies limit the annual coverage to $1,000 and the lifetime coverage to $25,000.

In general, commercial fee-for-service health insurance policies are one of three types:

- ***Basic Plans.*** These plans are inexpensive but they offer only a bare minimum of health insurance coverage. They may pay only for limited services performed in a hospital, as well as X-rays, lab tests, some drugs, and sometimes a few outpatient doctor visits. Basic plans typically have low or no deductibles.
- ***Major Medical Plans.*** These plans are designed to pay for most services in the case of a major illness or injury, but they usually do not cover minor health problems or regular office visits.
- ***Comprehensive Medical Plans.*** These plans are the top of the line in the sense that they offer the highest level of medical coverage. They pay for nearly all services on a fee-for-service basis, including doctor's office visits, X-rays, lab tests, inpatient and outpatient hospital services, psychiatric benefits, and sometimes extra items such as chiropractic treatments, acupuncture, and eye examinations.

Two Methods of Reimbursement

Let's clarify some confusing aspects about how insurers reimburse healthcare providers in fee-for-service plans. In general, two methods are used:

Usual, Customary, and Reasonable (UCR) Method

Under this often used method in fee-for-service healthcare, the insurer pays the provider the lowest of the following three amounts:

- ***Usual fee.*** The amount the physician normally charges for a service, which insurers keep track of using records collected over the years.
- ***Customary fee.*** This amount based on a percentile of fees charged by all providers within the same specialty area in the same geographic location for a specific service.

- ***Reasonable fee.*** This fee is the lesser of the usual fee and the customary fee, or it may be another fee that can be justified under special circumstances.

Here's an example of how these three fees would be applied by an insurer. Assume that Doctor A submits a claim and the usual fee is $220, but the customary fee in that area is $225. In this case, the reasonable fee will be $220, because it is the lower amount of the usual and the customary. Meanwhile, if Doctor B submits a bill for $250 as her usual fee, but the customary fee is $225, she will receive the customary amount of $225. (However, in both cases, the doctor will receive only a percentage of the fee and the patient will need to pay his or her co-insurance amount.)

One flaw with UCR is that it creates inflationary pressure on fees because the system encourages doctors to consistently increase their fees to ensure that their *usual* fees are higher than the *customary* range, which slowly raises the customary fee.

Fee Schedule Method

As mentioned earlier, many insurance companies create a specific fee schedule for doctors who agree to participate in a certain plan. The fee schedule includes a set payment for each and every possible procedure that doctors may perform. The physician is not allowed to charge patients above this fee and must write-off any difference.

Blue Cross and Blue Shield

Most people know the names Blue Cross and Blue Shield, but don't know much about them, so let's go over this. Blue Cross originated in 1929 when a group of teachers contracted with Baylor Hospital in Texas to provide hospital care at a fixed monthly cost. This type of arrangement was new in the history of healthcare and differed from the existing plans based on fee-for-service. Then over the next decade, Blue Cross plans became popular in many other parts of the country. Similarly, Blue Shield was devised in 1938 by the American Medical Association as an insurance method to cover doctors' services for a fixed prepaid amount per month.

Over the years, Blue Cross and Blue Shield organizations were established in just about every state in the U.S. Each one had a national association.

In 1986, the two associations merged to form the Blue Cross and Blue Shield Association to manage the various state insurers and compete directly with commercial insurers, although in some states the two organizations have remained separate.

Most Blue Cross/Blue Shield plans are set up as not-for-profit. To obtain this status, they are forbidden by state law from canceling coverage for individuals and are required to obtain approval for rate increases.

Blue Cross and Blue Shield plans were pioneers of prepaid plans that became the basis for managed care today. In addition to their standard individual and group policies, many Blues negotiate contracts with providers in an area to become part of a network. The providers have to accept payment according to the fee schedule determined by the Blues, often 10% lower than what the company pays other providers who are not participating. In exchange, the providers are paid directly rather than having to seek payment from patients. In some contracts, the doctors are penalized if they refer patients to specialists who are not part of the Blue's network.

Managed Care Health Care

Fee-for-service commercial health insurance plans are often regarded as the cause of the past decade's skyrocketing costs of healthcare, as doctors continually try to increase their fees. As a result, more and more commercial insurance companies, self-insured plans, and Blue Cross/Blue Shield insurers have moved toward closely-controlled "managed care" programs.

The most common term you will hear in the context of managed care is HMO, or Health Maintenance Organization. Although HMOs originated in the 1930s as a way to cut costs, they did not take off until the mid-1980s. There are now perhaps over 1000 HMOs, although an accurate count is difficult because there are many types of HMO operations. In general, there are five distinguishing characteristics of HMOs:

- Providers are prepaid on a *capitation* basis, meaning that they receive a fee for each person under their care regardless of whether the patient comes in or not.
- Patients pay only a small co-payment per visit, such as $10, but do not pay co-insurance.
- Care is highly controlled; patients must see a primary physician first who authorizes visits to a specialist if needed.
- Care done by providers outside the HMO network is not covered unless medically necessary; if patients go outside the HMO, they must pay a large co-insurance or receive no reimbursement at all.

- The HMO tries to cut costs through preventative care; patients may see doctors at no additional cost for regular checkups in order to catch illnesses before they become aggravated.

HMOs can be operated in many different ways. In some cases, the HMO is owned by an insurance company, so belonging to this type of HMO is synonymous with being insured. In the other cases, the HMO is an independent business with which numerous private insurers have contracted to serve their subscribers. In other types, doctors are employees of the HMO and work solely at its facility with no ability to see patients on their own. In some HMO networks, affiliated doctors are allowed to maintain their own fee-for-service practice as well as being part of the HMO network.

PPOs are similar to HMOs but follow looser rules. A PPO is usually a network of physicians who have contracted with an insurer to accept patients under certain plans at negotiated rates. Patients in PPOs can choose from among an extensive list of providers who are part of that PPO and in return, they receive a lower fee-for-service rate. If they see a doctor who is outside of the PPO, they must pay a higher co-insurance rate or even the entire fee on their own.

Recent years have brought new forms of managed care structures, such as:

- ***IPA (Independent Practice Association).*** Under this arrangement, the HMO contracts with many independent physicians or associations to care for its subscribers. Many IPAs are prepaid plans on a capitation basis. In some IPAs, physicians may see their non-HMO patients on a fee-for-service basis, whereas in others, physicians organize their own association and approach HMOs for contracts.
- ***EPO (Exclusive Provider Organization).*** An extreme version of a PPO, almost like an HMO. To obtain coverage benefits, patients must see only those doctors who are inside the network selected by the insurer or else they pay 100% of costs. Providers are reimbursed according to predetermined fee-for-service rates.
- ***POS (Point of Service Plan).*** A hybrid PPO / HMO, this plan requires patients to see a primary care physician who oversees their care and determines whether specialist visits are necessary. When a patient visits a participating provider, only a co-payment is required and there is no need to file a claim. However, care provided by out-of-network providers is billed to the patient.

- ***MSO (Managed Service Organization).*** These are managed care arrangements formed by hospitals that want doctors to see patients in their own offices but use the hospital for lab work, x-rays, and so on.

Managed care will continue to evolve over the next decade. According to 2006 statistics, nearly 78 million Americans belong to some type of HMO and 81 million have PPO coverage. The following table shows a breakdown of the number of Americans involved in various managed care programs in 2006. For example, of the 43 million Americans who have Medicare, 6.1 million (14.2%) of them have a Medicare managed care policy. Of the 166 million Americans who have commercial health insurance, nearly 75% of them (124 million) have some form of managed care policy.

Managed Care Penetration in 2006

(#'s in millions) **Segment**	**Total U.S.**	**Percent U.S.**	**Managed Care #**	**Managed Care %**
Medicare	43.0	14.3%	6.1	14.2%
Medicaid	45.4	15.1%	28.6	63.0%
Commercial insurance	166.0	55.1%	124.3	74.9%
Uninsured (4)	46.6	15.5%	NA	NA
TOTAL (5)	301.0	100.0%	159.0	52.8%

Public Health Insurance Programs

The two largest public health insurance programs are Medicare and Medicaid. Public health insurance also includes Tricare (formerly called CHAMPUS – the Civilian Health and Medical Program of the Uniformed Services), Veterans Medical Care, FEHBP (Federal Employees Health Benefits Program), and various other local government-run plans. Here are some details about these programs.

Medicare

You cannot perform medical billing without knowing and understanding Medicare. Medicare began in 1965 to help elderly and disabled citizens with the rising costs of medical and hospital care. The 1965 Social Security Act established both Medicare and Medicaid and made the former the responsibility of the Social Security Administration (SSA), while Federal assistance to the State Medicaid programs was administered by the Social and Rehabilitation Service (SRS). SSA and SRS were originally agencies in the Department of Health, Education, and Welfare (HEW). In 1977, the government created the Health Care Financing Administration (HCFA) under HEW to coordinate Medicare and Medicaid. In 1980, HEW was divided into the Department of Education and the Department of Health and Human Services (HHS). The most recent change came in 2001, when HCFA was renamed the Centers for Medicare & Medicaid Services (CMS). More than 44 million Americans were covered by Medicare in 2007, and this will grow by several million each year as the baby boomer generation ages and becomes eligible for Medicare benefits.

Medicare's Two-Part Coverage

Medicare coverage is divided into two parts:

- **Part A** covers hospitalization, skilled nursing facilities, home healthcare, and hospice care, and is free of charge for almost every American over the age of 65 and the permanently disabled. It is financed through payroll taxes for Social Security. If a subscriber is hospitalized, Part A requires that the individual pay a deductible amount first, then Medicare pays the remaining bill for 60 days of inpatient hospital care that occurs during each benefit period. In general, medical billing services are not involved with filing claims for Part A services because hospitals themselves process their own claims through Medicare "intermediaries" in each state.

- **Part B** pays for *inpatient* or *outpatient doctor's* services performed in a hospital, clinic, doctor's office, or home. It also covers surgical services and supplies, diagnostic tests, laboratory tests, x-rays, ambulance transportation, physical and occupational therapy, blood (after 3 pints), outpatient mental health services, artificial limbs, and durable medical equipment (abbreviated DME).

  Part B of Medicare is optional and requires Medicare subscribers to pay a monthly premium just like commercial insurance. Because of its low cost, most Americans sign up for Part B and allow the premium to be deducted from their Social Security check.

  Part B covers subscribers in most cases for 80 percent of what Medicare determines to be the "allowable" charge in a given geographic area and specialty, according to its own fee schedule. The beneficiary is responsible for an annual deductible and 20% co-insurance for each service.

One of the primary markets for professional independent billing services are providers with many Medicare patients because these doctors must file claims for Part B services for their patients. These claims are now required to be processed electronically to Medicare via various intermediary companies that handle the work for CMS.

Medigap Insurance

Many Medicare subscribers supplement their Medicare coverage with an additional policy called Medicare Supplement Insurance, usually referred to as Medigap because the coverage fills in the "gaps" left in Medicare for deductibles, co-insurance, and non-covered services. However, people in Medicare + Choice Plan, such as a Medicare Health Maintenance Organization (HMO) don't need a Medigap policy. Medigap policies are available from lots of regular commercial insurance companies, and also from the American Association of Retired Persons (AARP).

Medigap coverage has been regulated by the federal government to avoid having insurers fraudulently oversell insurance to the elderly. Medigap policies are standardized with 10 choices called Plans A-J. Every insurer that sells Medigap policies must offer Plan A that provides basic coverage for deductibles and some co-insurance that patients would have otherwise had to pay themselves. Insurers can also sell any of the higher level plans they want. The chart below summarizes the 10 plans.

Medigap Plans

All Medigap plans must cover certain basic benefits. These basic benefits are as follows:

Medicare Part A coverage:

- Coinsurance for hospital days 61-90 ($256 in 2008) and 91-150 ($496 in 2007)
- Coinsurance for each day 91-150 ($512 in 2008) (up to 60 days in your lifetime).
- Cost of 365 extra hospital days in your lifetime, once you've used all Medicare hospital benefits

Medicare Part B coverage:

- Generally, all coinsurance and co-payment amounts after your meet the $135 (in 2008) yearly deductible for Medicare Part B
- The first three pints of blood

Medigap Plan A
- Basic Benefits

Medigap Plan B
- Basic Benefits
- Medicare Part A Hospital Deductible: $1,024 in 2008 for each benefit period for hospital services

Medigap Plan C
- Basic Benefits
- Medicare Part A Hospital Deductible
- Skilled Nursing Home Costs: Your cost ($128 in 2008) for days 21-100 in a skilled nursing home
- Medicare Part B Deductible: Yearly deductible for doctor services ($135 in 2008)
- Foreign Travel Emergency
    - 80% of the cost of emergency care outside the U.S.
    - Up to $50,000 during your lifetime
    - You pay a yearly deductible of $250

Medigap Plan D
- Basic Benefits
- Medicare Part A Hospital Deductible
- Skilled Nursing Home Costs
- Foreign Travel Emergency
- At-Home Recovery
    - Help for activities of daily living, such as bathing and dressing, if you are already receiving skilled home care covered by Medicare.
    - Help for up to eight weeks after you no longer need skilled care
    - Will pay up to $40 per visit, seven visits per week, or a total of $1,900 per year

Medigap Plan E
- Basic Benefits
- Medicare Part A Hospital Deductible
- Skilled Nursing Home Costs
- Foreign Travel Emergency
- Preventive Care: Up to $120 per year for preventive services not covered by Medicare

Medigap Plan F*
- Basic Benefits
- Medicare Part A Hospital Deductible
- Skilled Nursing Home Costs
- Medicare Part B Deductible
- Medicare Part B Excess Charges: Pays 100% of the difference between your doctor's charge and the Medicare approved amount, if your doctor does not accept assignment
- Foreign Travel Emergency

Medigap Plan G
- Basic Benefits
- Medicare Part A Hospital Deductible
- Skilled Nursing Home Costs
- Medicare Part B Excess Charges: Pays 80% of the difference between your doctor's charge and the Medicare approved amount, if your doctor does not accept assignment
- Foreign Travel Emergency
- At-Home Recovery

Medigap Plan H
- Basic Benefits
- Medicare Part A Hospital Deductible
- Skilled Nursing Home Costs
- Foreign Travel Emergency

Medigap Plan I
- Basic Benefits
- Medicare Part A Hospital Deductible
- Skilled Nursing Home Costs
- Medicare Part B Excess Charges: Pays 100% of the difference between your doctor's charge and the Medicare approved amount, if your doctor does not accept assignment
- Foreign Travel Emergency
- At-Home Recovery

Medigap Plan J*
- Basic Benefits
- Medicare Part A Hospital Deductible
- Skilled Nursing Home Costs
- Medicare Part B Deductible
- Medicare Part B Excess Charges: Pays 100% of the difference between your doctor's charge and the Medicare approved amount, if your doctor does not accept assignment

- Foreign Travel Emergency
- At-Home Recovery
- Preventive Care

Medigap Plan K**

- Basic Benefits
    * 100% of Part A coinsurance plus coverage for 365 days after Medicare benefits end
    * 50% hospice cost-sharing
    * 50% of Medicare-eligible expenses for the first three pints of blood
    * 50% Part B coinsurance after you meet the yearly deductible for Medicare Part B, but 100% coinsurance for Part B preventive services
- 50% of Skilled Nursing Home Coinsurance
- 50% of Medicare Part A Hospital Deductible
- Annual out of pocket limit of $4,440 in 2008.

Medigap Plan L**

- Basic Benefits
    * 100% of Part A coinsurance plus coverage for 365 days after Medicare benefits end
    * 75% hospice cost-sharing
    * 75% of Medicare-eligible expenses for the first three pints of blood
- 75% Part B coinsurance after you meet the yearly deductible for Medicare Part B, but 100% coinsurance for Part B preventive services
- 75% of Skilled Nursing Home Coinsurance
- 75% of Medicare Part A Hospital Deductible
- Annual out of pocket limit of $2,220 in 2008.

*Plans F and J also have a "high deductible option." If the subscriber chooses the "high deductible option" on Medigap Plans F and J, he or she will first have to pay a $1,900 deductible in 2008 before the plan pays anything. This amount can go up every year. High deductible policies have lower premiums, but if the subscriber gets sick, the costs will be higher.

**The basic benefits for plans K and L include similar services as plans A-J, but the cost-sharing for the basic benefits is at different levels. The annual out-of-pocket limit increases each year for inflation.

In addition to the A-L standard Medigap policies, Medicare SELECT is a type of Medigap policy that can cost less than standard Medigap plans. However, subscribers can only go to certain doctors and hospitals for care. They need to check with their state insurance department to find out if Medicare SELECT policies are available.

Understanding Medicare and Medigap is critical to a billing service. Doctors and billing services must have in their records the full information about each patient's Medicare/Medigap coverage. For most people over 65, Medicare is their primary coverage, while the Medigap policy, if they have one, provides "secondary" coverage. In many states, the claims are filed electronically first to Medicare which pays its share and then it forwards the claim electronically to the Medigap secondary insurer for payment on any remaining portion. The patient does not need to pay the doctor and the billing service only needs to file the claim once. That's progress!

Medicare coverage can be confusing though. You must make sure that the person has only one Medigap coverage to avoid duplication of benefits. Another glitch can be finding out that some people do not have Medicare as their primary insurer. This can happen if the person is still employed and has health coverage from their employer, which becomes primary while Medicare becomes secondary. Similarly, Medicare can be secondary if the claim involves a workplace injury, automobile or other accident, and in a few other circumstances.

Participating vs. Non-Participating Providers

Another element to understand about Medicare is the distinction between *Participating* and *Non-participating* providers, referring to the fact that providers may accept Medicare's fee schedule or not.

Once per year, doctors must decide either to participate in Medicare, thus becoming a PAR physician by "taking assignment," or to not participate, called a NON-PAR.

- ***PAR.*** Taking assignment means that the doctor accepts the allowable fee determined by Medicare as his or her full payment for services rendered to the Medicare patient. This means that he or she cannot charge the patient a higher fee. In return, Medicare sends its check directly to the provider in a reasonably quick time frame. However, remember that Medicare usually pays the physician only 80% of the allowable amount, so the provider must bill the patient for the remaining 20% co-insurance.
- ***NON-PAR.*** Doctors can also choose not to participate in Medicare. They must still file claims for their patients but they can charge patients up to 15% more than Medicare allows (this is called the *limiting charge*). However, they are subject to a penalty for not participating in the sense that Medicare sends the reimbursement to

the patient and the physician must collect the fees directly from the patient.

Medicare HMOs

In the late 1990s, Medicare began using the HMO model as a way to cut costs and so contracted with various HMO facilities around the country. The Medicare-HMO model has several advantages for subscribers. Although they pay the Medicare Part B premium, they no longer pay any deductibles for Part A services or co-payments for Part B services. This saves subscribers money, and for some people, allows them to avoid purchasing a Medigap policy.

In addition, Medicare HMOs provide without charge many routine preventative checkups, eye examinations and glasses, hearing aids, and discounted prescription drugs. Because of the lower costs to patients and the extra benefits, millions of Medicare enrollees opt to join a Medicare approved HMO rather than continuing to see independent physicians on a fee-for-service basis.

Medicare HMOs usually require patients to see only doctors within the HMO network. These plans are called "lock-ins" and hold patients to receiving all care through a primary physician who then refers them to specialists if needed. A few Medicare HMO plans operate with more flexibility, letting patients go outside the network, particularly if they live in different states at different times of the year as many seniors do.

Medicaid

Medicaid is administered jointly by CMS and state governments according to guidelines established by federal law. Medicaid assists people of any age whose income is below a certain level determined each year. In 2007, more than 40 million people used Medicaid. Note that many Medicare members who cannot afford Medigap secondary insurance are allowed to receive Medicaid to pay their deductibles and co-payments. These people are often called *Medi-Medi* crossovers. (Note if you are doing electronic claims filing: Just as Medicare can send secondary claims electronically to Medigap insurers, it can also forward claims electronically to Medicaid carriers.) However, some states do not accept a HCFA form on a secondary claim, such as Ohio, which has a separate form 6780 which is designed so you don't have to attach the Medicare EOB.

Medicaid claims are processed differently in each state, sometimes through an insurance carrier like a Blue or through a computer service company that is contracted to handle claims for CMS. Medicaid regulations are very strict regarding what kinds of services are covered and what they deem allowable fees.

Tricare (formerly called CHAMPUS)

Tricare is a healthcare program for active and retired military personnel and their families. It was formerly called CHAMPUS, which stood for Civilian Health and Medical Program of the Uniformed Services. People covered by Tricare are allowed to use civilian doctors rather than military personnel for their medical care, while having a portion of any services provided paid for by the federal government. At age 65, Tricare beneficiaries are transferred to the Medicare program.

Workers' Compensation

Worker's Compensation covers medical expenses and disability benefits when an illness or injury results directly from a person's work. In most states, employers who employ more than one employee are required to carry worker's comp insurance. The employer pays the insurance premium. If an employee is hurt while working on the job, he or she is entitled to medical coverage.

Worker's comp differs from state to state. But many states are regulating the benefits of worker's comp policies to protect corporations from having exorbitant costs due to overuse. For example, some states, such as California, limit the number of visits an employee may have with a chiropractor after being hurt on the job. This is now causing some doctors to find ways of saving money on their overhead due to the decrease in revenues they receive from Worker's Comp claims.

When you submit insurance claims for worker's comp, you must always submit them with documentation, such as charts or operative notes, in order to receive payment. The claim must be billed at the worker's comp rate, not the usual and customary fee. Processing claims in this manner will expedite your payment. You also have to bill with an approved diagnosis code and use the same code for every claim after the first one.

Filing worker's comp claims is much more complex than standard claims, as they require second opinion reviews and many types of medical reports to verify the injuries. If you do billing for a doctor who treats worker's comp injuries, it is recommended that you charge more because filing these claims takes a lot longer.

Dental Health Insurance

You also want to know about dental health insurance because dentists use billing services as well. As with heath insurance, dental insurance is offered in many forms: fee-for-services, PPO, HMOs, and pre-paid plans. Fee-for-service and PPO dental insurance plans function just like their counterparts in health insurance, with an annual deductible, a co-pay, and/ or patient co-insurance (often 20%).

The largest difference between health insurance claims and dental claims is the claim form used and the type of documentation required. Dental claims are filed on a form published by the American Dental Association (ADA) and often require supporting documentation to substantiate the need for the service. Supporting documents may include a "narrative" from the dentist along with radiographs (X-rays), photos of the teeth involved, or sometimes plaster models. Dental claims are reviewed at the insurance company by dental claims examiners who adjudicate the claim and determine what benefits, if any, to pay.

Some dental claims require more time to file and appeals because dental insurers can ask for documentation. Some dental insurance policies are very restrictive in what they cover, excluding all cosmetic work as well as repair or restorative work such as fillings and crowns that replace other work that the insurance company does not believe should have been replaced. Some policies have long waiting periods for crowns, such as one year.

However, filing electronic dental claims is improving fast and is a market you can explore for your business. Most of ClaimTek's business packages include *DentOffice*®, a specialized software program that allows you to file dental claims.

3 The Inner Workings of a Doctor's Office

How a billing service works is directly linked to how a doctor's office works. If you're not familiar with medical office procedures and functions, this chapter will help you gain some perspective on their day-to-day operations and how those intersect with your billing and practice management responsibilities.

Most healthcare practitioners (and dental offices) have one or more office personnel who handle the reception work, some patient support, and perhaps claims filing, billing, and accounting functions. If there is a single person, he or she may be called "office manager," "receptionist," "business assistant," or "medical assistant" – or there may be one of each of these. These personnel can be key allies to your getting a contract with the provider – or they may become your nemesis. We'll review how you will want to cultivate these office personnel when we get to the marketing chapter, but for now, be aware that these people are pivotal to your success.

The Basic Patient Forms

Assuming the doctor's office is independently run (that is, it is not a staff HMO model), the following background typically occurs for each patient visit.

1. If the patient is new, he or she is asked to fill out a PATIENT REGISTRATION FORM. This requires the patient to provide his or her formal name, address, phone number, date of birth, sex, marital status, employer, driver's license, primary insurer company name, insurance plan ID number, secondary insurer ID if applicable, and so on. It is important to know that the patient may not be the "responsible party" for his or her own medical payments. For example, an individual may be covered under another person's insurance, and that individual is known as the "guarantor." The

guarantor is thus the actual holder of the health insurance policy and the biller must get the guarantor's information from the Patient Registration form to file the claim. Figure 3-1 shows a typical patient registration form.

Figure 3-1

Patient registration form

PATIENT INTAKE FORM
CONFIDENTIAL PATIENT INFORMATION

DATE OF ILLNESS: ____/____/____ *IF ACCIDENT ?:* AUTO ____ WORK INJURY____ SLIP & FALL____
DO YOU HAVE A LIVING WILL/ADVANCE DIRECTIVE? ____YES ____NO IF NOT, WOULD YOU LIKE MORE INFO?
____YES ____NO PHYSICIANS GROUP DOES NOT HONOR LIVING WILLS/ADVANCE DIRECTIVES: IN THE EVENT OF A LIFE THREATENING EMERGENCY, 911 WILL BE CALLED. TRANSFER TO A HIGHER LEVEL OF CARE WILL BE INITIATED.

PATIENT DATA

NAME____________________ HOME PHONE:( )__________ WORK PHONE:( )__________
MAILING ADDRESS:____________________ CITY:__________ STATE:______ ZIP:______
AGE:______ BIRTHDATE:____/____/____ SOCIAL SECURITY #:______-______-______
____ WHITE ____ BLACK ____ ASIAN ____ HISPANIC ____ OTHER
OCCUPATION:____________________ EMPLOYED BY:____________________
BUSINESS ADDRESS:____________________
DRIVERS LICENSE #:____________________ STATE:__________
IN CASE OF AN EMERGENCY PLEASE CALL ____________________ ____________
NAME & PHONE NUMBER RELATION TO PATIENT

PAST MEDICAL HISTORY

NAMES OF MEDICATIONS YOUR ARE ALLERGIC TO:____________________
ILLNESSES FOR WHICH YOU NOW ARE RECEIVING TREATMENT:____________________
PRIOR INJURIES WITH DATES:____________________
PRIOR SURGERIES WITH DATES:____________________
CURRENT MEDICATIONS:____________________
INCLUDING OVER THE COUNTER & HERBAL SUPPLEMENTS:____________________
(If any of the following are relevant to your medical history, please check the accompanying box)

( ) POLIO	( ) DIABETES	( ) RHEUMATISM	( ) SCARLET FEVER	( ) DIGESTIVE DISORDERS
( ) ANEMIA	( ) BACKACHE	( ) CONCUSSION	( ) HEART TROUBLE	( ) HIGH BLOOD PRESSURE
( ) ASTHMA	( ) ARTHRITIS	( ) CONVULSIONS	( ) GERMAN MEASLES	( ) MUSCULAR DYSTROPHY
( ) CANCER	( ) DIZZINESS	( ) HIV POSITIVE	( ) RHEUMATIC FEVER	( ) OTHER ______
( ) NEURITIS	( ) NUMBNESS	( ) TUBERCULOSIS	( ) VENERAL DISEASE	______
( ) EPILEPSY	( ) HERPES	( ) HEPATITIS (A,B,C)	( ) MULTIPLE SCLEROSIS	

SOCIAL HISTORY

MARRIED? ____ SINGLE? ____ DIVORCED? ____ NUMBER OF CHILDREN ____ GRANDCHILDREN ____
TOBACCO USE - __________ PACKS PER DAY ALCOHOL USE - __________ DRINKS / BEERS PER DAY

FAMILY HISTORY

FATHER ALIVE? ______ AGE ____ ILLNESSES____________________
MOTHER ALIVE? ______ AGE ____ ILLNESSES____________________
NAME, AGES, ILLNESSES OF BROTHERS AND SISTERS:____________________

PATIENT'S SIGNATURE ____________________ DATE __________

2. As part of the patient registration form (or on a separate form), there is also a RELEASE & ASSIGNMENT OF BENEFITS FORM wherein the patient grants the doctor permission to release information about

The Importance of the Patient Registration Form

The registration process is actually critical to proper medical billing to prevent fraud. Believe it or not, some patients will actually try to use someone else's insurance or Medicare card to receive benefits. Some will even use someone else's social security number. Many medical offices are cracking down on this fraudulent abuse of the medical system and are asking for photo identification. This can become especially critical when a doctor's office has 20 or 30 patients with the same last name, and sometimes also sharing the very same first name. This is one reason why *MedOffice®* allows you to store a photograph of each patient. In addition, you might add a "Name Alert" to the patient, which automatically triggers a warning message that this patient has the same name as other patients. Then, each time you access the patient's chart and see the alert, you can be prompted to ask for the date of birth to confirm that you are dealing with the correct patient.

his or her diagnosis and treatment to the insurance company. It also lets the patient authorize the insurance company to pay the provider directly. Patients must sign the Release and Assignment of Benefits form.

3. In some cases, the patient may also fill out a PRE-AUTHORIZATION FORM (also called a Pre-Certification Form), which is used if the insurance policy requires the provider to obtain approval in advance for certain procedures. If the physician fails to obtain the approval in advance, he or she may be denied payment. Many insurance companies have set up 800 phone numbers and Internet sites where physicians can get immediate authorizations if needed. It is expected that the future medical office will use the Internet or "smart cards" to determine a patient's eligibility, coverage benefits, and any pre-authorizations required. Note that obtaining pre-authorizations is a service that you may be able to provide your clients.

4. Since 2001, another form that patients are commonly asked to sign is the HIPAA PRIVACY FORM. This acknowledges that patients have been informed of their right to privacy and confidentiality regarding their medical records. The form also includes permission for the medical provider or the office staff to leave messages on the patient's answering machine. Unless the patient specifically grants this permission, providers are not allowed, according to HIPAA, to leave messages for the patient on an answering machine. If you are the

billing company, you need to be aware of the policy in your client's office in case you ever need to leave a message for the patient.

5. Patients whose insurance policy is based on a PPO or HMO may be required to pay a co-payment for the visit at this time. The co-payment is typically required under PPO policies when patients see specialists, and the remaining fee is covered by the insurance company. If a co-pay is made, patients often want a receipt, so some medical offices handwrite a receipt or print out a "walk-out" statement that summarizes the day's charges and payments.

6. The next form used in medical offices is the ENCOUNTER FORM, often called a *superbill*, routing slip, fee ticket, visit slip, or charge form. The encounter form is a paper document used to record the patient's diagnosis and the medical procedures performed by the provider. This form is what you, the billing company, must receive in order to key in the claim and transmit it to the patient's insurance company. Physicians use preprinted paper encounter forms that list the most common diagnostic and procedure codes used in their office. The doctor simply checks off the codes that pertain to each patient. The form also contains a few blank spaces if the provider needs to write in codes that are not preprinted. The use of diagnostic and procedure codes is now required by all insurers to denote each patient visit. A copy of the encounter form can also serve as a receipt for patients who must submit their own claims to their own insurance company. Figure 3-2 shows a typical encounter form for a medical doctor of internal medicine. Note that superbills for every medical specialty will display completely different codes, so there is no standard superbill.

Some medical practice management software, such as ClaimTek's *Med-Office,* allows the physician's office to design and print their own encounter forms directly from the software. Each provider in the office can have their own default encounter form or they can design a brand new one at any time. Some medical offices have done away with paper encounter forms in favor of small mini-computers called "Tablet PCs" that the provider carries around for patient visits.

Filing Insurance Claims

In most medical offices, the encounter forms are collected at the end of each day (or after several days) and forwarded to the billing person. What

Figure 3-2

Patient encounter form

PHYSICIANS GROUP SIGN-IN & FEE SLIP

NAME (Printed): ____________________ DATE: ____/____/____

Patient's Date of Birth: ____/____/____

	CODE	CPT	PROCEDURE	FEE	UNITS
			E & M NEW PATIENT EXAM		
( )	NE0	99000	Exam - No Charge	$0.00	
( )	NE1	99201	Problem Focused Exam	$130.00	
( )	NE2	99202	Expanded Problem Exam	$165.00	
( )	NE3	99203	Detailed Exam	$230.00	
( )	NE4	99204	Comprehensive Exam	$280.00	
			E&M ESTABLISHED PATIENT		
( )	EE1	99211	Established Visit, Minimal	$85.00	
( )	EE2	99212	Established Visit, Focused	$125.00	
( )	EE3	99213	Established Visit, Expanded	$175.00	
( )	EE4	99214	Established Visit, Detailed	$230.00	
			OFFICE CONSULTATION		
( )	C1	99241	Minimal Consultation	$290.00	
( )	C2	99242	Expanded Consultation	$415.00	
( )	C3	99243	Detailed Consultation	$545.00	
( )	C4	99244	Comprehensive Consultation	$670.00	
			CONFIRMATORY CONSULTATION		
( )	2OP1	99271	Minimal Confirmatory	$290.00	
( )	2OP2	99272	Expanded Confirmatory	$415.00	
( )	2OP3	99273	Detailed Confirmatory	$545.00	
( )	2OP4	99274	Comprehensive Mod. Complex	$670.00	
			THERAPIES		
( )	IST	97012	Mechanical Traction	$45.00	
( )	ICE	97010	Cold Packs	$40.00	
( )	HEAT	97010	Hot Packs	$40.00	
( )	IF	97014	Electrical stimulation	$45.00	
( )	US	97035	Ultrasound (1 unit per 15 min)	$56.00	____
( )	USR	97035	Ultrasound (1 unit under 15 min)	$48.00	____
			THERAPEUTIC PROCEDURES		
( )	TA	97530	Therapeutic Activities	$64.00	____
( )	FTIC	97140	Manual Therapy Techniques (-52)	$68.00	____
( )	TE	97110	Therapeutic Exercises	$64.00	____
( )	MAS	97124	Massage (1 unit per 15 min.)	$56.00	____
( )	MASR	97124	Massage (1 unit under 15 min.)	$48.00	____
			CHIROPRACTIC MANIPULATIVE TREATMENT		
( )	CMT1	98940	Chiro. Manip. Tx., 1-2 regions	$70.00	
( )	CMT3	98941	Chiro. Manip. Tx., 3-4 regions	$80.00	
( )	CMT5	98942	Chiro. Manip. Tx., 5 regions	$90.00	
( )	CMTE	98943	Chiro. Manip. Tx., extraspinal	$65.00	
			INJECTIONS		
( )	TPI	20552	Trigger Pt. (1 or 2 muscles)	$245.00	
		Macro	includes J1030 & J2000		
( )	TPIM	20553	Trigger Pt. (3 or more muscles)	$395.00	
		Macro	includes J1030 & J2000		
( )	SJI	20600	Small Joint Injections	$145.00	____
		Macro	includes J1020 & J2000		
( )	AEW	20605	Ankle, Elbow, Wrist Injections	$170.00	____
		Macro	includes J1030 & J2000		
( )	HKS	20610	Hip, Knee, Shoulder Injections	$195.00	____
		Macro	includes J1040 & J2000		
			SUPPLIES / OTHER		
( )	TT	64550	Tens Unit & Instruction	$120.00	
( )	SUPP	99070	Supplies - Medical	____	

	CODE	CPT	PROCEDURE	FEE	UNITS
			CERV, THOR, LUM, CHEST, PELVIC		
( )	XC1	72020	Single view, cervical	$52.50	
( )	XC2	72040	Two Views, cervical	$105.00	
( )	XC3	72040	Three views, cervical	$157.50	
( )	XC4	72050	Four views, cervical	$210.00	
( )	XC5	72050	Five views, cervical	$262.50	
( )	XC7	72052	Complete, cervical	$362.50	
( )	XT1			Single vie ####	
( )	XT2	72070	Two views, thoracic	$125.00	
( )	XTS	72072	Three views, incl. Swimmer's	$187.50	
( )	XCS	71010	Single view, chest	$62.50	
( )	XTC	71020	Two view, chest	$125.00	
( )	XL1	72020	Single view, lumbar	$62.50	
( )	XL2	72100	Two views, lumbar	$125.00	
( )	XL4	72110	Four views, lumbar	$250.00	
( )	XL6	72114	Six views, includes bending	$375.00	
( )	XP1	72170	Single view Lumbopelvic	$62.50	
( )	XPS	72020	Single view Spot	$52.50	
( )	XP3	72190	Three views Lumbopelvic	$187.50	
			UPPER EXTREMITY X-RAYS		
( )	XMR	70030	Eye, Detect Foreign Body	$57.50	
( )	XCL	73000	Clavical Complete	$57.50	
( )	XSC	73010	Scapula Complete	$115.00	
( )	XACJ	73050	A-C Joints, Bilat	$115.00	
( )	XHU	73060	Humerus Min. Two Views	$115.00	
( )	XS1	73020	Shoulder Single view	$57.50	
( )	XS2	73030	Shoulder Two views (-25)	$115.00	
( )	XS3	73030	Shoulder Three views	$172.50	
( )	XE2	73070	Elbow Two views	$105.00	
( )	XE3	73080	Elbow Three views	$157.50	
( )	XFO	73090	Forearm, 2 Views	$115.00	
( )	XW2	73100	Wrist Two views	$105.00	
( )	XW3	73110	Wrist Three views	$157.50	
( )	XD2	73120	Hand Two views	$105.00	
( )	XD3	73130	Hand Three views	$157.50	
( )	XFI	73140	Finger, 2 Views	$105.00	
			LOWER EXTREMITY X-RAYS		
( )	XH1	73500	Hip One View	$62.50	
( )	XH2	73510	Hip Two Views	$115.00	
( )	XFE	73550	Femur Two Views	$125.00	
( )	XK2	73560	Knee Two Views	$115.00	
( )	XK3	73562	Knee Three Views	$172.50	
( )	XK4	73564	Knee Complete	$230.00	
( )	XTF	73590	Tibia / Fibula, Two Views	$125.00	
( )	XA2	73600	Ankle Two Views	$105.00	
( )	XA3	73610	Ankle Complete	$157.50	
( )	XF2	73620	Foot Two Views	$105.00	
( )	XF3	73630	Foot Three Views	$157.50	
( )	XTOE	73660	Toes, Two Views	$105.00	
			DIAGNOSTIC / OTHER PROCEDURES		
( )	UA1	81002	U/A Dipstick	$20.00	
( )	UA2	81025	U/A Pregnancy	$30.00	
( )	NCVM	95903	Motor Nerve Conduction	$200.00	____
( )	NCVS	95904	Sensory Nerve Conduction	$150.00	____
( )	HRF	95934	H - Reflex	$125.00	____
( )	EMG1	95860	EMG, 1 Extremity	$200.00	
( )	EMG2	95861	EMG, 2 Extremities	$400.00	
( )	EMG3	95863	EMG, 3 Extremities	$600.00	
( )	EMG4	95864	EMG, 4 Extremities	$800.00	

I hereby certify that the above ____ procedures and services were provided to me on the above date.

PATIENT SIGNATURE: ______________________________

happens next depends on whether the office intends to send the insurance claims on paper or electronically. Even though your business as a medical biller will be based on filing mostly electronic claims, let's look at a comparison of paper claims filing vs. electronic claims filing just so you can be familiar with the difference between the two methods.

Figure 3-3

CMS 1500 claim form

1500
HEALTH INSURANCE CLAIM FORM
APPROVED BY NATIONAL UNIFORM CLAIM COMMITTEE 08/05
PICA PICA
1. MEDICARE (Medicare #) MEDICAID (Medicaid #) TRICARE CHAMPUS (Sponsor's SSN) CHAMPVA (Member ID#) GROUP HEALTH PLAN (SSN or ID) FECA BLK LUNG (SSN) OTHER (ID)
1a. INSURED'S I.D. NUMBER (For Program in Item 1)
2. PATIENT'S NAME (Last Name, First Name, Middle Initial)
3. PATIENT'S BIRTH DATE MM DD YY SEX M F
4. INSURED'S NAME (Last Name, First Name, Middle Initial)
5. PATIENT'S ADDRESS (No., Street)
6. PATIENT RELATIONSHIP TO INSURED Self Spouse Child Other
7. INSURED'S ADDRESS (No., Street)
CITY STATE
8. PATIENT STATUS Single Married Other
CITY STATE
ZIP CODE TELEPHONE (Include Area Code) ( )
Employed Full-Time Student Part-Time Student
ZIP CODE TELEPHONE (Include Area Code) ( )
9. OTHER INSURED'S NAME (Last Name, First Name, Middle Initial)
10. IS PATIENT'S CONDITION RELATED TO:
11. INSURED'S POLICY GROUP OR FECA NUMBER
a. OTHER INSURED'S POLICY OR GROUP NUMBER
a. EMPLOYMENT? (Current or Previous) YES NO
a. INSURED'S DATE OF BIRTH MM DD YY SEX M F
b. OTHER INSURED'S DATE OF BIRTH MM DD YY SEX M F
b. AUTO ACCIDENT? PLACE (State) YES NO
b. EMPLOYER'S NAME OR SCHOOL NAME
c. EMPLOYER'S NAME OR SCHOOL NAME
c. OTHER ACCIDENT? YES NO
c. INSURANCE PLAN NAME OR PROGRAM NAME
d. INSURANCE PLAN NAME OR PROGRAM NAME
10d. RESERVED FOR LOCAL USE
d. IS THERE ANOTHER HEALTH BENEFIT PLAN? YES NO *If yes, return to and complete item 9 a-d.*
READ BACK OF FORM BEFORE COMPLETING & SIGNING THIS FORM.
12. PATIENT'S OR AUTHORIZED PERSON'S SIGNATURE I authorize the release of any medical or other information necessary to process this claim. I also request payment of government benefits either to myself or to the party who accepts assignment below.
SIGNED DATE
13. INSURED'S OR AUTHORIZED PERSON'S SIGNATURE I authorize payment of medical benefits to the undersigned physician or supplier for services described below.
SIGNED
CARRIER
PATIENT AND INSURED INFORMATION
14. DATE OF CURRENT: MM DD YY ILLNESS (First symptom) OR INJURY (Accident) OR PREGNANCY(LMP)
15. IF PATIENT HAS HAD SAME OR SIMILAR ILLNESS. GIVE FIRST DATE MM DD YY
16. DATES PATIENT UNABLE TO WORK IN CURRENT OCCUPATION MM DD YY FROM TO MM DD YY
17. NAME OF REFERRING PROVIDER OR OTHER SOURCE 17a. 17b. NPI
18. HOSPITALIZATION DATES RELATED TO CURRENT SERVICES MM DD YY FROM TO MM DD YY
19. RESERVED FOR LOCAL USE
20. OUTSIDE LAB? YES NO $ CHARGES
21. DIAGNOSIS OR NATURE OF ILLNESS OR INJURY (Relate Items 1, 2, 3 or 4 to Item 24E by Line)
1. 2. 3. 4.
22. MEDICAID RESUBMISSION CODE ORIGINAL REF. NO.
23. PRIOR AUTHORIZATION NUMBER
24. A. DATE(S) OF SERVICE From MM DD YY To MM DD YY | B. PLACE OF SERVICE | C. EMG | D. PROCEDURES, SERVICES, OR SUPPLIES (Explain Unusual Circumstances) CPT/HCPCS MODIFIER | E. DIAGNOSIS POINTER | F. $ CHARGES | G. DAYS OR UNITS | H. EPSDT Family Plan | I. ID. QUAL. | J. RENDERING PROVIDER ID. #
1 NPI
2 NPI
3 NPI
4 NPI
5 NPI
6 NPI
25. FEDERAL TAX I.D. NUMBER SSN EIN
26. PATIENT'S ACCOUNT NO.
27. ACCEPT ASSIGNMENT? (For govt. claims, see back) YES NO
28. TOTAL CHARGE $
29. AMOUNT PAID $
30. BALANCE DUE $
31. SIGNATURE OF PHYSICIAN OR SUPPLIER INCLUDING DEGREES OR CREDENTIALS (I certify that the statements on the reverse apply to this bill and are made a part thereof.)
SIGNED DATE
32. SERVICE FACILITY LOCATION INFORMATION a. NPI b.
33. BILLING PROVIDER INFO & PH # ( ) a. NPI b.
PHYSICIAN OR SUPPLIER INFORMATION
NUCC Instruction Manual available at: www.nucc.org
PLEASE PRINT OR TYPE
Printed on Recycled Paper
APPROVED OMB-0938-0999 FORM CMS-1500 (08/05)

Paper Claims Filing

In the olden days, filing health insurance claims meant that the entire process was done using paper claim forms that were typed out on a typewriter. The claim form that became the standard form used was called the HCFA 1500, pronounced *Hick-fah fifteen hundred.* However, the form is now called the CMS 1500 form, though many people still call it the HCFA form. This form was created by Medicare and eventually adopted as the standard

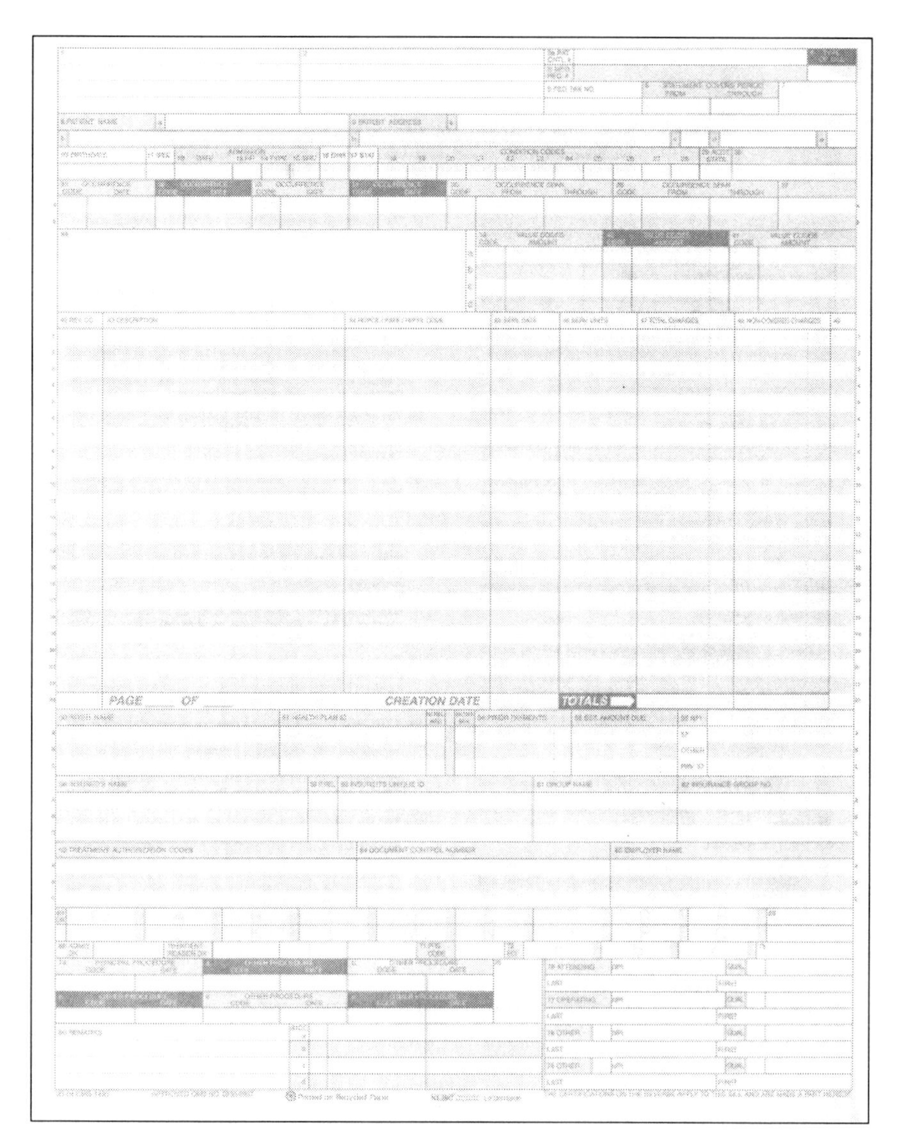
PAGE ___ OF ___

CREATION DATE

TOTALS

Figure 3-4

CMS 1450 form

claims form by nearly every insurance company in the U.S. for medical encounters, other than hospital and emergency room claims, which are filed on a form called the CMS 1450 (nicknamed the UB) and dental claims (filed on a form produced by the American Dental Association).

The CMS 1500, CMS 1450 and ADA forms are shown in Figures 3-3 through 3-5. Note that the CMS 1500 form was just updated in 2005 and became effective in 2007. These new forms carry a date identifier at the bottom that reads 08/05. Note also that the dental form has similar fields required in the CMS 1500 form, but also has spaces for the dentist to provide a verbal description of the procedures performed.

Figure 3-5

ADA claim form

Dental Claim Form
©American Dental Association, 1999 version 2000

1. ☐Dentist's pre-treatment estimate Specialty (see backside)
☐Dentist's statement of actual services
2. ☐Medicaid Claim Prior Authorization #
☐EPSDT
3. Carrier Name
4. Carrier Address
5. City 6. State 7. Zip

PATIENT
8. Patient Name (Last, First, Middle) 9. Address 10. City 11. State
12. Date of Birth (MM/DD/YYYY) / / 13. Patient ID # 14. Sex ☐M ☐F 15. Phone Number ( ) 16. Zip Code
17. Relationship to Subscriber/Employee ☐Self ☐Spouse ☐Child ☐Other
18. Employer/School Name Address

SUBSCRIBER / EMPLOYEE
19. Subs./Emp. ID/SSN# 20. Employer Name 21. Group #
22. Subscriber/Employee Name (Last, First, Middle)
23. Address 24. Phone Number ( )
25. City 26. State 27. Zip Code
28. Date of Birth (MM/DD/YYYY) / / 29. Marital Status ☐Married ☐Single ☐Other 30. Sex ☐M ☐F
39. I have been informed of the treatment plan and associated fees. I agree to be responsible for all charges for dental services and materials not paid by my dental benefit plan, unless the treating dentist or dental practice has a contractual agreement with my plan prohibiting all or a portion of such charges. To the extent permitted under applicable law, I authorize release of any information relating to this claim.
X
Signed (Patient/Guardian) Date (MM/DD/YYYY)

OTHER POLICIES
31. Is Patient covered by another plan ☐No (Skip 32–37) ☐Yes: ☐Dental or ☐ Medical 32. Policy #
33. Other Subscriber's Name
34. Date of Birth (MM/DD/YYYY) / / 35. Sex ☐M ☐F 36. Plan/Program Name
37. Employer/School Name Address
38. Subscriber/Employee Status ☐Employed ☐Part-time Status ☐Full-time Student ☐Part-time Student
40. Employer/School Name Address
41. I hereby authorize payment of the dental benefits otherwise payable to me directly to the below named dental entity.
X
Signed (Employee/subscriber) Date (MM/DD/YYYY)

BILLING DENTIST
42. Name of Billing Dentist or Dental Entity 43. Phone Number ( ) 44. Provider ID # 45. Dentist Soc. Sec. or T.I.N.
46. Address 47. Dental License # 48. First visit date of current series 49. Place of treatment ☐Office ☐Hosp. ☐ECF ☐Other
50. City 51. State 52. Zip Code 53. Radiographs or models enclosed? ☐Yes, How many? ☐No 54. Is treatment for orthodontics? ☐Yes ☐No
If service already commenced:
55. If prosthesis (crown, bridge, dentures), is this initial placement? ☐Yes ☐No If no, reason for replacement: Date of prior placement: Date appliances placed: Total mos. of treatment remaining
56. Is treatment result of occupational illness or injury? ☐No ☐ Yes Brief description and dates
57. Is treatment result of: ☐auto accident? ☐other accident? ☐neither Brief description and dates

58. Diagnosis Code Index (optional)
1. 2. 3. 4. 5. 6. 7. 8.

59. Examination and treatment plan — List teeth in order

Date (MM/DD/YYYY)	Tooth	Surface	Diagnosis Index #	Procedure Code	Qty	Description	Fee	Admin. Use Only

ADA®

60. Identify all missing teeth with: X

Permanent		Primary		
1 2 3 4 5 6 7 8	9 10 11 12 13 14 15 16	A B C D E	F G H I J	Total Fee
32 31 30 29 28 27 26 25	24 23 22 21 20 19 18 17	T S R Q P	O N M L K	Payment by other plan

Max. Allowable
Deductible
Carrier %
Carrier pays
Patient pays

61. Remarks for unusual services

62. I hereby certify that the procedures as indicated by date are in progress (for procedures that require multiple visits) or have been completed and that the fees submitted are the actual fees I have charged and intend to collect for those procedures.
X
Signed (Treating Dentist) License # Date (MM/DD/YYYY)
63. Address where treatment was performed
64. City 65. State 66. Zip Code

©American Dental Association, 1999
[illegible] (Same as ADA Dental Claim Form) – [illegible]
To Reorder, call 1-800-947-4746

A Brief History of the CMS 1500 Form (Like You Really Want to Know)

The story behind the HCFA 1500 form is actually quite interesting. In the early days of health insurance, claims filing was a nightmare. Nearly every commercial insurance company, as well as Medicare, Medicaid, and Blue Cross/Blue Shield had its own unique paper claim form. Keeping track of which form was to be used for which insurer was a major task. Every form had its particular requirements for reporting the doctor's diagnosis, the procedures performed, and the fee.

In the early 1980s, the American Medical Association established a task force to develop a standardized form that would be acceptable to the government as well as to commercial insurers. The result of their work was the Uniform Health Insurance Claim Form, called the HCFA 1500, issued originally in 1984. In 1990, the form was revised to eliminate the spaces where doctors would handwrite explanations of unusual services or circumstances to justify their fees. The new version, called the Red Form (since it is printed in red ink) allows only for standard diagnosis and procedure coding. (Only small additional notes are permitted on the form in Block 19, where doctors have up to 50 characters to add descriptive information. For example, if a patient is transported in an ambulance, there might be a note on his condition in the ambulance. Chiropractors may use the space to describe the pain level of the patient. It can also be used for extra diagnosis codes, beyond the usual four codes).

The HCFA 1500, now called the CMS 1500, requires patients to provide information about any secondary insurance carrier so that the primary carrier does not duplicate any benefits that might be paid by a secondary insurer.

How does the CMS 1500 form get filled out? It begins when the encounter form from the medical provider is transmitted to the billing service, which takes the data from the encounter form and keys it onto the paper form. This data includes the patient's name, address, sex, date of birth, marital status, insurance information, and diagnostic and procedure codes. Of course, today's medical practice management software facilitates this process of keying claims, though as you can imagine, mistakes are still quite possible (and they do happen) when typing in detailed data.

In offices that do not use electronic claims, the next step is that the claims are printed out on the paper CMS 1500 form (or ADA dental form) and mailed to the appropriate insurance company. Upon arrival at the insurer's office, they are opened, screened, assigned a control number, microfilmed for record keeping, and then manually entered into a computer by a claims examiner.

If a claim contains no errors, the claims examiner may pay the claim and, in general, the physician receives payment in about 30-90 days, depending on the speed and reliability of the insurance company. When a claim has no errors and is approved, the insurer sends out a document called an Explanation of Benefits (EOB) to the patient with a copy to the physician. For Medicare, an Explanation of Medicare Benefits (EOMB) is mailed out, and the physician receives a computerized report of the payments along with the check.

However, if the claim contains errors such as missing information or an incorrect or unacceptable code, it is denied and returned to the doctor's office via US mail for correction. This denial may end up taking several months before the doctor's office or billing service can correct the claim and resubmit it, largely because they are dealing with paper forms that must be reviewed by humans.

Another problem with paper claims is the fact that insurance companies often lose them and can take months to "find" them. Many billers suspect that insurance companies intentionally lose claims to avoid paying them.

Once a patient's primary insurance has paid, don't forget that if the patient has secondary insurance, it means that another paper CMS 1500 form must be prepared and submitted. This form must be accompanied by a copy of the EOB from the primary insurer showing how much was already paid so the secondary insurer does not duplicate payments. It might take another 30 days to receive the remainder due from a secondary insurer.

The above steps describe the billing and accounting operation of many medical offices that are either not computerized at all or are only partially computerized because they still print and mail paper claims.

Electronic Claims Filing

Filing claims electronically significantly reduces the steps discussed above for paper claims and has truly become the most efficient and error-free way to file claims and obtain reimbursement. This is why becoming a knowledgeable medical biller who specializes in electronic claims filing has become one of the leading new businesses of this century.

The steps to electronic claims filing demonstrate its advantages in efficiency and reduced errors. We will explain these steps fully, including an overview of setting up your software, so that you can understand the whole process at this time. The most significant contrast in the two methods of insurance billing happens toward the end of the process when you file the claims via modem or over the Internet rather than on paper forms.

Note that Chapter 7 provides complete details on billing procedures, showing you how to start billing for a doctor once you have your first client, including screen shots from MedOffice software to exemplify specifically how medical billing and practice management software works. In this chapter, our goal is to give you an overview of the claims process so you can understand it in the context of electronic vs. paper claims. Chapter 7 will explain the process in detail.

Step 1. The first step in electronic medical billing is setting up your software. This is perhaps the most time consuming phase for a medical billing service, but once it is done, electronic claims processing and patient accounting takes considerably less time than paper forms. The best medical billing software programs today can be easy to use (especially ClaimTek's *MedOffice*). In general, you see a "main menu" of basic functions from which you select your commands. Each main menu command then leads to "sub-menus" with more detailed commands. To help you visualize a medical billing program, Figure 3-6 shows the main screen for MedOffice.

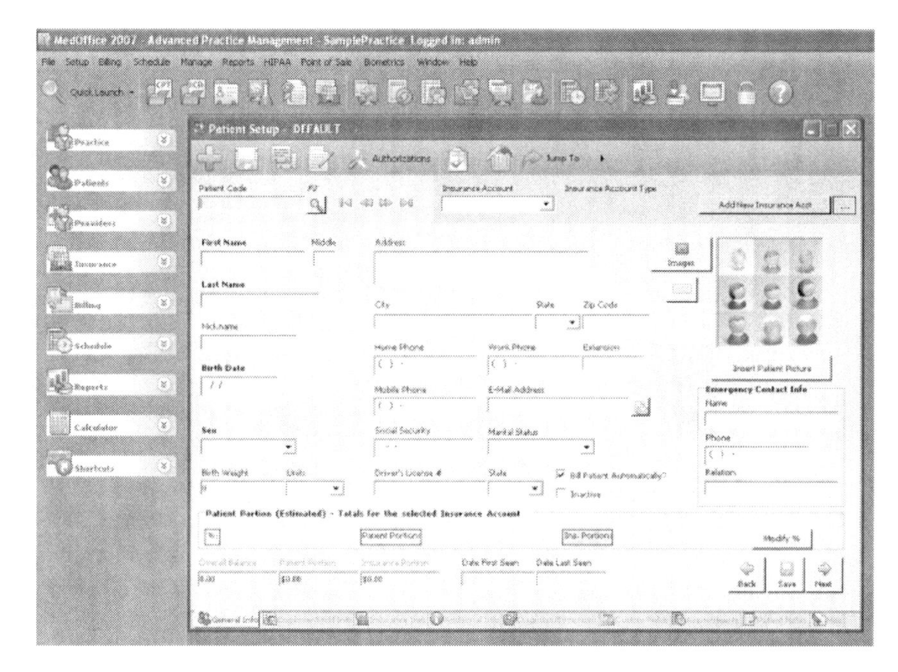

Figure 3-6

Main Screen in MedOffice

Whichever software product you use, the set up procedures are similar because billing always needs to store specific information about each patient, as well as the providers in the practice and the insurance companies to be billed. You must also input (or import) the list of commonly-used diagnostic and procedure codes for each practice for which you do billing. (This is less daunting than it sounds, because most medical offices use only a few dozen codes or a hundred codes, not hundreds of them.)

In addition, if the software you are using performs full practice management, the set up procedure also requires entering existing account balances for each established patient or importing data from a current software product being used. Figure 3-7 shows the screen from MedOffice where data for a typical patient is keyed.

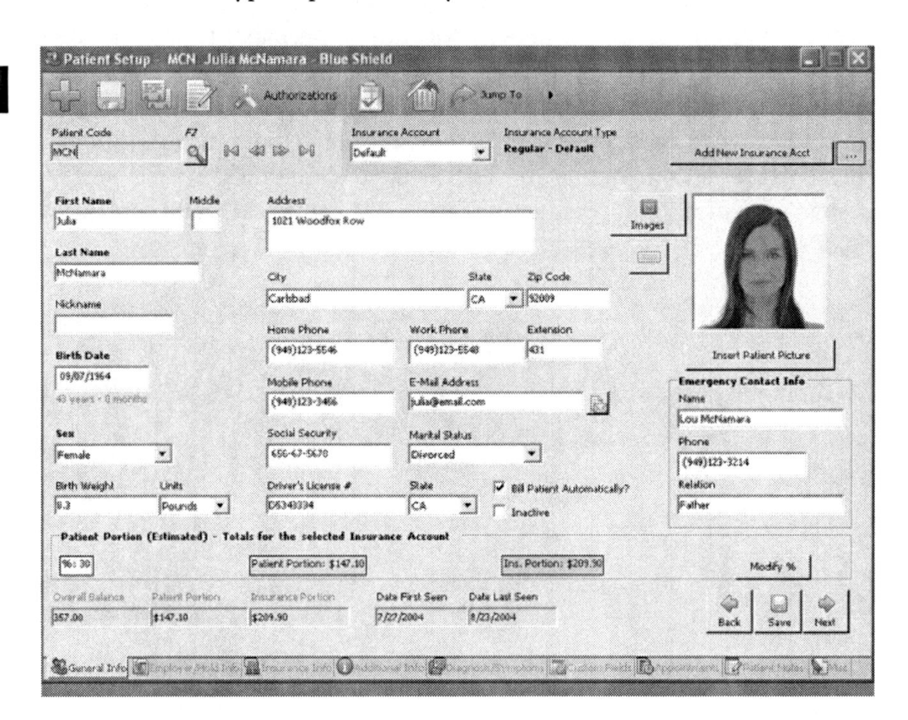

Figure 3-7

Basic patient data screen in MedOffice

In MedOffice, keying patient data is fast and efficient. You type in the data for each field, then tab to the next field. Each patient has one centralized screen on which to enter personal data, followed by other screens where the patient's insurance and employment information is stored along with other data.

As mentioned earlier, medical billing software reduces the risk of errors when entering data. For example, most software is programmed to block you from keying in an alphabetic character if the field only accepts numeric characters, or to signal you if only nine digits have been entered where ten are expected.

Let's assume that you have set up your database for a doctor's office that has become a client of yours. Here's your next step?

Step 2. In order to perform insurance claims filing, the medical billing service must receive copies of the daily encounter forms from each medical office for which he or she does billing. Many billing services get the encounter forms by asking their clients to mail or overnight them. Some billers have their doctors use a courier delivery service. If there are only a few encounter forms, some offices simply fax the encounters forms to their biller. Depending on the volume, the encounter forms can be sent each and every day, or once per week, or at whatever interval is appropriate to prevent the claims process from falling behind. Some billers provide personalized service by traveling to their local client's offices to pick up copies of the encounter forms. They use this time as an opportunity to schmooze and network with the office personnel to learn more and potentially get some new contacts.

MedOffice and MedOffice Remote

Another way that the data can be transmitted to your billing company is by using ClaimTek's MedOffice and MedOffice Remote software. These two programs work together; MedOffice Remote resides in your doctor-client's office while MedOffice is your software. The medical office uses MedOffice Remote to key their own encounter forms into the system, but each day, you use MedOffice to log onto your client's computer to download the data so you can perform the next steps of the process, as explained below. Another method will be to offer your doctor clients online access to MedOffice as a hosted application. We will discuss this process later in the book, or you can visit our web site at www.claimtek.com and click on Software to read about MedOffice Remote.

Step 3. Once you have the encounter forms, the next step is to key in the data for each patient. Believe it or not, this work takes about 30 seconds to 1 minute per established patient – that is all. (Of course, if the patient is new, you need to first set up a new record for that patient, but for any established patient, you only need to bring up the claims entry module and select an existing patient.) In chapter 7, we will show you details of how this is done.

Step 4. In this step, you will now begin to see the difference between paper and electronic claims. We are at the point where all the claims for a batch of encounter forms have been keyed. Gone are the days at this point of printing out dozens if not hundreds of CMS 1500 forms and sorting them by insurance company, then inserting each insurer's batch into an envelope and mailing them.

Instead, in this step, you simply open the menu command in your software to process electronic insurance claims. This process varies in the details from software to software product, but in general, submitting electronic claims is usually simple and fast. In general, you just click on a command in your software to find all insurance claims that have not yet been sent, and the software will search for these claims and then "batch" them together for transmission.

You may be wondering how a large batch of claims can be sent all at once if they are going to different insurance companies. The answer is that billing companies, as we have briefly discussed, use "clearinghouses," that is, businesses that accept all claims from billers nationwide for reprocessing and forwarding to individual insurers. In this way, each billing company does not need to separate their claims into dozens of separate batches corresponding to the dozens of insurance companies they may need to bill. They can transmit a large batch of claims all at once and the clearinghouse forwards them to the respective insurers. (We'll talk more about clearinghouses in Chapter 7 as well.)

However, in some cases, billers need to "filter" their claims to divide them into different segmented batches according to various parameters. For example, you may need to submit certain claims directly to a specific insurance company over the Internet or by modem, so when batching your claims, you would need to segregate those claims from all others. Another common scenario is separating secondary claims from primary claims. (And there are indeed some claims that must be sent on paper, which you need to segregate from the electronic claims. For example, some local health and welfare plans and worker's compensation claims may be exempt from electronic claims and so require you to separate them out and send them on paper).

As you develop your billing business, you will find various circumstances where you need to filter a large batch of claims into smaller groups, so be sure your software has this feature. For example, MedOffice allows you to filter claims in many ways: by primary/secondary/ or tertiary claim filing, by insurance company, by provider, by patients, by location, by patient type, and more. Chapter 7 explains this process in greater detail.

Note that when you are preparing claims for transmission in this step, you may need to tell your software what "format" to use in transmitting the claims. In prior years, there were only two formats: paper claims vs. a digital format that essentially captured the text image of the paper claim files; the text was then what you transmitted to insurers or your clearinghouse. However, new federal regulations added another digital format that is increasingly required for most claims, called ANSI. This format uses binary code in a compressed format that improves the speed of the electronic transmission. Thus your last action in batching your claims is to select the format in which you want to prepare the claims. Once you choose the format, you simply save the file you have created and you are now ready to move on to Step 5.

Step 5. This step in claims filing is the actual transmission of the claims via modem or Internet to your clearinghouse or individual insurance companies. This step is roughly equivalent in complexity to sending an e-mail. You tell your software that you are ready to transmit a batch of claims, then you select the file you want to transmit, and hit *Send.* Your software initiates the modem transmission in a few seconds and the claims are sent.

Step 6. After receiving the claims, the clearinghouse notifies you, usually within minutes while online, that your claims have been received. You may also receive a report about any claims that contain errors and need to be reprocessed. You can then make a paper copy of this report, called an Audit/Edit report or Sender Log, for your records. In many cases, you can make an immediate correction on certain rejected claims and resubmit them the same day.

However, if an error is due to coding, you are best advised to confer with your doctor's office before resubmitting the claim. In fact, it's against federal regulations for an offsite biller to change any coding. (Note: If you are certified medical coder and you have access to patient records to verify documentation, you may change the coding per your business agreement with the doctor's office. But if you are not a certified medical coder, don't even think of it. Remember: you're the biller, not the doctor.)

As you can see, electronic claims are simpler and more efficient to create and process than paper claims. Compare the two charts in Figure 3-8 to see how the two processes differ:

Figure 3-8

Comparison of Paper vs. Electronic Claims Flow

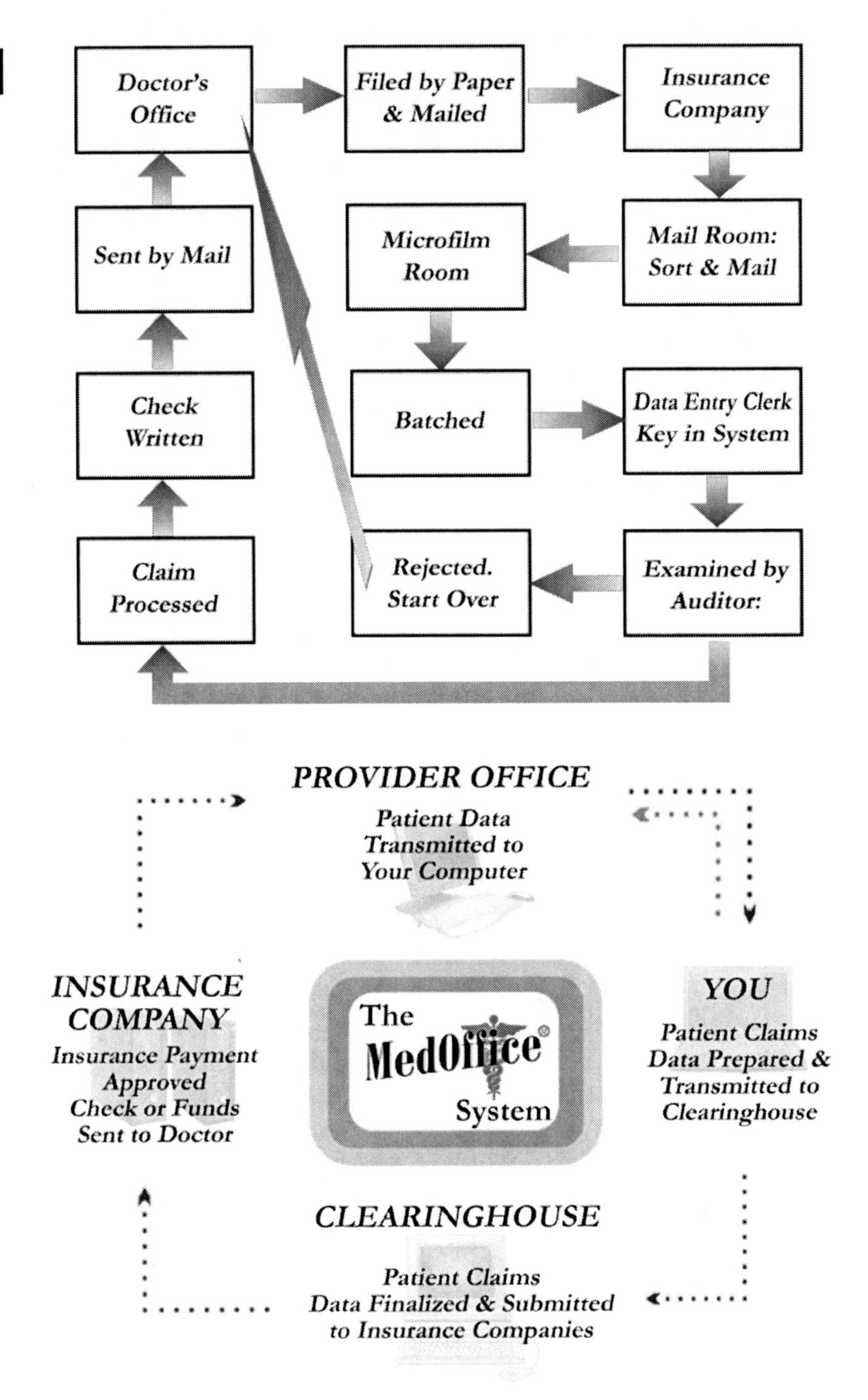
Doctor's Office
Filed by Paper & Mailed
Insurance Company
Sent by Mail
Microfilm Room
Mail Room: Sort & Mail
Check Written
Batched
Data Entry Clerk Key in System
Claim Processed
Rejected. Start Over
Examined by Auditor:
PROVIDER OFFICE
Patient Data Transmitted to Your Computer
INSURANCE COMPANY
Insurance Payment Approved Check or Funds Sent to Doctor
The MedOffice System
YOU
Patient Claims Data Prepared & Transmitted to Clearinghouse
CLEARINGHOUSE
Patient Claims Data Finalized & Submitted to Insurance Companies

What's more, electronic claims get paid faster than paper claims because the data arrives at insurers already in digital form. Commercial insurance companies will process and pay clean electronic claims within as little as 24 hours, while Medicare will process and issue a check for electronic claims within 14-19 days for providers. Furthermore, because of the error checking that occurs in both the keying-in phase and when you are online with the clearinghouse, filing claims electronically is significantly faster and less prone to mistakes than paper claims. Fewer claims are rejected, and those that are rejected can be investigated, fixed, and resubmitted quickly.

Electronic claims are also very advantageous for patients who have secondary and tertiary insurance coverages. Electronic claims make it far less time consuming to process the primary claim, get paid, and then process any secondary claim. In the case of Medicare, in fact, you can often process the primary claim to Medicare which forwards the claim electronically to a Medigap secondary insurer that has been stored on file (as long as you have the patient's permission to do so). You can often receive the check from the secondary insurer even before Medicare has paid its share.

A Note on Dental Claims

Dental claims are keyed and submitted almost exactly like electronic health claims as described above. The occasional difference is that dental claims may require backup supporting documentation. If the documentation is simple, such as a "narrative" from the dentist describing the patient's need for the services, the claim can still be sent electronically. If the supporting documentation is a photo or a tooth model, however, the claims must be printed on paper and mailed. However, dental claims filing is moving increasingly towards electronic claims, and thus dentists still represent a market for professional billing services. It is expected that in the future, x-rays and teeth photos will be able to be sent electronically along with the claim form.

Managing Receivables: Insurance and Patient Payments

The first part of this chapter has covered only a portion of the story concerning the operation of a medical office. Registering patients, recording the medical transaction on encounter forms, and processing insurance claims are just the first half of the entire process. Of course, the goal of all this is to obtain compensation for the medical provider from a combination of payments from the insurance companies and the patients.

The second part of the process is therefore to perform the follow-through required to record payments and send out statements to patients. In most medical offices, the receivables process works as follows.

After claims are submitted to insurers, each insurer reviews the claims and decides how much to pay for each procedure code listed. This reflects the fact that a vast majority of medical care in the US today is fee-for-service, where each and every procedure is evaluated and paid separately. In this way, a single claim for a patient may consist of one or more procedure codes and each code must be reviewed and paid on its own merits.

Once the insurer determines how much to pay for a claim, it mails the provider's office the Explanation of Benefits (EOB). If multiple claims were submitted in a batch to the same insurer, and they were paid at the same time, many insurance companies will batch process the payments into a single check along with one long running EOB for the entire batch. (Of course, each patient receives a copy of the EOB as well.)

Whenever a claim is paid and the physician receives the EOB and a check, you must track each patient's account. Many billing services do this by arranging for the office staff to forward them copies of all EOBs that come in each day, so they can key in the payments and update the balances. In the case of Medicare, the local carrier for Medicare sends providers a long list showing all claims processed in the most recent batch. The list summarizes each claim, including the original fee billed, the allowable amount, the amount paid, the co-insurance, the deductible (if any), and the required write-off. This is called a remittance notice. Figure 3-9 shows what this report looks like.

Your first step is therefore to key in all the data from the EOBs and Medicare remittance lists. This is done in the accounts receivable module that your full practice management software contains. You begin by looking up each patient's record and keying in the amount paid based on the EOB or the Medicare remittance notice. Most medical billing software automates a portion of this record keeping function, such as calculating the 20% co-insurance payment and the write-off once you enter the amount paid. Chapter 7 explains how MedOffice records insurance receivables in detail.

Many industry experts expect that electronic funds transfer of claims payments from insurance companies right into a provider's bank account will soon become standard. If so, this improvement may substantially automate the posting of payments and write-offs. You may not even need to

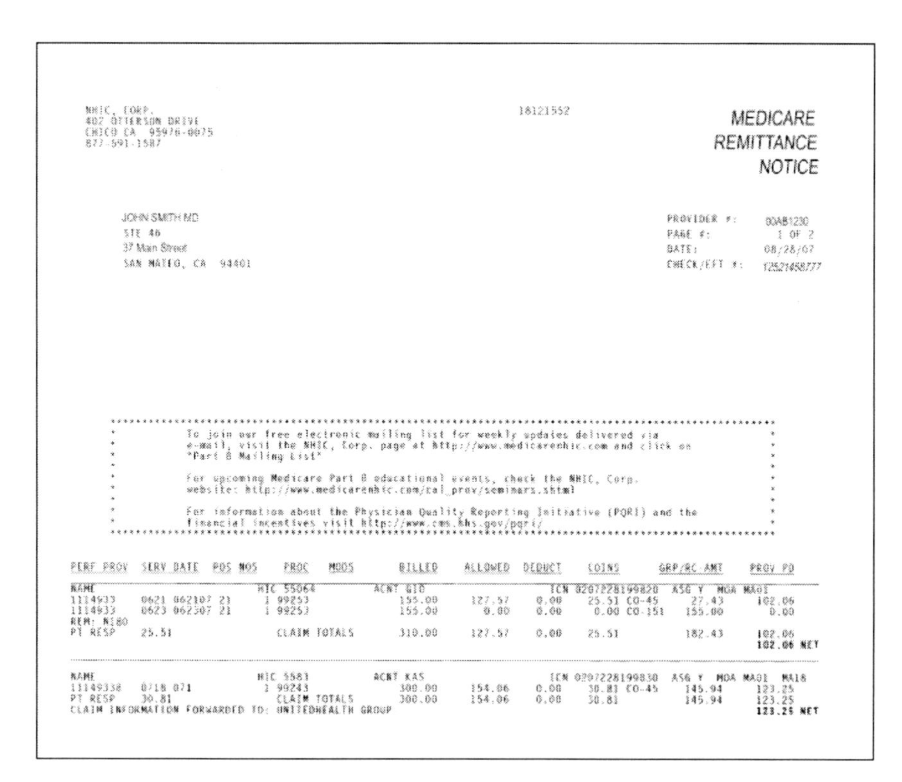

NHIC, CORP.
402 OTTERSON DRIVE
CHICO CA 95976-0075
877-591-1587

18121552

MEDICARE
REMITTANCE
NOTICE

JOHN SMITH MD
STE 46
37 Main Street
SAN MATEO, CA 94401

PROVIDER #: 00AB1230
PAGE #: 1 OF 2
DATE: 08/28/07
CHECK/EFT #: 12521458777

To join our free electronic mailing list for weekly updates delivered via e-mail, visit the NHIC, Corp. page at http://www.medicarenhic.com and click on "Part B Mailing List"

For upcoming Medicare Part B educational events, check the NHIC, Corp. website: http://www.medicarenhic.com/cal_prov/seminars.shtml

For information about the Physician Quality Reporting Initiative (PQRI) and the financial incentives visit http://www.cms.hhs.gov/pqri/

PERF PROV	SERV DATE	POS NOS	PROC	MODS	BILLED	ALLOWED	DEDUCT	COINS	GRP/RC-AMT	PROV PD
NAME			HIC 55064		ACNT GID			ICN 0207228199820	ASG Y MOA MA01	
1114933	0621 062107	21	1 99253		155.00	127.57	0.00	25.51	CO-45 27.43	102.06
1114933	0623 062307	21	1 99253		155.00	0.00	0.00	0.00	CO-151 155.00	0.00
REM: N180										
PT RESP	25.51		CLAIM TOTALS		310.00	127.57	0.00	25.51	182.43	102.06
										102.06 NET
NAME			HIC 5583		ACNT KAS			ICN 0207228199830	ASG Y MOA MA01 MA18	
11149338	0718 071		1 99243		300.00	154.06	0.00	30.81	CO-45 145.94	123.25
PT RESP	30.81		CLAIM TOTALS		300.00	154.06	0.00	30.81	145.94	123.25
CLAIM INFORMATION FORWARDED TO: UNITEDHEALTH GROUP										**123.25 NET**

Figure 3-9

Medicare Remittance Notice

key in the amounts; updating the accounts receivable records will be done automatically when you log on to capture the notification of payments to your doctor's bank account.

As discussed throughout this chapter, a billing service offering complete practice management will be involved in many additional functions related to the doctor's claims and cash flow. These can include:

- Following up on rejected or underpaid claims by contacting the insurance company and filing an appeal. In some cases, such as when claims are rejected due to lack of supporting documentation, the claim can be re-filed with the correct documents. In other cases, the billing company may need to query the medical provider to fix or correct a code on the claim that caused its rejection. We will talk more about how billers file claims appeals in Chapter 7.
- Printing out monthly statements for patients showing their past payments and balances due. Most software programs make this process fast and easy. You can often add a customized comment, such as "Balance due over 60 days; please remit today."

- Preparing financial reports for doctors showing the status of their cash flow and analyzing the major factors of their business, including aged balances (showing which patients are delinquent in their payments for 30, 60, and 90 days or more), and insurance aged balances (showing which insurance companies are delinquent for 30, 60, and 90 days or more). Many doctors also like to get reports showing things like which procedures generate the most income, which clients see them most frequently, what percentage of their fees are generated from referrals, and so on. Most current state-of-the art billing software allows you to provide a variety of financial reports, as well as visual data in the form of pie charts, bar graphs, and so on.

- Advising the doctor about the correct use of diagnostic and procedure codes that determine how much reimbursement the physician receives. Many doctors code incorrectly, or unintentionally "downcode" meaning that they use a code that pays them less than they could be receiving for a service. In addition, doctors do not have the time to keep up with the changes in coding that Medicare and other insurance firms regularly implement, and in many cases, the doctor's staff also does not stay abreast of new coding requirements. The professional billing service that stays current with coding procedures can play an important role in ensuring that doctors are properly reimbursed for their services.

- As stated throughout this chapter, another important practice management function for a billing service is analyzing the doctor's practice and making recommendations to improve its profitability and cash flow, such as dropping out of certain HMOs and PPOs or joining others that pay higher fee schedules. Some billing services even become involved in preparing bids on behalf of their clients to take over the patients of a certain HMO. Most qualified billing services will prepare for their clients various financial analysis reports that compare income derived from capitated plans versus fee-for-service plans, so the provider can decide if it's worthwhile to stay a member of an insurance company's capitated plan.

As you can readily see, a professional billing service offering full practice management can alleviate many problems for a medical practice. Working hand in hand with the doctor's office staff, a knowledgeable billing service serves the interests of both the doctor and the patients. This explains why billing services are increasingly able to easily attract healthcare providers who simply can no longer keep up with the ever-changing health insurance world. A good billing company allows the doctor to be a doctor and do what he or she does best, while the billing company does what they do best!

4

A Crash Course in Coding for Medical Billers

In the last chapter, we referred to two sets of coding used by insurance companies and Medicare that act as a kind of shorthand for the doctor's diagnosis of the patient's problems and for the services provided. These coding systems are critical to medical billing and so you have to be familiar with them. You don't need to become an expert in coding because your job as a medical biller does not involve doing coding yourself. But you need to know the ins and outs of coding so you can be helpful to your clients should they make mistakes in their coding or if they are not as familiar with it as you.

In fact, many medical billers learn enough about coding that they can sell a coding review to their clients. In a coding review, they help their doctors improve their coding choices in order to receive better insurance reimbursements.

Let's do a brief review of the two coding systems used in insurance billing and then come back to talking about how you can learn to sell a coding review.

All about Diagnosis Codes (ICD)

Through much of the 20th century, the healthcare and insurance industry used long handwritten notations to indicate a patient's symptoms and diagnosis. However, in 1988, the Medicare Catastrophic Coverage Act implemented a coding system known as the ICD, which stands for the International Classification of Diseases.

Note: the ICD codes are currently in their 9th Revision, and are sometimes called the ICD-9. The next version of the codes, ICD-10 is available, but has not yet been mandated to become the official coding system that doctors must use. When the 10th revision becomes official, there will be a two-year phase-in period, so the ICD-9 will be around for several more years. This book therefore refers simply to the ICD-9 codes, since the transition may begin to occur some time in the near future.

The coding system was originally set up by the World Health Organization to help with statistical record keeping of diseases, though the first set of codes was actually adapted for use in the United States. The World Health organization produces a major update of the codes every ten years, but Medicare (CMS) and the US. Public Health Service issue annual changes and addenda. The ICD-9 codes are most often printed in two volumes.

- **Volume 1** is a numerical list of codes beginning with 001.0 and extending through 999.9, along with some additional codes such as the "V" codes for vaccinations and certain types of exams and treatments, and a section of "E" codes that indicate the causes of external injuries such as traffic and boating accidents. Most codes are either 3, 4, or 5 digits; the larger the number of digits, the more specific the code is about the diagnosis.
- **Volume 2** is an alphabetic listing of diseases.

As you might expect, the diagnosis codes greatly facilitate the automation of insurance claims because computers can read the codes and match them to common and expected procedures and fee schedules. If a medical provider lists a diagnosis code with a procedure that does not match the diagnosis, the insurer can automatically kick out the claim and return it to the sender for an error.

As a result, doctors must follow very strict requirements in their coding. One of the most rigorous rules is that the healthcare provider must use the most specific level of coding possible, most often a 4- or 5-digit code rather than a 3-digit code. As the ICD-9 code book states:

> "claims submitted with three- or four- digit codes where four- and five-digit codes are available may be returned to you [...] for proper coding. It is recognized that a very specific diagnosis may not be known at the time of the initial encounter. However, that is not an acceptable reason to submit a three digit code when four or five digits are available."

Healthcare professionals should also not use a broad-based generic codes based on probable, suspected, or questionable diagnoses. (In the past, this was called a Rule-Out, but it caused problems because billers would often accidentally bill for the code that the doctor was ruling out.) So if the physician does not know the diagnosis, he or she is required to use a code that represents a description of the symptoms or a "family history of" classification. Insurers also require that the first code on the claim form should be the patient's primary diagnosis, that no more than four diagnosis codes are used for any one line item (representing a specific procedure) on the claim form, and that certain codes are used to indicate the late effects of a no-longer acute situation. There are also standard codes to indicate where the medical service was performed, the frequency of the service, and the level of services provided.

All about Procedures Codes (CPT)

The procedure coding system is related to diagnosis codes in that these codes represent the services performed by the healthcare provider. In other words, the procedure codes are what the doctor does, whereas the diagnosis codes are what is wrong with the patient.

Throughout much of the 20th century, there were more than 120 different procedure coding systems in the US because nearly every insurance company had its own set of codes. This was one reason why doctors often had patients submit their own claims; back then, it was simply too much for them to keep track of all the codes.

Around 1983, Medicare adopted a specific coding system based on recommendations from the American Medical Association (AMA). The AMA coding system is now used by all healthcare providers. Just as with the diagnosis codes, this system is fairly complex and rigorous in its usage requirements.

The system is divided into three levels of codes. The top level is the most utilized of the three levels. Called the CPT-4, which stands for Current Procedural Terminology, Fourth Edition, it lists literally thousands of codes representing services performed by medical personnel of all kinds. The AMA updates the CPT codes at least once per year to account for new procedures. Many billers buy a new book once per year and subscribe to a service that provides them with the new codes during the year.

The main portion of the CPT codes is divided into six sections, with each one representing a broad field of medicine and containing hundreds of specific procedures, each with a unique five-digit *numeric* code. An overview of these six sections is shown here:

Evaluation and Management Codes	99200 to 99499
Anesthesiology Codes	00100 to 01999
Surgery Codes	10000 to 69999
Radiology, Nuclear Medicine, and Diagnostic Ultrasound Codes	70000 to 79999
Pathology and Laboratory Codes	80000 to 89999
Medicine Codes	90000 to 99199

Healthcare providers seldom use more than a few dozen of these codes because they specialize in just one or two fields of medicine. The average doctor may work with only about 100 CPT codes on a regular basis and those are the ones they pre-print on their standard encounter form. For example, a chiropractor may use only about a dozen codes, while a pediatrician or family practice may use hundreds.

Using the procedural codes is fairly straightforward, but as a biller, you need to be aware of a few coding issues that are critical for doctors to code correctly. The most important one of these is the use of modifiers, which are two-digit supplemental codes added to the CPT codes for certain types of procedures and services such as special prolonged time with a patient, concurrent care (more than one doctor attending), or repetitive services for chronic condition. Using the right modifiers can add to a doctor's income because insurers sometimes pay a higher fee for some services, and conversely using the wrong modifier can cause the claim to be completely rejected. So it's important that you learn as much as you can about procedure coding, because it can significantly increase the perception of your expertise as a professional medical biller.

Level II and III Procedure Codes

As mentioned, the CPT codes are the top level procedural coding, and below them are two additional sets of codes. Those two sets of codes are collectively referred to as the HCPCS (pronounced HicPics) codes, an acronym that stands for **H**CFA **C**ommon **P**rocedure **C**oding **S**ystem.

The Level II codes are used to bill insurers for certain types of items not listed in the CPT codes, including some medical supplies. The Level II codes were created because the CPT codes had only a few dozen codes used for billing supplies; as a result, there are actually thousands of codes in the Level II book for supplies like gauze pads and syringes, as well as drugs, injections, and durable medical equipment (DME) sold or rented to patients. All these items must be coded for insurance reimbursement. The Level II codes use 5-digits and are alphanumeric, ranging from A0000 to V5999. Here is a list of Level II codes:

Transportation Services A0000-A0999
Chiropractic Services A2000
Medical & Surgical Supplies .A4000-A5500
Miscellaneous & Experimental A9000-A9300
Enteral & Parenteral Therapy B4000-B9999
Dental Procedures. D0000-D9999
Durable Medical Equipment (DME) E0000-E1830
G Codes for Procedures G0001-G0062
Drugs Administered Other Than Oral Method J0000-J8999
Chemotherapy. J9000-J9999
Orthotic Supplies L0000-L4999
Prosthetic Supplies L5000-L9999
Medical Services M0000-M9999
Pathology & Laboratory. P0000-P9999
Temporary Codes Q0000-Q9999
Diagnostic Radiology R0000-R5999
Vision Services. V0000-V2799
Hearing Services V5000-V5900

The codes are revised each year with hundreds of additions, deletions, and changes. This means that billers must usually purchase a new edition of the HCPCS book and stay abreast of various Medicare bulletins and books on coding changes.

The third level of procedure coding is called the HCPCS Local Level 3. These codes are alphanumeric, ranging from W0000 to Z0000, and they are created by the local Medicare office in each state and can vary. Local codes are used to describe new procedures that one Medicare office may recognize. Local codes are seldom used because of standardization of coding.

A billing service that knows coding has a significant advantage in the market. Be sure you stay up to date with Medicare especially. The agency is an ever-changing operation, and its need to control costs results in more and more documentation to justify medical procedures. A billing service must therefore maintain an ongoing knowledge of Medicare, not just learn it once. As you operate your business, be sure to read the Medicare bulletins, and attend the Medicare and Medicaid conferences.

Dental Codes

Dental treatment uses a set of dental codes similar to those used in the CPT. These codes go from D0000 to D9000, and are called the *Code on Dental Procedures and Nomenclature.* Any claim submitted on a standard paper or electronic dental claim form must use these dental procedure codes. The current version of the Dental Code has been in effect since January 1, 2007. You can find this code in the ADA publication entitled *CDT-2007/2008.* Here is an example of the dental codes.

D0110 - INITIAL ORAL EXAM
D0111 - EXAM & PREPRATION
D0112 - INITIAL EXAM PERIO
D0120 - PERIODIC ORAL EXAM
D0125 - ORAL EXAM BY ORAL SURGEON
D0130 - EMERGENCY ORAL EXAM
D0120 - LIMITED ORAL EXAM
D0150 - COMPREHENSIVE EXAM
D0160 - EXTENSIVE ORAL EVALUATION
D0210 - COMPLETE SERIES X-RAYS
D0220 - PERIAPICAL-FIRST FILM
D0222 - PERIAPICAL-TWO FILMS
D1110 - PROPHYLAXIS-ADULT
D1111 - ADULT PROPHY AND SCALING
D1112 - PROPHYLAXIS-CHILD
D1201 - TOPICAL FLUORIDE & PROPHY-CHILD
D1202 - TOPICAL FLUORIDE & PROPHY-ADULT
D2110 - AMALGAM-ONE SURFACE, PRIMARY
D2120 - AMALGAM-TWO SURFACES, PRIMARY
D2160 - AMALGAM-THREE SURFACE
D2161 - AMALGAM-FOUR OR MORE SURFACES
D2510 - GOLD INLAY-ONE SURFACE
D2520 - GOLD INLAY-TWO SURFACES
D2540 - ONLAY-METAL, PER TOOTH
D2542 - METALIC ONLAY - TWO SURFACES
D2543 - ONLAY, METALLIC - THREE SURFACES
D3110 - PULP CAP-DIRECT
D3120 - PULP CAP-INDIRECT

How Much Should You Know about Coding?

As I've stated, your role as the billing service is not to do any coding on behalf of your clients. Only healthcare professionals and certified coders can code patient encounters.

But you do need to know enough about codes to enhance your professionalism because potential clients will immediately believe that you don't understand their business if you are not familiar with their coding. Some doctors may even ask you about their coding when you first market to them and go for an interview. This means that before you walk into a potential client's office, you should always become familiar with the types of codes they commonly use.

This is not to say that you need to memorize the codes, but initially, it is well worth your time to study the codes that go with the specializations you intend to cover. For example, if you are going to specialize in chiropractors, pediatricians, or neurology doctors, we advise you to look at typical encounter forms from those professions as you prepare to launch your business. Learn the common diagnostic and procedure codes that your clients use and look up the codes so you know what they are.

Are You Allowed to Change Codes When You File Claims?

This question comes up a lot among new billers. What if you find a code that you think has been done incorrectly? What should you do?

The answer, call the provider's office and discuss the coding. Never attempt to change any coding yourself from the encounter form to the claim; this could open you up to a malpractice suit. However, go ahead and discuss any coding issues you recognize with your clients and offer whatever advice you can to help them do better coding. Let them make the final decision though.

If your client agrees to any coding change you've recommended, be sure to obtain the change in writing and keep it as a record in your system.

How to Sell a Coding and Superbill Review to Clients and Potential Clients

Over time, you will actually come to know by heart most of the codes you frequently work with simply because you will key them time and time again for your clients. And with further study, many billing services learn coding so well that they often become coding consultants for their clients.

Once a year, for a fee, they review their client's encounter form, checking all the codes in use to ensure that they are up to date in order to maximize the billing reimbursements. Some codes are paid higher than others, as you will learn over time.

You can charge a fee for this service if your review is extensive, but many billers simply offer it as a courtesy to their clients and as a way to keep their contract year after year. Some billers also use the coding review as a marketing technique to get in the door of a potential client, by offering a "free" review with every appointment.

The importance of this service is more powerful than you may think. Physicians often don't know much about coding or how to maximize their reimbursement. Magazines for doctors constantly have articles offering advice about better coding. For example, in an article in the February 2006 issue of Physicians Practice, a magazine aimed at educating doctors to improve their own practice management, doctors are advised to stop relying on their superbill so much. The article points out that many physicians completely overlook reimbursement opportunities for the following reasons:

- They perform procedures on patients that are not even listed on the superbill and then fail to bill for them.
- They rely on circling one code rather than adding additional codes when multiple services were provided.
- They close themselves off to having their billers ask questions about incomplete coding.
- They overlook the use of modifiers that could help them receive greater reimbursements.
- They fail to update their superbill annually with new CPT and ICD codes.
- They use add-on codes incompletely by failing to bill for multiple services.
- They use the wrong modifiers that cause multiple procedures to be paid at less than full. They don't fight insurance companies who routinely deny payment for separate procedures.
- They undervalue their time and code incorrectly for time spent counseling patients.

As a professional medical billing service, you can provide a potentially very cost-effective review of a doctor's superbill and coding practices to show them where they are incorrectly coding and losing income. Of course, this means that you need to know the proper coding and be familiar with the types of situations where insurance companies will attempt to downgrade or deny coding. For this reason, begin making efforts to improve your knowledge of coding. If you work with ClaimTek, we can help you learn how to do a professional coding and superbill review.

For Those Who Want to Solidify Their Knowledge and Advance Beyond the Basics

As you've been reading the last few chapters about health insurance, the daily operation of a medical office, and all the coding information, you may feel that you'd like to learn a lot more about the medical business. It's a fascinating field and we agree that the more you know, the more valuable you can be to your clients. The more you know, the more earning power you have too.

We're not saying that you have to go out and read dozens of other books or take courses, but if you are inclined to do so, here are some ideas.

Medical Billing Courses. Many community college and adult education schools have courses or workshops in medical billing and coding. In some cases, these courses are intended to train people who want to work in the front office of a physician's practice, but other courses are specifically targeted to entrepreneurs. If you enjoy a classroom atmosphere, this type of training may be for you. These courses are usually inexpensive, but they are typically quite limited in scope. If you are eager to get your business underway, taking college courses one at a time may prolong the amount of time it takes to learn what you need to know. Shy away from most Internet-based courses because there are several unqualified companies that offer automated online training. Such courses often use a simple training manual broken into segments, each followed by a quiz. Despite the certificate you may receive, such courses are shallow and will usually fail to provide you with the deep training you need to succeed.

Coding Courses. You might want to take a coding class at your local college. You can usually find a course that lasts a half-day on Saturdays. A coding course will help you become familiar with procedure and diagnosis coding. While you don't need this to start a medical billing business, knowing coding will set you apart from others. Some of you might also be interested in becoming an accredited professional coder. Coders work in hospitals, universities, and clinics. These jobs are usually full-time, but you might run a medical billing business on the side.

Books. Dozens of books are around to teach you more about practice management and coding. Find a medical bookstore in your city where you can purchase coding manuals and other reference books. The ICD-9 code book is available from the US. Government Printing Office and the CPT code book can be purchased directly from the American Medical Association. You can also obtain both these books from various private publishing companies which republish them under license in special easy-to-use formats intended for medical offices. One such publisher is Ingenix (www.ingenixonline.com or call 800-464-3649). Another generalized book you may wish to read is *Understanding Medical Insurance: A Step-by-Step Guide* by JoAnn C. Rowell.

Intern at a Doctors' Office. If you're taking classes at a college on medical billing, try to arrange an internship where you can go into a medical office or a billing company and work for a while learning the business. Internships average about 160 hours. This is not a paid position, but you can learn a huge amount by doing this.

5

Setting Up Your Business and Getting Ready

Now that you've learned about health insurance, coding, and the procedures used in medical offices, let's take a look at the tasks you must begin accomplishing in order to launch your business. Like any business, there are quite a few preliminaries that you have to get out of the way. Here's a short list of what you must take care of at this time:

- Choose your medical billing / practice management software or buy a business opportunity that helps you get started professionally
- Name your business
- Decide on a business structure, file your DBA, and get any business licenses required
- Brand your business with a great logo, business cards, and stationery
- Set up your office
- Purchase a computer (if you don't have one)
- Buy office supplies
- Create a web site

This chapter will help you through all these important business steps. In general, these are easy things to get accomplished, but they take time and thinking. Many of them are not actions you can just go out and get done in a day. Allow yourself a month or more to get all of these done. If you are uncertain or confused about doing any of these, ClaimTek can help you.

Choose Your Medical Billing Software or Buy a Business Opportunity Package

This decision is the first one you need to make. Why do we recommend this? Because it really helps to know which medical practice management or billing software you are going to use – or if you prefer to buy a business package from a company – before you do any of the other steps listed in this chapter! Here's why.

If you are going to buy medical practice management software on your own, you want to test out various software products and make sure you are comfortable *working* with one. Researching this type of software and reviewing demo copies will help you assess much more realistically whether this is the right business for you. You will also learn a lot more about the business by talking with software companies.

For many of you, you might prefer to buy an entire business opportunity package that includes the software, training, marketing, and support. As stated in our Introduction, we would be pleased if you work with *ClaimTek Systems*, which offers three different programs for entrepreneurs seeking a complete turn-key operation, including software, professional training, marketing materials, and tremendous support in order to get into business. Naturally, we are biased that ClaimTek offers you the best business program you can find anywhere. Our software, *MedOffice*®, is the most advanced and easiest-to-use full medical practice management on the market. We invite you to visit www.claimtek.com to evaluate the numerous benefits of our business opportunity programs and to request a demo copy of our software. If you are exploring other business opportunity companies, contact us and we will be happy to explain how our program compares to others.

Should You Buy Software Only?

If you already have extensive knowledge of medical office operations and practice management, you may feel comfortable purchasing just a medical billing and practice management software program rather than a full business opportunity package. That decision is up to you and has worked for some people with a professional background as a medical insurance specialist in the medical field.

If you are in this category, the question is, what software should you buy? There is no single answer to this question. Each medical software program has its unique design that creates both advantages and disadvantages for a business. In addition, software is an ever-changing product, with producers adding new features from time to time, so reviewing a software program in a book like this would be out of date rapidly.

Again, we hope you will visit www.claimtek.com to learn about *MedOffice* if you are interested in just the software. ClaimTek spent years developing *MedOffice*, our premier practice management software, with numerous advanced features that make it easy to learn, easy to use, and very versatile for medical billing and practice management.

If you look at other software programs, here are some general guidelines about what to look for:

- True billing service capability. Because you'll probably want to do full practice management for many medical offices, you need to be sure your software has true billing capability so you can manage multiple practices. Some software programs are intended to handle a single practice only and are not appropriate for a professional billing service.

- Claims only vs. Practice Management Software. Some software programs allow you to submit electronic claims, but don't contain all the operations you need to do full practice management, including patient records, claims filing, accounts receivable, patient statements, point-of-service inventory and sales capability, clearinghouse set up, unlimited number of practices, and many others.

- Ability to handle all types of claims. Be sure your software can record and file claims not just for common medical providers on standard CMS 1500 forms, but also for all those providers whose claims filing has special needs such as chiropractors, podiatrists, durable medical equipment, and ambulance services. Your software should also give you the capability of filing the CMS 1450 (UB) form used by hospitals and several other types of health care facilities.

- Line item accounting. Because Medicare and other insurers sometimes pay only some of the CPT codes on a claim, or just a portion of them, you must be able to record payments and link them to the specific line item charges billed. That way, if you need to question a denied claim, or bill the patient for the difference, you can tell which specific charges were paid vs. not paid. You must also be able to write off and make adjustments on unpaid portions, which requires line item accounting for accuracy.

- Multiple fee schedules. With the growth of managed care plans such as PPOs and HMOs, doctors increasingly need to have multiple fee schedules. They are required to accept one set of fees for Medicare patients, another set of fees for patients under a certain PPO plan, and yet another set of fees under a different PPO plan. This means that your software should be able to store many fee schedules. The software should also be able to handle capitated plans because you need to log reimbursements for these differently.
- Pop up windows for common data sets. Some sets of data, such as insurance companies, procedure and diagnostic codes, and fees are annoying to have to retype over and over again. To facilitate this, be sure your software product has pop-up windows that make it easy for you to point and click on items you want instead of typing them every time.
- Clearinghouse flexibility. Does the software allow you to work with several clearinghouses of your choice, or are you forced to use the clearinghouse required by the software vendor?
- Multiple ways to enter data. Since people have their own preferences when it comes to entering data. Some prefer to use the keyboard, others to click on icons to access the various parts of the software, and others love using the Tab key to go from field to field, while others prefer to use the mouse. It helps if your software offers many methods of entering data.
- Reports. One of the critical features of a quality practice management software is that it offers many types of reports for clients and that these can be customized. For example, one of your clients may want a simple printout report, while another may prefer graphics such as pie charts and bar graphs. In addition, your clients often have different needs in practice management in terms of the frequency of the reports. You may have one doctor who wants a report once per week, while another doctor wants reports once per month. Thus, you should make sure your software offers many kinds of reports, printed in different styles, and easy to produce without a lot of effort.
- Demo copy. Be sure you can get an up-to-date demo copy of any software you are interested in purchasing.

Your decision in choosing a medical billing business opportunity company or just the software is an important one – and worth taking some time researching. Let us say that we wouldn't write this book if we did not believe that ClaimTek's software, MedOffice, and business opportunity are not the best you can choose for your business. We have been in business since 1993 and have invested many years developing our MedOffice software. We have built our business opportunity programs to offer the most comprehensive and long-lasting support on the market, because we know this business inside and out and are committed to helping readers like you succeed.

Should You Choose a Web-based Medical Billing Software Application?

As you search for medical billing and practice management software, you'll find several companies aggressively promoting a web-based application. They may call it an "ASP" application, but if it requires a browser to run, it is actually web-based. ASP stands for Application Server Provider, and usually refers to running an application remotely on a server, not using a web browser.

As this can be confusing for the average user, we would like to explain the three methods that software applications in this business can be accessed.

- The application is installed locally on your computer or on your local network.
- The application is installed on a server and you access it remotely via Direct Connection to the Application Service Provider site (ASP). This is called a server-based ASP.
- The application is web-based accessed via a browser at an Application Service Provider site (ASP). This is called a browser-based ASP.

What makes the difference between a server-based ASP versus a web-based ASP is that server-based ASP applications run just as if they were on your local computer while web-based ASP applications are limited because they must be accessed using a web browser. The browser thereby limits what you can do with the application, just like it limits what you can do with any Internet site. We'll give some examples below of such limitations.

But the point to remember is that MedOffice can run either locally on your computer, just like any software product or we can run it on our server as an ASP application for you. Our competitors offer web-based ASP applications, which have many disadvantages that we will detail. Here is a list of why web-based systems are not as useful as desktop software or formal ASP operations, despite the claims of other vendors.

1. **Web-based applications offer a limited user interface (UI) and screen access.** In a busy billing service, it is essential that you are able to open several screens at once so you can "multi-task" (i.e. run a report while posting payments, looking up a patient chart while entering a claim, etc.). For example, you might be working away entering new patients when you receive a call from an insurance company in response to an inquiry you placed earlier. You need the ability to jump to different screens at the same time to look up the information without interrupting your existing work flow. Most medical billers are used to keyboarding fast and jumping between screens. The problem is, this functionality is eliminated when you are working on a web-based ASP application. In contrast, desktop or server-based ASP applications like ClaimTek's MedOffice provide you with the rich user-interface that allows you to access many parts of the system simultaneously and quickly.

2. **Web-based applications lack versatile billing functionality.** The majority of web-based applications can do billing only on the CMS-1500 insurance form. But as a professional billing service, it is critical that you be capable of doing billing for all or most specialties, even those that require other insurance forms, like the new CMS-1450, also called the UB-04 or the Medicare "Part A" form for hospital claims. (This form was formerly called the UB-92 until 2007 when a new version was phased in. This form is also used for mental health, home health, and some types of physical therapy.) Your software should also be able to handle DME (Durable Medical Equipment) and dental billing, as well as a host of specialties. This factor is important to keep in mind when deciding on your software purchase. When you are starting up your business, it is unlikely you can predict what medical specialties you may sign up or what types of clients you may be referred to. If your software has limited capabilities, you will be restricted in the scope of services you can offer. To maximize your chances of success, you need to be able to handle comprehensive services. For example, if you do not have a fully capable system, but happen to get a referral from an existing client for a specialty in need of expanded billing functionality, you'll end up turning away a potential client and miss out on a new revenue

opportunity. You're in business to satisfy needs and make money! You need to be ready to accept all clients.

3. **Web-based applications lack performance and speed.** Web-based applications can be affected by many factors beyond your control that result in slow data entry or interruptions, such as a lost Internet connection from your ISP (Internet Service Provider), or slow traffic on the Internet. If the system goes down, you have no choice but to wait until the hosting company fixes the problem. A great deal of your business reputation and success lies in the hands of others.

4. **Web-based applications can lack security.** While security on the web is becoming more enhanced, news reports still come out from time to time about serious security breaches among major institutions including the big banks! Information on the web is simply not as secure as it needs to be. Even if you do not mind the possible security issues yourself, you'll find that many of your potential doctor-clients will object to your service being web-based, and that means you can lose potential customers.

5. **Web-based applications lack local data backups.** With web-based applications, you do not have control of your data. While the hosting company may have backup measures in place, you cannot backup anytime you want or have the data in your own local possession. And if the company suddenly goes out of business, what happens to your data? The best a company can do is to provide you with your data in raw format on CD (usually for a price). But what will you do with it? How can you convert it to another system? This is an area of deep dark waters.

6. **Web-based applications often have on-going fees & restricted options for claims and patient statement processing.** Web-based applications typically process claims and patient statements through their own channels and charge you per transaction fees. This is how they make their money. It is a good business model for them, but this factor restricts your ability to choose a different clearinghouse if you do not like their service. To our knowledge, some competitors charge 75 cents per transaction! With ClaimTek's MedOffice software, you can submit your claims to any clearinghouse you decide to work with. We recommend several clearinghouses, and you are free to choose any other clearinghouse you want. Also, the clearinghouse fees for a web-based company may go up, and you'll be forced to pay it because

your web-based application is tied into them. Without choices, you're not in control of your business. Remember, you'll be in this relationship for the long haul. You need independence, flexibility, and control as you grow your business. Isn't this one of the main reasons you wanted to start your own business anyway?

7. **You may incur additional fees as you expand your business.** With web-based applications, you'll incur additional costs as you add new clients and create new accounts (databases) to your growing business. Our MedOffice software allows you to create multiple databases at no charge, so you can grow your business without worry.

8. **Web-based applications have very limited customizability.** Many necessary functions may not be customizable in web-based applications (i.e. custom patient statements, custom reports, data import and export, data-transfer from one database to another or exporting reports in several formats to PDF, Excel, Access, RTF, etc.). Our MedOffice system gives you full control to customize many aspects of your business according to what your clients want.

9. **Web-based applications are difficult to integrate with other applications.** Most web-based applications do not allow integration with other systems like QuickBooks for accounting, Outlook for e-mail, or Electronic Medical Records (EMR) like Medinotes or others. All of these enhanced functions are available in our MedOffice software!

10. **Web-based systems do not offer lucrative software resale opportunity.** Selling software like MedOffice to doctors who insist on handling their own billing can be a valuable ancillary to your own practice management and billing services. Remember that you are trying to build relationships with healthcare providers. Selling software as an option helps you in that regard. This way you maintain a professional business relationship with your client. Besides being a lucrative area, you may be able to convert such relationships down the road into billing clients. Sooner or later healthcare providers suffer from instability in the staffing area and may look to outsource. Your startup medical billing business from home or small office will naturally progress towards this stage (software sales) once you are established and have gained good working knowledge of the system and the medical industry in general. It is an option that's worth

having. Web-based systems do not offer you significant potential in this arena.

11. **Web-based applications are not technologically cost effective.** An idea promoted by web-based medical billing vendors that web-based applications save you the cost of hardware upgrades and maintenance may seem appealing at first. But if you study this in depth, you'll realize that web-based applications are simply not as robust as they need to be. In contrast, ClaimTek is keeping up with the latest technologies and plans to offer a robust web-based option only when it is up to the standards that it needs to be. Additionally, hardware today, while highly reliable, is not a major investment factor anymore. Great computers today cost only a few hundred dollars! Advanced desktop-based and client/server applications like *MedOffice* offer better technological solutions and more robust, feature-rich, versatile functionality for medical billing services.

    If you need the flexibility of remote access, however, MedOffice is available online as a server-based ASP application, which is not the same at all as a web-based application. In this type of ASP, the full functionality of the software is available, but it simply runs off of a server. It does not require a web-browser or HTML to work. Instead, using our dedicated servers, you can run MedOffice as a "service" accessible via the Internet from any computer in the world! We can arrange remote access for you and your doctor-clients giving you full program accessibility, versatility and control. In essence, this gives you the best of both worlds; you can have MedOffice installed on your computer, or you can access it as a hosted application.

In short, you must consider the drawbacks and shortcomings of web-based ASP applications. We believe that our MedOffice system offers more secure ways to file claims while keeping you in complete control of your data. Web-based applications may work well for basic functionality, but for a busy, growing medical billing service, they just do not cut it today!

The table below compares the three options of accessing software – as a local application, or a remote running as an ASP, or as a web-based application – and summarizes the points made above.

	Local Application (Installed on your Desktop/Laptop)	**Remote Application Accessed via Direct Connection to an Application Service Provider site (ASP)**	**Web-based Application (Browser-based ASP)**
Who Offers?	MedOffice	MedOffice	Some of our competitors
Technology	Native - resides on your desktop	**Native – resides remotely on a server and accessed via the Internet** (all the benefits of a desktop without installing it on your machine)	Based on HTTP / HTML displayed inside a web browser
User Experience	**RICH** Running software on your desktop or laptop offers the highest quality user experience and speed	**RICH** Running software via an ASP connection simulates the complete user experience as if you were running the software on your own machine. You can open multiple screens and are not limited to a specific page flow.	**POOR** You are limited to the quality of web browsers and web technology, so the application is not as rich as a full software experience. For example, you are limited to viewing one screen a time, you are tied to one-page-at-a-time flow, and you can lose transactions if you mistakenly hit the back button or your computer locks up.
Accessibility	**Local or Remote** Software is stored on your desktop or laptop. You usually work on it locally, but you can also access it remotely using any desktop connection or communication software such as GoToMyPC or PCAnywhere, etc.	**Remotely via an Internet connection** You access the software via a direct Internet connection. Note that this is not the same as accessing a web site.	**Remotely via a specific website** Must be accessed through an Internet browser to a specific website.
Backup	**YES** You back up your own data.	**YES** Company backs up your data.	**YES, BUT...** Company back ups your data. Applications cannot be run locally.

	Local Application (Installed on your Desktop/Laptop)	**Remote Application Accessed via Direct Connection to an Application Service Provider site (ASP)**	**Web-based Application (Browser-based ASP)**
Who Offers?	MedOffice	MedOffice	Some of our competitors
Multi-tasking	**YES** You have full control over application, allowing for unlimited multi-tasking (such as opening more than one window at a time)	**YES** You have full control over application, allowing for unlimited multi-tasking (such as opening more than one window at a time)	**NO** You do NOT have control over multi-tasking, so you can open only one screen at a time.
Portability	**YES** You can move your data to a new machine at any time.	**YES** If you choose to run the application locally someday, you can move your data to your local computer	**NO** If someday you wish to move your business to your own computer, your data cannot be easily converted to a local application.
Customizability	**YES** You can customize the application in many ways.	**YES** You can customize the application in many ways.	**DIFFICULT** You cannot easily customize the application.
Integration with other applications	**YES** You can integrate MedOffice with many other applications such as QuickBooks.	**YES** You can integrate MedOffice with many other applications such as QuickBooks.	**NO** Web-based applications do not allow integration with other systems like QuickBooks for accounting, Outlook for email or Electronic Medical Records (EMR).
Program Updates	**YES** Updates downloaded to your computer.	**YES** Company performs updates.	**YES** Company performs updates.
Clearinghouse	**MANY** You can use multiple clearinghouses.	**MANY** You can use multiple clearinghouses.	**ONE** You usually have only one choice of clearinghouse.
Costs	**One time cost** Possible periodic costs for upgrades and support.	**Monthly cost** Includes upgrades and support fees.	**Monthly cost** Includes upgrades and support fees.

Naming Your Business: What Do You Want to Present to the World?

Naming a new business is never easy. A lot of people agonize over their business name for weeks and months. There's a sense that this is your first really important business decision – and that's absolutely right!

A good business name helps distinguish your company from the competition. A cool, attractive-sounding, and memorable name draws in potential clients, while a bad business name seems to turn people off.

Given this, please don't rush into naming your medical billing business. Give it time and thought. Come up with a variety of possible names and ask people around you. Get opinions. Visualize yourself telling others, "Hello, I'm so and so and my company is such and such." What is the reaction you get when you say the name? Do you picture yourself heartily shaking hands and the other person nodding their head with curiosity and interest? Or do you see yourself cringing as the person says to you two or three times, "What did you say the name of your company was?"

As you consider possible business names, think about the nature of the services you intend to offer and aim to have your business name reflect your strengths. For instance, you might name your business according to one of the following parameters:

- The quality of your service – "Reliable Medical Billing"
- Your Location – "[name of your town] Medical Billing"
- The Types of Services You offer – "Johnson Practice Management and Medical Consulting"
- A personalized approach – "Neighborhood Medical Practice Management"

These examples are meant only to demonstrate the variety of meanings your business name can suggest, so don't simply choose one of these above. Give your name some thought, and exercise your own creativity and professionalism in finding your company name.

Also make sure people understand what your company does from its name. This means that it helps to recognize that you will likely do full practice management and to name your company as though you were going to do only claims can be a mistake.

Another criterion to consider when you name your business is the number of words you use. It is recommended not to use more than four words; otherwise it's simply too long. Also, some day, you may decide to sell your business, so if you are using your personal name, it may be harder to sell.

As you come up with ideas for your business name, be sure not to infringe on a name already in use or trademarked in your area. The worst decision you can make is to select a name and print your business cards, stationery, and brochures, and then find out that the name is already in use. This is a costly error.

To investigate if your desired name is in use, first look in the phone book and Yellow Pages, checking for names that are exact duplicates or similar. But you don't want to stop there, as not all companies advertise in the Yellow Pages. Go to your county clerk's office, or to the Internet and check out your city or county's web site (most cities and counties now maintain a web site for businesses to check registration, licenses, and tax regulations). Such web sites often allow business owners to research a database of already registered business names. If you find the same business name on the database, you will need to select a different name. Don't risk using the same one just because it's located elsewhere. If the name is used in your county, you need a different name.

However, if you search your entire state and discover that your selected business name is used in another county, you still may be able to use it as long as the owner has not registered it in your county. But this can backfire on you. If your business grows and your name is eventually used on a statewide basis, you won't be able to incorporate your business because the name is already used in another county. The best action then might be to incorporate immediately using the name you want. Consult a trademark lawyer if you have questions about using a name that another business is already using and keep in mind that incorporating your business is always done at the state level, so you cannot use a business name intended only for local use.

Decide Which Business Structure Fits Your Dream

Are you thinking about staying a small home-based business and being able to process claims in your pajamas? Or are you considering growing your company into a mega-billing and practice management firm that expands across your state, if not several states? Or is your dream something in between, and you're just not sure yet?

All of these options are possible, because as a new entrepreneur in this field, the world is your oyster. You can stay small if you prefer to enter the business for extra income as a part-time job or because you want to create a full-time business while working from your home. Or you can initiate your business with the goal of expanding it to the point where you need employees to handle all the doctors you will be serving, while you go out and continue marketing and being visible in the field.

Your vision of your business influences how you set up your legal business structure. You have four main options to choose from, and in most cases, the choice is completely up to you, based on your needs. They are:

- sole proprietorship
- general partnership
- corporation
- Limited Liability Company (LLC).

Here's some basic information to help you understand these choices. But please remember, I am not a lawyer and the following descriptions are for general information only. If you have questions, speak to your own lawyer or CPA about which business structure is best for your individual situation. There are advantages and disadvantages to each structure when it comes to legal protection and taxes. Your specific circumstances play a role in determining which structure fits your needs, so obtain advice from your own professional team.

A **sole proprietorship** is perhaps the most common business legal structure used by new entrepreneurs starting out. The sole proprietorship form of business is the easiest way to get a business off the ground with the lowest costs in legal fees. In a sole proprietorship, you and you alone are the owner of your business. You are legally responsible for any and all legal issues that might arise. When it comes to taxes, you file under your own social security number (rather than using an Employer Identification Number or EIN) and your business income is reported directly to the IRS on Schedule C, Profit or Loss from Business (Sole Proprietorship). Note that owning a sole proprietorship does not mean you cannot have employees. It only refers to type of business structure under which you operate.

Starting a sole proprietorship is straightforward. If your company uses your full name as its official business name (such as Steve Johnson Medical Billing Service), you do not need to file a fictitious business name statement, also known as a "DBA" (Doing Business As). You can open your doors for business once you get any business licenses necessary in your county or state.

However, if you choose a business name that doesn't contain your personal name, you need to file a DBA with your local county, city or town, and publish that name in a local newspaper between three to five times (determined by your local laws). You can obtain the forms for filing a DBA from your local or county government office, or you can search the Internet to find those newspapers in your area that handle DBA filings for business owners. Many local newspapers offer a fixed fee package in which they will file all the paperwork for you and advertise your business name in their classified section the requisite number of times.

By the way, be prepared to receive a lot of unsolicited mail once you declare and file a DBA because many companies search county records each week to identify new businesses – and then they blast you with promotional and marketing materials. Within days of filing your DBA, you will likely receive mail from lawyers, plumbers, electricians, printers, and many other companies seeking your business.

Sole proprietorships must usually obtain a business license from their city or county. Even if you plan to work from home, some cities may require you to have a business license and pay a local business tax. (When you apply for your license, keep in mind that if you work from your home, and you do not expect to have clients coming to your house, you do not need to worry about having parking spaces available or needing to petition your local government for an exemption from any parking regulations that small businesses must sometimes have.)

Note that you may need to file for a sales tax license with your state if you intend to sell any products or if your state requires you to add tax to your services. In general, medical billers do not need to add sales tax because yours is a service business rather than a product business, but you should check with your state because some states do charge sales tax on service businesses.

A second common business structure that some entrepreneurs use is the **general partnership,** which is necessary if you are going to work with a friend or partner. (If you intend to work with your spouse, there is no need to form a partnership and it is actually better not to do so.) Partnerships are easy to form. You begin by creating a partnership agreement – and don't think that you won't need an agreement if you are working with your "best" friend. Many partners begin as friends, but business tends to take a toll on friendships. Over time, the partners can experience stress, money problems, jealousy, or unpredictable life changes that split them apart and make them no longer want to work together. A partnership agreement can prevent problems and a nasty breakup. Your agreement should spell out the responsibilities and duties of each partner, the financial split of income, and the termination options in case you decide to sever the partnership.

A partnership is also slightly more complicated than a sole proprietorship from a tax point of view. This is due to the fact that a partnership files its own tax return, indicating its profits or losses and how those are allocated percentage-wise to the partners. Each partner then files his or her own tax return, showing any "passed through" profit or loss, which then becomes part of his or her own personal income. You may wish to use an accountant for filing a partnership tax return or at least use tax software. Like sole proprietorships, partnerships also need to file a DBA as discussed above and get a license with their local or county government.

The third type of business structure is the **C corporation**. (There is also a type of corporation known as the **S Corporation**, but this becomes far more complicated and is usually reserved for businesses having many owners. If you need to know about S Corps, consult your CPA.) Many business owners decide to incorporate because it increases their credibility and appearance of professionalism.

The main disadvantages of corporations are that it costs money to incorporate and corporations are effectively taxed twice – the corporation itself pays tax on its profits and those who receive dividends from the corporations are taxed on their personal income taxes. This can be avoided by paying the owners working in the business a reasonable salary, rather than giving them dividends. The salaries are deducted from the corporate profits, thereby minimizing or completely eliminating the corporation's taxes. However, the owners must pay taxes on their salaries.

The advantage of incorporating is that it provides certain legal protections for the owners in the event of lawsuits or liabilities. In the corporate form of business, the corporation – not the owners – is responsible for business debts and liabilities incurred. If you go out of business or get sued, a creditor or plaintiff who wins a law suit against you can sue only the corporation, not the owners personally.

If you think that incorporating is right for you, do some investigating as to whether you might want to incorporate in Delaware or Nevada, two states that are known to offer tax advantages to corporations. But you may need to pay taxes in your own state if you derive income there, so check with your CPA.

The fourth type of business structure used by entrepreneurs is often considered a hybrid between the partnership form of business and the corporation. It's called the **Limited Liability Company,** or LLC for short. This form of business offers the advantages of a corporation in terms of the legal protections it provides for owners in the occurrence of a lawsuit. But tax-wise, it is more like a partnership in that profits are passed through to the owners on their own income tax returns.

Setting up an LLC or corporation takes far more effort than establishing a sole proprietorship or general partnership, but you can use many online legal services to help you form one of these types of businesses. Such legal service companies handle many of the steps that you would otherwise have to perform yourself, including:

1. Validating your business name and ensuring that it does not infringe on any other trademarked name.
2. Filing your state's paperwork, such as the "articles of incorporation" for a corporation or the "articles of organization" for an LLC.
3. Paying the filing fees, which may range from $40 to $900 depending on your state.
4. Writing the operating agreement that sets out the rights and responsibilities of the owners or directors. Even if you are the only owner, you still need to create an operating agreement.
5. Publishing the notice of your DBA if necessary.

Whichever type of legal structure you decide is right for your business, it's best to check with your CPA to confirm the advantages and disadvantages given your particular situation. It's possible of course to change legal structures, such as going from a sole proprietorship to a partnership or incorporating as a C Corp or LLC, but changes cost time and money. If you change your legal structure, you're going to need new stationery, checks, business cards, and so on. So it's better to think the decision through carefully when you first start out, projecting years ahead to where you'd like to be.

For some of you, your dream may be to start small and stay small – and there is nothing wrong with that. There's great joy in being a small home-based business where you can pick up your kids after school, file claims at night in your pajamas (or during the day in your PJs), and only dress up once in a while when you visit a client's office.

For others, you may want to test the waters by starting out as a sole proprietorship or partnership before incorporating or forming an LLC. Many entrepreneurs that I've worked with did not intend to grow large and discovered over time how easy the medical billing business could be for them. Almost unconsciously, they grew and grew, racking in more clients month by month, until one day they realized they had five clients, then seven, then 10, then 18, then 25. Many of them incorporated and hired one employee, then another, then three or five employees. Some of them have gone on to hire 10 employees and grow into fairly large enterprises.

In short, anything is possible in medical billing and practice management – and it's your dreams and efforts that will determine what you become.

Should You Hire Employees?

As long as we are on the subject of hiring employees, here's a short discussion of some pros and cons of hiring them.

If you are first starting out, it is recommended that you not waste your resources hiring any employees. After all, you either have no clients to start or perhaps you land one or two clients quickly, but you can handle the work on your own and not bother paying an employee.

However, there are advantages to hiring someone on a part-time basis as soon as you can afford to do so. One is that you will gain more freedom to spend your time marketing and building your business. Having an employee who does the data entry means that you can get out and network and follow all the suggestions we make in Chapter 6 on marketing and business building. Meanwhile, another advantage is that the employee will learn how to use the software and claims filing along with you. The value of this is that if you end up growing rapidly, you won't experience any time lag should you need to hire an employee quickly and train them when you really need them to be up and running immediately. If you can afford to do this, it can be worthwhile to begin training someone as soon as possible.

If you hire an employee, be sure to learn about your state's requirements for payroll and benefits for employees. You will need to withhold federal tax, social security, your state's tax, your state's worker's compensation program, and possibly local taxes. Check with your accountant regarding your state's payroll requirements. There are also professional payroll services that will work with small businesses having as few as one employee. These payroll services can alleviate much of the learning curve if you are thinking of hiring.

Brand Your Business with Your Logo, Business Cards, and Stationery

While you're on the subject of naming your business, this is also the time to think about your stationery and business cards. When you think about these, you must begin considering your logo, which includes two elements:

- the layout, color, and font of your business name when it is spelled out, and
- a symbol or image used to accompany the name.

Some companies don't bother with a symbol or image to accompany their business name; they just use a distinctive typeface for the design of their name, and this becomes their main logo. Think of IBM, Dell, Microsoft, and Oracle. Other companies use typography and an image in their logo. Whenever you see the company name spelled out, it always appears in the exact same font and typestyle along with an image that accompanies the spelled out name.

What's the importance of your logo?

Frankly, a great deal. The power and attractiveness of your logo has a big impact on getting potential clients to read your marketing materials. If your brochures and stationery don't indicate that you are a professional company with good taste and a high quality image, it's not likely they will give your correspondence and marketing materials much time. Materials that look unprofessional are quickly tossed.

Don't forget that one of the rules of thumb in marketing is that it takes seven impressions for your business to make an impact on a targeted potential client. That means you have to send, on average, seven pieces of literature to potential clients to get them to pay attention to you and seriously consider your services. This is, of course, an average. Some clients can be landed after the first or second letter or brochure, because your materials resonated with them and they needed your services, while other clients may not sign up with you for months and months or even years. But, on average, you will find that you have to communicate with potential clients about seven times to generate business if that client is interested.

The importance of this marketing rule is that you're better off having a great logo and company name that is memorable. Your goal is to design stationery and business cards that don't look like ordinary or run-of-the-mill mail order businesses. You don't want a doctor's office to receive materials from you that gives them a sense they are receiving mass mail from a humdrum company.

In terms of going about getting your logo, if you're good at graphics, you may be able to design it yourself. What some people do is find another quality logo and imitate it. If you use another company's logo as the basis for your own, be sure to change it extensively in color, size, shape, etc, so that the other company won't sue you for copyright infringement.

If you have no design skills, the best choice is to have your company logo designed by a professional. You can do this at a very reasonable price using any number of Internet-based graphic design shops or a local graphic artist in your town. There are design firms on the Internet that will design a corporate logo for $100-$200. You don't have to spend thousands to get a good logo. Your main criteria are that it is attractive, distinctive, memorable, and unique. And don't be afraid to use color in your logo (both the typeface and image) because color attracts the eye.

While designing your logo, keep in mind that you need different sizes. You must have one size that fits on your stationery, another size for your business cards, and another size to put on any marketing materials you send out. You might also want different sizes in JPEG or GIF format for your web site. Most design shops will give you a whole range of sizes and formats that you can use on your printed products, your business cards, your web site, in email correspondence, and so on. Be sure to get the files from your designer so you can store them on your computer and have access to them any time you need them. You will probably want color-separated versions (CMYK), as well as JPEG and GIF formats.

Concerning printing stationery and business cards, you can find numerous national printing companies on the Internet, as well as your local printers. Be sure to use quality letterhead paper, not the regular plain white laser printing paper used in everyday business. In fact, don't be afraid to use a colored paper because that often stands out more. This doesn't mean use screaming red paper or even a dark violet. A nice light blue, cream, or grey can be good. Be sure the color of your paper won't prevent type from being readable. Also, make sure whatever paper you choose is compatible with your printer. You don't want paper that won't sit flat in your laser printer.

You don't need to spend tons of money, but if you skimp, it will show. With so many printing companies available on the Internet, you can find full color bleed business cards with PMS colors on quality paper for less than $100 for 1000 cards. Some people like to place their photo on their business card so that when they walk in a client's door, there's recognition of their face.

How many sheets of stationery should you print? The answer partially depends on the extent and degree of marketing you will choose to do. We are going to discuss marketing in great detail in the next chapter, so it might be best if you hold off on making a decision right now. But here's a clue: it is probably larger than you expect. Marketing is vital in this business, so some medical billing companies print up a few thousand pieces of letterhead stationery and 3,000-5,000 business cards. But once you read the marketing chapter, you can fix your print quantities. Don't forget that you can always go back for more.

Some Important Office Supplies You Can't Live Without

While electronic claims have altered the medical billing world enormously in decreasing the amount of paper that will go across your desk, nevertheless medical practice management remains somewhat of a paper-intensive business. You can end up with paper when you receive encounter forms from your doctors and EOBs from insurers. You also handle paper if you are going to be sending out patient statements.

The point is, when you have paper around, you need a variety of office supplies to help sort, file, and store the paper. You also need things like rubber stamps to mark items and lots of other fun stuff. All this gives that sense of being in business. Besides, it's fun to go over to Office Depot, Staples, Office Max, or wherever you shop and browse the aisles for business goods.

Here's a list of some of the items you'll want to have on hand and an explanation about why.

Colored Folders. Colored folders are very useful to store paper documents from your doctors. We will explain in Chapter 7 how you can use a color-coded file system in which you assign each doctor a separate color to make it easy to identify which client you are working on at any given time. Right now, you don't know how many colors to buy since it depends on how many clients you will have. For now, you might get a box of folders of a single color to use for your first client. Then, as you add clients, you can buy boxes of different colors.

Color Highlighters. You will want to have yellow, pink, light green, and other color highlighters to use when you send out secondary claims and need to highlight information on the primary EOB that is sent as backup information with the claim.

Rubber Stamps. It is very useful to purchase a number of rubber stamps to use in stamping documents with an indication of their status. Here are some of the stamps that come in handy in a medical billing business:

- **ENTERED**. Use this stamp on encounter forms (superbills) once you have entered the data into your software. This helps you avoid being confused if you forget to file the encounter forms. By the way, if you have employees, you may want this stamp to have a small blank line next to it so that the employee can initial his or her work on the document after it's been stamped.
- **FILE.** Use this stamp to indicate a document that needs to be retained in your files.
- **CONFIDENTIAL.** Given the HIPAA privacy laws, most medical data is confidential, but you don't need to stamp every piece of paper that comes across your desk if it is not being sent out. Use this only under special circumstances: when you are mailing a document out and need to remind the recipient that the data is confidential.
- **FAXED.** Use this stamp on a document that has been faxed, so you won't be confused in case you can't recall whether it was faxed or not.
- **POSTED.** Use this stamp on EOBs to indicate that you've posted the payment to the doctor's A/R in your software.
- **BILL SECONDARY.** Use this stamp on EOBs to remind yourself that you need to bill the patient's secondary insurance company.
- **PATIENT RESPONSIBILITY.** Use this stamp on EOBs and patient statements to indicate that the patient must pay that specific portion of the payment.
- **TRACER.** Use this stamp on claims that you send to insurers when you resubmit them on paper for the second or third time. This alerts the insurer that you've already filed the claim and that this document is simply a tracer.
- **PAST DUE.** Use this stamp on patient statements when a patient has not paid and you want to give the patient a gentle reminder.
- **DATE STAMP.** Get a date stamp with changing dates so you can stamp any documents that come in from your clients. That helps you know your timing on when everything should be processed.
- **YOUR BUSINESS NAME AND ADDRESS STAMP.** In addition, get a rubber or impression stamp with your business name and address that you can use on any mailing you send out when you don't want to run an envelope through your printer. For example,

patient statements are always mailed out in window envelopes so that the patient's address shows through and you can avoid printing a mailing label. A rubber stamp helps you avoid running all the patient statements through your printer just to print your return address.

Clasp Envelopes. You will need a box of 9" x 12" clasp envelops for sending out to insurers any claims that require attached chart notes or operative reports that cannot be folded.

Window Envelopes. If you do full practice management, you will be sending statements out to your doctor's patients. This means that you absolutely want to use open window envelopes for both patients and insurance companies to which you send correspondence. An open window envelope saves you the trouble of printing labels.

HCFA Envelopes. These are small envelopes without windows that patients use to return their payments to the doctor's office or to you.

Rollaway Cart. Depending on your office space, some people purchase and use one of those three-drawer plastic rollaway carts that they move around their office as they work. The drawers come in handy to store your "work in progress" files rather than cluttering them all around your desk and trying to find them constantly. A cart also makes it easy to remove all your office clutter if you are working from home and you need to clear out your office space to use as a family space in the evenings. When you are a small business, one rollway cart is usually sufficient, but larger businesses often have multiple rollaway carts for each employee who is in charge of one or more doctors.

You can buy a cart that either has drawers or one that has racks for hanging files. If you use files, you can section the files according to client, and within each client, you would have tabbed green hanging folders for the following:

- Incoming claims to be processed
- Incoming EOBs to be posted
- Follow up for claims that are pending

Postage Scale. It can be worthwhile to invest in a small and accurate postage scale because you are going to need to weigh mailings that contain claims with backup documents. No point wasting postage.

Paper Shredder. You must have a professional quality shredder that can be used to securely dispose of personal documents that contain any private patient or doctor information and data.

PO Box. You probably want to have a post office box (or better yet, a physical address with the equivalent of an office address) so that your home address is kept private and also so that patients recognize you as a professional business. Companies like the UPS Store, Postal Annex, and other executive suites offer real addresses that can be helpful in portraying a serious image.

Postage Machine or Printer. You have several options when it comes to obtaining postage or printing out your own to avoid going to the post office:

1. You can buy stamps by phone or on the Internet from the US Post Office. If you do this, be sure to buy many denominations of stamps so you can make up the right postage you need for different weighted envelopes.
2. You can print your own postage from an approved vendor for the US Post Office such as Stamps.com. They provide you with software that lets you print your own coded stamps acceptable to the US Post Office. Stamps.com has a free trial program that even provides you with a digital scale and free supplies.
3. You can purchase a postage machine from a company such as Pitney Bowes. Postage machines are great but there are pros and cons. On the pro side, the machine prints the postage for you and you don't need to log onto the Internet, nor drive to the post office. You can print exact postage and not waste money as you sometimes do with stamps. On the con side, you need to lease some machines and that means a monthly fee and possibly a multi-year lease that cannot be cancelled without penalty. Be careful about such leases.

Preparing Your Office for Healthcare Security Regulations

Since we are discussing issues related to setting up your office, you should be aware that maintaining the security and privacy of healthcare records is a responsibility that you also need to consider, even if you are a home-based business. According to the federal government's Health Insurance Portability and Accountability Act, referred to as HIPAA (and pronounced *hip-pa*), medical office personnel and medical billers must adopt various office procedures to ensure the security and privacy of patient's rights. For example, you must make a secure location in your home or office for all your medical business files. This can be either a private room with a door that can be locked or simply lockable file cabinets – one or the other is fine, as long as you can guarantee the privacy and security of any records in your possession.

In addition, you also need to ensure that you have or use the following:

- Password protected software;
- Backup computer files that are stored offsite and can be obtained in case of emergencies, disasters, or computer crashes;
- If you have employees, you must require them to sign a non-disclosure agreement that they will maintain the confidentiality of all patient records with which they come in contact.

Workspace Furniture

The workspace you need for a medical billing business is largely the same as for any professional business, but there are some special procedures we will discuss here. Here is what you need.

Desk. It is very desirable to have a desk that offers you a large work area. One great option, if you have the space in your office, is to use a large dining room table, although the disadvantage here is that you won't have a keyboard drawer, which may be better for your posture. Alternatively, get a desk that has a large surface area. Or buy one that has a "return," meaning the type of desk that is in two-pieces in U or L-shape. You're going to handle a lot of paperwork and so this really helps to have the surface area available to keep the files you are working on each day.

Credenza. Having an extra surface area and storage area right behind your desk is also useful. If you have the space, buy a credenza that has drawers and cabinets where you can store your office supplies and put your current paperwork. You might use the credenza for your personal / business files (for your own company) and use the rollaway cart for your clients' medical billing files.

Chair. You will be sitting a lot, so make sure you have an ergonomically correct chair that you *love* sitting in.

Fax machine / Printer / Scanner Combo. Purchasing a combination machine has many advantages in saving room on your desk (instead of three machines) while providing you with three vital business functions. You definitely need good fax capability because some clients may fax you their encounter forms and other documents rather than mailing them to you. Be sure to get a fax machine that has memory so you can receive faxes even when you are out of paper and one that automatically tells when it is out of ink. A scanner comes in handy from time to time when you may need to scan a paper document that becomes part of an electronic patient record.

Filing Cabinets. You need significant filing storage space to keep your clients' encounter forms (superbills) and other paper records they send you. As mentioned, the HIPAA law requires you to maintain the privacy and security of all medical records in your keeping, so if you don't have a private lockable office, your filing cabinets must be lockable. A great style of filing cabinet to buy are the ones called "vertical file cabinets" such as the type you see in doctors offices where the files are standing up vertically with the edges of the files visible. This allows you to label the edges of the files so you can view from the side without having to lift them up out of a drawer. If you have a lockable office, these can be open files, or get files that have a door that pulls down to secure them.

As your business builds, you may need more filing cabinets and eventually a fireproof storage facility for older records. You must keep paper data and records you receive from your doctors and insurers for a period of six years and nine months, even if you go out of business, unless you've arranged in your contract for the doctor to store the files. But if the doctor's office doesn't maintain copies of the records, it will become your responsibility. Be sure that your contract with the doctor specifies who must keep the files, including encounter forms, backup documentation, and EOBs.

Imaging Technology

As long as we're discussing filing cabinets, let's point out that many professions are now scanning all their documents given the quality and speed of today's imaging technology. Medical offices are increasingly using scanners for patient records and billing data. You can take advantage of imaging too, by scanning in all your superbills and EOBs for storage rather than keeping the paper copies in filing cabinets or offsite in boxes. You might hold onto original paper documents for a year, then scan them and store them on CDs after that. If you decide to use imaging technology, get a high quality rapid scanner and scanning software. See Chapter 8 on Additional Services for information about how you can offer imaging to doctor's offices.

Technology for Your Office

Technology is the heart of most businesses today, and medical billing is no different. So here's what you need to know about your technology needs:

Computer and Monitor. It's not a rule that you must have the latest and greatest computer, but we do recommend that you have the best small business computer you can afford. Fortunately, the price of hardware has come down enormously and it's amazing the computing power you can purchase these days for less than $1000. So if you have a good computer already, one that is relatively new, you're probably fine. If your machine is old and it's obvious that you must buy a new one, it's truly worthwhile to purchase the most powerful and up-to-date machine you can so you won't need to upgrade for a few years. Get the fastest chipset and most memory you can afford and be sure it is installed with the latest version of Windows. Anything less than these requirements will prevent you from maximizing the latest medical billing and/or practice management software such as my company's program, MedOffice. Keep in mind that software programs tend to get more and more sophisticated so it is better to be prepared for increasing computing power.

If you're wondering about purchasing a Macintosh computer, they are great machines but not for a medical billing business, unless you have the new Mac which runs both Windows and MacOS. The reason is that almost all medical practice management and billing software is written for PC machines.

Monitor. If you can, get a 17 or 19 inch flat panel monitor to reduce the space it takes up on your desk. Most new computers come with flat panel monitors these days. The size matters because a large monitor gives you ample screen space to view multiple windows at once. For example, you might need to simultaneously use your practice management software, write a business document on Word, check a web site on the Internet, and review your accounting all at once. Rather than having to keep closing or minimizing windows, the larger screen area enables you to keep many windows open at once.

Computer Network. If you employ people, you'll want to set up multiple computers networked together. If you have more than three computers, you may need a standalone server that is not accessed by employees for entering data.

Business / Productivity Software. You will need the following general office programs for many of your business functions:

- MS Word or other word processor
- QuickBooks or another bookkeeping program
- Excel

Backup Capability. There are several ways you can back up a single computer system.

1. You can buy a 2nd hard drive onto which you do your backups.
2. You can use CD's to store your backups. To keep costs down, use CD-RW format disks which allow you to rewrite them over and over. If you do this, follow this process. Label one CD for each day of the week – so you will have five or seven CD's, depending on how many days you work. To begin, back up each day once through the first cycle of CD's using one CD per day. In the next week, on Monday, rewrite Monday's disk, and on Tuesday, use Tuesday's CD, and so on. This procedure is vital to protect your data. If you have a computer virus or failure that goes undetected for several days, but you were backing up just to one disk over and over again, you would risk losing all your data because your backup disk would likely be infected too. For example, say that your computer got a virus on Thursday but you didn't know it until the following Monday. If you are using just one CD for backups, your CD would be worthless. But with this system, at least you have several days of valid backups before the virus happened. An alternative is also to use flash drives in the same manner as well. The cost of flash drives has come down dramatically.
3. You may wish to have an off-site backup system in case of fire, especially if you have many providers and lots of data to protect. One of the best ways to get an off-site backup service is via ClaimTek's Remote Backup System, described in detail in Chapter 8. This service provides automated off-site backup via the Internet. Even better, you can also sell this service to your clients.

What Type of Internet Service Do You Want?

It is possible to operate a medical billing business using just a dialup modem to transfer your claims. This is good for people who live in parts of the country where dialup is your only choice. Claims can also be submitted when connected to the Internet by logging onto the web site of a clearinghouse and uploading your files. This method can also tolerate dial-up access rather than high speed. However, as a professional business in today's world, it would be preferable to have high speed access via DSL or cable modem. The higher speed allows you to send your claims and pull back your reports in a shorter amount of time with less frustration. High speed also makes it easier to do research and use the Internet for accessing insurance carriers to follow up on your claims.

Easy, fast access to the Internet is quickly changing how people do business in medical billing. For example, in former times, billers could spend hours on the phone with insurance companies trying to get answers on the status of previously filed claims. Today, a lot of insurers have web sites where billers can go to check on whether a claim has been paid or not. Another change is the use of email. Doctors today often want to email their biller about various issues or to check on a claim, especially on claims for high dollar values that have not been paid yet. For example, surgeons may do multiple surgeries on the same patient and they want to make sure that a claim has been paid before they perform another surgery.

So the point is, if you can afford high speed service, it is likely to pay off for you in your efficiency and ability to provide fast customer service.

Your All-Important Telephone System

Even if you are running a home office, it is best to have three phone lines: one for your family's personal home use, a separate line for your business calls to ensure your family does not answer business calls, and a third line that serves as your fax line and, if you don't have cable modem, then it also doubles as your Internet access line (dialup or DSL, as discussed above). A third line is important to ensure you can have constant open access to incoming faxes. For example, there will be times when your doctor's office may want to speak with you while they are faxing you information to review. If it's necessary to keep your startup costs down, you can probably get away with just two lines, where your second line doubles as both a fax and voice line, as well as your DSL line.

As your business grows, you may eventually want to have a multiphone line system, or if you take on employees, you will need several phones. When you reach five or more employees, you may want to get a dedicated line for each employee, given that each one may have responsibility for certain accounts. Some phone systems require you to have a T-1 or partial T-1 lines, which are fast and can save you money when you reach this level. But keep in mind that some phone systems are quite costly and so they tend to be rented to businesses using a lease option. If you do this, bear in mind that lease options are a contract which you are responsible to pay over many years, so be careful about signing a long-term lease.

As for having a cell phone, you should have one because you may have clients who won't appreciate not being able to reach you whenever they need to. It's simply expected these days that business people have a cell phone that provides 24/7 access to them.

Do You Need a Web Site?

In today's world, it is pretty much a necessity to have a business web site. Many potential customers judge a business's professionalism by whether or not they have a web site. From a practical point of view, web sites are also great advertising tools because potential customers can read about your company on your site, and you can post various marketing materials online rather than mailing them as documents. Your web site is also useful to mention on any marketing and advertising materials you publish and distribute.

Some of you may be able to build your own web site with one of the easy-to-use software web design tools available that provide choices of many business templates to select. You simply enter your company's name and address information and write your own text in the blocks provided, upload the template to your web host, and within hours, you can have a nice looking simple one or two page web-site. These templates are not sophisticated, but at least you have a web presence.

Many Internet provider services also offer subscribers a free small web site that allows you to compose a few pages of information using a template they provide. These can be easy, but the problem is, you don't usually have your own domain name. Your web address is a sub-address of your web host, and this is not as professional as you might want.

However, if you work with ClaimTek, we offer you an extensive pre-built web site that you can have up and running within hours. We provide you a choice of 20 template designs to choose from, varying in colors and styles. Your web site comes complete with nearly 20 pages of pre-written content about medical billing services and other services that your company may offer. If you purchase our medical billing opportunity, the web site is part of your package. Once you've named your company, and provide us with your data (address, phone number, fax number, etc.), we customize your choice of template to reflect your business. We also show you how to go into the pages and change the text yourself, should you desire to further customize it. We give you full control of your site so that you may change the content and design as you wish. In addition, we guide you on search engine optimization sources so that your web site can be quickly found when potential clients search for you.

ClaimTek's pre-constructed web site options save new billing companies a lot of headache, time, and expense. We know how important a web presence can be to a medical billing company, so we have put a lot of effort into creating our sophisticated but easy-to-use templates that you can choose from as well as extensive, well-written pages that will look like you wrote them.

Do You Need Business Insurance?

If you are working from a home office, it's a good idea to add liability insurance to your home policy or renter's insurance. If a client, employee, or anyone comes into your home, you want to be covered. You should also disclose to your homeowner's policy that you are running a business. Make sure that your policy covers any of your office equipment in case of fire or theft. You may also want to purchase "errors and omissions" (E&O) business insurance as well, which covers you in the event of a lawsuit claiming your errors created a loss for the plaintiff. (Typically, E&O insurance is not required unless you handle coding matters.)

If you are in a commercial office space, you will need to get business insurance, which typically includes liability insurance that holds harmless the landlord, as well as coverage for all your office furniture, computers, and any equipment on the premises. Some landlords or lease companies want to see a copy of your policy to prove they are covered in case of a loss.

Do not confuse business insurance with worker's compensation insurance, unless you have specifically added this into your policy. If your employees are driving their own vehicle on the job, even for something as simple as going to the post office to get stamps, you can be liable as a business owner. This coverage can be included in your worker's comp provided it has been disclosed to the insurance carrier.

Tracking Your Money Using Accounting Software

Running your own business – whether you're a sole proprietor, partnership, or LLC – means that you must maintain annual accounting records of your income and expenses. This is necessary both to file your taxes and to determine if your business is profitable.

You can maintain your accounting records in any of several ways. Some people use manual accounting journals in which they simply handwrite their income and expenses. Other people use an Excel spreadsheet. But many business people now use dedicated accounting software for small businesses, such as QuickBooks. This last approach is the best choice if you're serious about running your business in a professional manner. Small business accounting software is easy to use, accurate and an efficient way to maintain accounting records. If you don't know much about accounting, programs like QuickBooks make recording data easy because they automate a lot of the basic accounting operations.

Another reason to use accounting software right from the start is that you won't have problems later if your business grows quickly. By not having your records already in an accounting program, you can end up unprepared for your increase in business. It's worthwhile to launch your business with growth in mind, setting up good procedures and policies for the future.

Don't Forget to Create a Great Working Environment for Yourself

A lot of people get so wrapped up in getting their office ready for business that they neglect decorating the walls, hanging some nice artwork, and adding little touches that personalize their workspace. A few months later, when their business gets off the ground and their office is scattered with paperwork, they come into their work space and wonder why it is so drab and uninspiring.

So, if you're just starting out in a new office, don't neglect to spend some time and money creating a great work space for yourself. You'll benefit with greater happiness, productivity, and efficiency. You'll enjoy coming to your office and tackling your work, no matter how hard it is. You'll feel inspired, refreshed, and happy each and every day.

That's why you're in business for yourself, isn't it?

6

Marketing, Sales, Contracts, and Pricing Your Services: Big Questions, Big Answers

As you embark on a medical billing and practice management business, you may be wondering how someone goes about finding and getting in touch with healthcare providers to sell them your services. If you are new in this business or your background is not in a medical area, you may even feel confused about the steps to take to get your business off the ground.

Well, have no fear! We have written this chapter with loads of powerful, targeted techniques that are proven to work. We will walk you through dozens of ideas on developing a marketing campaign, creating print and electronic marketing materials, making calls and visits to doctors' offices, networking, and developing your image and reputation in your community as a professional medical billing service. We will guide you through the best way to speak to a doctor when you are in the actual appointment with him or her making your pitch, complete with do's and don'ts that will help you land the sale. We will also teach you how to price your services and write a contract. And finally, we will end the chapter with information about how to write a short business plan (which requires knowing about your marketing and pricing).

Seven Factors to Consider When Building Your Marketing Program

Before we get into the fine details about marketing programs, we need to let you know about seven very important factors to take into account as you think about your marketing. These issues are generic to any program you decide to create and undertake, so it's useful to keep them in mind at all times.

1. Marketing is Personal

The first factor to understand about marketing, especially for a small or home-based business, is that it is up to you to decide what type of marketing programs you want to undertake. There are many methods of marketing, but each entrepreneur has to select the ones that seem right for him or her.

We don't mean to suggest that you can ignore reality. For example, your industry has an impact on your choices in marketing. The methods most appropriate to reach doctors are not going to be the same as those that work to attract restaurant owners. Another factor is your budget. Even though you may *want* to send out a mailer and free promotional gift to thousands of doctors in your area, you won't be able to choose this method unless you have the cash to pay for the materials. Time is yet another factor that you have to take into account beyond your personal wishes. If you're in a hurry to get clients, you may be willing to make choices that you wouldn't otherwise select.

In general though, as you read through this chapter, you can decide which marketing methods may work best for you given your personality, experience, interests, and skills. We've researched and tried every one of the methods we're going to present to you and we know they work in getting clients for medical billers. So, as you read the marketing ideas presented here, think about which ones are the best choices for you. Each requires different talents and skills, and each has its pros and cons. What worked for some people may not work for you, based on several factors such as location, individual personality, prior experience, skills and personal preferences.

2. Marketing is Elusive and Ever-changing

Marketing consists of a lot of strategies at different times. It's elusive, not one-dimensional or fixed. You have to be flexible and willing to try many different techniques. You have to be willing to hit the market from many angles. It's like being a politician for public office who runs a varied campaign consisting of talk shows, bumper stickers, mailers, town hall meetings, etc. You also have to be proactive. You can't just send out direct mail letters and then wait by the phone. If you do this, your chances of getting a client are not very high compared to a biller who conducts a professional campaign.

3. You Need Both Marketing and Sales Skills

We define marketing as the process of making your company's products and services known to your possible clientele and gaining their interest in you. Sales is the process of landing the deal and getting the contract signed. In operating a medical billing and practice management business, you need to be successful at both of these, especially when you are first starting out. No one wants to become the greatest marketing wizard but have no sales skills and no clients.

The difference in these terms is important to keep in mind because in the medical billing field, you always have to build your marketing campaign with an eye to the future, even once you get clients. In other words, once you become successful, it doesn't mean you can stop marketing. You have to choose and launch your marketing programs knowing that clients may come and go, and so you need to be prepared to replace them or to grow your business beyond your original expectations. Of course, you especially need to have the tools in place to help retain clients. There are several ways that ClaimTek can teach you to cement relationships with your clients that help ensure their loyalty.

4. You Must Reinforce Your Branding at all Times

You've probably heard the word branding many times in recent years. If you're not familiar with it, it refers to the idea that the marketing message or image your business puts out to the world must be very clear, distinctive, and purposeful. Everything you send out must reinforce that same message. You want your potential clients to develop a specific image of your company each time they hear from you.

One reason why branding is so important has to do with what marketing experts have learned about how long it takes to get potential clients to pay attention to advertising. You've probably heard the research that a company has to put advertising in front of someone roughly six to eight times before a prospective client will take action to buy your product or service. In general, you can't expect to send out a single brochure and get business. While it may happen occasionally, you should plan on repeating your message many times to potential clients.

Paying attention to your branding is what helps you ensure that your messages all deliver the same impact to clients. You don't want to advertise or send out a brochure in week 1 that portrays your medical billing service as the "friendliest," then in week 2 send out more advertising that presents you as the "fastest." Each and every time you reach out to potential clients, it is far better to brand yourself in the same, consistent way over and over again so clients will really know what you stand for.

So, as you review the marketing methods we teach you in this chapter, keep in mind that you want to perform them in ways that reinforce and support your branding. For example, if you decide to send out direct mail pieces, ensure that every piece prominently shows your company logo and any promotional statement you have created to describe your services. If you also go to networking meetings, always introduce yourself with the same message and be sure the business cards you hand out also show your logo and your mission. And similarly, if you visit a doctor's office, make sure they will remember you by clearly stating the name of your company and your mission.

Once you start this branding process, all the marketing methods that follow in this chapter will fall into place to help you gain recognition throughout your community, your state, and even the entire U.S. if you so choose.

5. You Have to Be Totally Professional

The medical practice management business demands the highest level of professionalism you can muster. As we've said, healthcare has become one of the largest industries in the United States and the competition for business is rising. Many changes are happening in the insurance field and even doctors are being forced to alter their practices. In other words, there is so much going on in healthcare today that you just can't cut it unless you jump in with all your heart and soul and really understand the industry and commit to making your medical practice management company a professional player.

So how do you become a "professional?"

First, knowledge is an important element and you're already taking care of this by learning everything you can as you read this book. But you'll need to keep learning and be open to more and more education. You'll want to keep up to date on all the billing changes that Medicare and commercial insurers implement from year to year. You'll want to begin learning about the medical practices in your community, which PPOs and other insurance networks are popular among them, what doctors in your community are doing about changes in healthcare, and numerous other topics. If you enjoy working in the medical arena, all this will actually be fun. The healthcare field is fascinating, and if you make it your new career, you'll find that your desire to become a professional will drive you forward with pleasure and excitement.

The other main aspect to being as professional as you can is that, as you develop your marketing programs, go for the highest quality you can afford. Good marketing campaigns cost money, but you can't expect to compete if you don't have completely professional-looking business cards, stationery, brochures, fliers, and other marketing materials. If your printer tells you to use a higher quality business card stock that costs an extra $30 per thousand, it may well make the difference of a prospect keeping your card and calling you a few months later. In short, you can end up being "penny wise and pound foolish" if you try to take shortcuts or save a few bucks on marketing items that give you a professional appearance.

Don't forget that doctors have spent years and years in their own education and many of them take financial risks in opening their medical practices. They want to do business with someone who gives them confidence and assurance that their billing and practice management are going to be handled professionally. Sloppy marketing materials on plain white paper won't do that. Brochures that look home-made or slapped together in a day will simply get tossed in the basket.

That brings us to the third idea in enhancing your professionalism. Be sure to spend quality time on your marketing materials. Don't rush through the writing process if you compose direct mail letters or brochures. Once you've written a draft, let it sit for a few days, and then review your writing to see if you might find a better way to convey your message. In addition, get feedback from others on your marketing materials. Ask the opinion of your spouse, business partners, friends, and even a few doctors on any letters or brochures you produce. You may find what you have written to be perfect, but don't be defensive if someone suggests different wording. If you are in doubt, hire a professional copywriter to revise your brochures and direct mail pieces.

And finally, always proof and reproof whatever you write. We've seen cover letters written to doctors with grammatical errors and misspellings. Mistakes tell doctors that you are a person who does not pay attention to details – and that is not who they want to hire.

We'd like to interject here that if you decide to work with ClaimTek, you will get a big jump start in the professionalism department. We help train you and provide comprehensive education and support about medical billing procedures, insurance regulations, marketing, healthcare trends, and more. We also provide an extensive package of professionally designed and printed marketing materials, including an assortment of high quality brochures, fliers, PowerPoint presentations, and other marketing documents. After you read this chapter, we invite you to visit the ClaimTek web site (www.claimtek.com) to learn about the marketing materials you have access to using when you work with us.

6. It's Useful to Specialize Your Business at First

One additional factor that can impact your marketing is your decision about whether or not you are going to specialize in specific healthcare fields. This decision can impact the type of marketing you decide to do because your choices will be different if you are seeking chiropractors, internists, surgeons, or pediatric specialists.

If you are new to medical billing and practice management, it is best to take whichever type of clients you can get in the beginning to launch your business. As you gain experience though, you can think about focusing on a few specializations and learn as much as possible about how to process claims for just those specialties. It can be easier to become an expert in a few fields than to become a generalist and know all of them. Then as your business grows, you can expand into whatever medical areas you enjoy and add more types of medical practices to your practice management portfolio. Given that you are an established business, you can often rely on referrals and word of mouth to boost your marketing.

Many billers decide to focus on fields such as mental health, chiropractic, podiatry, psychology, or physical therapy when they first start their business. These fields are easier to learn and develop for your business because they use fewer procedures and diagnosis codes than internists, family practices, and general surgeons, and so filing claims for those specialties is easier. In addition, some types of specialties have high dollar value claims, so it is not likely that you will land a contract with certain types of doctors when you are new. For example, a surgeon who bills out a million dollars in claims is probably going to prefer an established, knowledgeable billing service. Compare this to a chiropractor who brings in $200,000 to $400,000 per year and who would be willing to hire a less experienced medical practice manager who nevertheless seems skilled and professional.

The Big Seven Marketing Categories

Now we're ready to present to you seven major categories of marketing and within each one, there is a huge range of individual options from which you can choose to create your overall marketing campaign.

Read the list of ideas below while thinking about your own special talents and interests. Consider your previous business experience and consider what marketing tools you're already familiar with. Ask yourself, "Have I done direct mail? Have I written catalogue copy or product specifications? Can I handle calling on doctors and can I put them at ease during a first meeting?" Perhaps you have a flair for design and copywriting, so developing a powerfully persuasive flier or brochure will be your lead into the office. Or perhaps you have the gift of a charming personality and easy conversation that enables you to approach the most surly office manager and quickly find out who you can talk to and when.

Category 1 - Tap into Your Own Resources

This first option is frankly the easiest way to begin getting clients because it is the marketing method right in front of your nose and the one that costs the least. We include it because even though it is obvious, many people neglect it. However, while it appears simple, it is not. Talking to your own resources such as your doctors, friends, family, and others still requires that you demonstrate knowledge and professionalism. Just because they know you already, don't expect that they will hand you their business unless they feel completely comfortable that you can handle their needs.

Here are some specifics about how to tap into your own resources.

Talk with Your Own Doctors

Your own doctors may be a good starting place for you to find clients. You have a relationship with their office and you are familiar with how they work simply because you already make appointments and get your patient statements. In fact, if you notice that your statements are always late or appear to be sloppy, this might give you a good reason to talk to them about switching their practice management to you.

You can approach your own doctors in several ways. You might call the office and talk with the receptionist or office manager indicating that you are a patient and tell them that you are starting a medical practice management business. Ask if they might be interested in talking to you further about their needs. Give them a clear sense of your background and the effort you are putting into getting your business off the ground. Be sure you have some brochures, fliers, and a good cover letter prepared in case they invite you to send written materials to them. Don't assume that because you are their patient, they will automatically say no to you, fearing a conflict of interest. They may consider you another business just like others that approach them.

However, note that it is not a good idea to contact your doctors and other doctors randomly to sound out the viability of starting your business unless you have already gotten trained and are ready to go. Many amateurs try to test the waters for their medical billing business this way, without having received any professional training in marketing. It is usually a mistake to talk to doctors prematurely unless you know what to say and how to be persuasive in their language.

You might also talk to your own doctors to find out if they can help you with referrals to others. Do they know any new doctors coming into their building who might need a medical billing or practice management company? Can they recommend any specialists with whom your doctor coordinates that you could call? If they give you any names, you have already made enormous progress, because you can call the other doctor and say that your doctor "referred you to them" which already sounds like an endorsement of your services.

There is actually an important principle of marketing to mention here related to this point: Get names to use as referrals as often as possible. The truth is, business is all about relationship building. Rather than approach a potential client cold, it always helps when you can tell them that you were referred by someone else to speak with them. The simple fact that you know someone in common gives them an assurance you travel in the same world as they do. You literally seem less foreign and more credible when you can say, Dr. So and So referred me to you.

We know many medical billing companies whose first clients were one of their own doctors or someone they contracted using a referral from their doctor. So if you feel comfortable with this option, give it a try. If you feel uncomfortable about talking to your own primary doctor, perhaps you might try this method with a specialist you visited years ago who may not really remember you, but which still allows you to say that you were once a patient of his or hers.

Ask for Referrals from Friends

Friends and acquaintances can often turn out to be sources of referrals for you. The fact is, you don't always know who your friends know and this makes it worthwhile to spread the word that you are going into the medical practice management business. You can talk to your friends directly or indirectly. You can simply tell them, "Hey, did you know I've just launched my new career in medical practice management?" Then see what they say in response. Or you can be more direct and follow your announcement with a query such as, "Do you know any doctors that you might be able to refer me to because I'm developing a mailing list of names and I may want to go into some offices to set up appointments?"

Don't push on friends to the point of jeopardizing your friendship. You may find some friends unwilling to share their information and there may be many reasons for that. Some may not want to share information that might reveal any medical conditions they have, and so you need to respect their privacy. If you talk with friends and acquaintances, always reinforce your professional attitude towards your new business. Don't let them perceive you as someone "just fishing" for referrals. While they may not have any names to give you now, it could very well happen that sometime in the future, they will get to see your success and may be more willing to give you some leads.

Category 2 – Network, Network, Network

Networking has become one of the most popular ways to market in recent years – and for good reason. As more and more people have become entrepreneurs starting their own business, they have realized that they can help each other. As we said, business is increasingly becoming a function of building relationships. Knowing and helping another business owner leads to them helping you.

Here are some ideas for how to get involved in networking. Some of them involve indirect networking, i.e., meeting people who are not specifically involved in the medical or healthcare field. Other ideas here are direct, in that your goal is to network specifically with people who are in the healthcare world.

Join a Business Networking Group

Just about every community has one, if not dozens, of business networking groups. There are women's groups, men's groups, breakfast groups, dinner groups, and even professional business referral networks. Some networking groups don't require you to join anything. You can come to individual meetings as your schedule allows and present yourself and your business to the group. If anyone knows a lead for you, they will share it. Other networking groups are much more formal and require you to join a specific set of people with whom you meet week in and week out to share leads. In some of these groups, you must bring in leads for other group members and essentially exchange your leads for theirs. Some of the most well known groups like this are Business Network International (BNI) and LeTip, both of which are national organizations that have local leads chapters in every major town and city.

Whenever you network, don't walk in expecting to get business within the day. It can take time to find the right leads for your medical practice management business. Some people go into these meetings and become selfish about making sure they get a referral for themselves. It is far better to show the good side of your personality and be patient about getting some leads. You never know when someone in the group may know doctors or have a friend who is a medical office manager to whom you can get referred.

What might you accomplish by going to general networking meetings or breakfast groups? Actually quite a lot! Such groups give you a chance to practice your speech about what type of medical practice management you do. The more you get up and talk about your business, the better you will get at delivering your talk so that when you walk into a doctor's office, you will feel completely polished and confident.

Networking groups also give you a chance to hand out your business card and begin getting your name out into the public. As we just said, one of the people you give your business card to might hand it over to a good friend who works in a medical office. In fact, you should never go to any networking event without taking 100 to 200 business cards with you.

A third value in going to networking groups is to collect cards from other people who could turn out to be useful to your business down the road. They may become suppliers for services you need or they may become sources of referrals. Be sure to store all the business cards in a way that helps you, such as scanning their names in to your computer or entering their contact information and email addresses into your email software.

If you join a formal leads group, don't forget that you will need to spend some of your time coming up with leads for other members. You may not want to do this if your focus is on your business, but on the other hand, such formal leads groups can prove to be educational and instructive if the members can help you with many of your marketing questions.

Join a Hospital Foundation

This suggestion is a form of networking that is both more direct than general networking because you get involved in the healthcare field. However, it is also more indirect because it requires time and patience since your goal cannot be to market your business in a blatant way, but rather to build professional relationships and become involved in your community.

Every hospital has a foundation that helps raise money for the hospital – and that foundation needs volunteers. So, since you are interested in healthcare, why not join and use this as a method of networking?

If this interests you, here's what to do. Call one of your local hospitals and ask about their foundation. Find out when it meets and how you can get your name on the list of activities and fundraisers in your community. You can sign up to attend certain events if you offer to contribute or to work as a volunteer, and that will begin giving you visibility in the foundation – and some future networking opportunities because of the fact that there are a lot of doctors at these events.

However, as we said above, be forewarned. When you are at these types of events, adhere to the unspoken protocol that you don't blatantly network or hand out business cards unless you are asked. Let people get to know you and ask about what you do on their own. As you become known and respected, you may also be invited to private functions in homes which is both fun socially and potentially useful for your business networking.

There is another possibility that you might explore once you get connected to the hospital foundation. Try to find out the name of the administrator who handles new doctors coming onboard with the hospital. If you are comfortable with this, you might approach that administrator and offer to give 10% of your profits back to the hospital foundation from all fees you earn for doctors that are referred through them.

Contact Your County Medical Society

Many counties have associations for doctors who are moving into the area and want support with their relocation. You can sometimes network with your county's medical society, which might be willing to give you the names of new doctors moving into your area. We have had ClaimTek billers find success in networking with their county medical society.

Use Your Community's Master Calendar to Find Networking Opportunities

Many communities have a website that lists all the events occurring within it. Many of these events are a great chance to meet other business people and network. Call your city or visit their website to find out if they maintain a master calendar. Then study it each month to select one or two events that might prove valuable to you. Don't forget to bring lots of business cards and be ready to introduce yourself with a tightly worded 30 second "commercial" about your business. Often called elevator speeches, these are one to three sentences you have rehearsed over and over again so that you can introduce yourself and quickly let people know what you do. Don't recite your elevator speech in a stiff way. Be natural and friendly – no one needs to know you've rehearsed it.

Employer Advisory Council

Many people are unfamiliar with this organization that can lead to interesting networking opportunities. The Employer Advisory Council is a national group throughout the United States that puts on meetings for employers to review new labor laws, cafeteria plans, health plans, and HIPAA issues. Doctors run businesses, so they often send their office managers to these meetings. By joining, you may have a chance to hook up with a medical office manager or two and do some networking that could lead to a contract or referral to another doctor.

Hold Your Own Office Manager Meetings

This idea follows the proverb "If you can't bring the horse to the water, bring the water to the horse." Rather than joining a networking group and hoping to meet people who can get you into a medical office, why not form your own group and invite office administrators to come to you. The idea is based on one practice administrator we know in California who put together a monthly meeting for office managers of doctor's offices. She invited as many office managers as she could find to come to her meetings, ostensibly to learn about issues such as HIPAA, NPI, and other trends. Many office managers accepted her invitation and the group took off. She then used the contacts she made among attendees for her own networking. Eventually some of them helped her land contracts for practice management.

If you don't feel qualified to run such a group yourself, you might consider inviting an expert speaker to come to your meetings. That person might talk about those areas you don't know but leave you time to speak as well. Aim to find someone who can benefit from your invitation as much as you can.

Tap Into Your Chamber of Commerce

Nearly every community has a chamber of commerce whose mission is to help business people grow their business. Chambers host numerous conferences, workshops, and networking events throughout the month and also have many committees you can join. Joining your chamber can prove to be one of your best methods of networking. Be sure to look into the different committees and find something to volunteer for that sparks your interest. Although you will have to donate effort to a chamber committee, it may be no more than two hours per month. The key is that the chamber offers you a major avenue to become visible in your community and to build relationships.

Category 3 – Try the World of Direct Mail and Print-Based Marketing

This category includes a wide range of individual options to do marketing using printed materials. The value of print is that it gives you a chance to put something visual in front of your potential clients which they can read, analyze, and think about. Many people simply prefer reading information about a company rather than meeting the owner or hearing a speech about what you do. Printed materials also have the advantage of being durable, meaning that people may keep them for a period of time, reviewing them as needed. Many medical practice management and billing companies have gotten business months after sending out a brochure or flier because the doctor kept the materials and consulted them when he or she finally needed someone.

The downside of printed materials is that the costs can add up. Sending out hundreds of direct mail pieces can become expensive in printing and postage fees, therefore you should budget and plan for how much you can afford to do each month. Always put your costs in perspective to the results you might achieve. It is said that the typical business spends up to 30% of its gross income on its marketing budget. So, if just one small doctor brings you $1,000 income per month ($12,000 per year), don't be afraid to spend a percentage of that to get the account.

Here are some options for printed materials that you can send out:

Conduct a Simple Postcard Campaign

Postcards are an easy and inexpensive way to alert a doctor's office to your new business. They offer a great advantage in that the recipient can read your message immediately as soon as the mail is delivered. A post card does not require anyone to open it. They can just pick it up and read it right on the spot. That makes postcards a fast way to get your logo and branding across.

If you are designing a postcard campaign, look for a design on one side that has a high degree of humor or curiosity about it. You want the recipient to look at the image on the front of the postcard and get drawn into reading the backside. Some businesses use a striking photograph, or a humorous cartoon, or a graphic message related to medical billing.

On the backside of your postcard, get the reader interested by posing a question, such as "Having problems with your accounts receivable? We can help bring in your cash." Another one is, "Is your cash flow nil? Give us a call, we'll show you the difference?" Then be sure to put your company's name, address, phone number, web site address, logo, and any phrase or motto used to brand your business.

You may be wondering how you obtain a mailing list so you can send out your postcards. One way is to walk around medical buildings and make your own list of suite numbers and names. Of course, this takes time, so many billers buy mailing lists of doctor's offices. One of the best places to buy a mailing list is from your state medical board, many of which sell mailing lists of doctors for less than $100. For the fee, you will receive all doctors' names on an Excel spreadsheet that you can print or transfer to mailing labels. In some states, you may even get mailing labels completely prepared. However, note that mailing labels are good for postcards, but as we will discuss later in this chapter, don't use mailing labels for direct mail envelopes, as labels clearly indicate a mass mailing. Labels are ok for postcards, but not on letters. (Note: ClaimTek supplies you with mailing lists with our packages.)

Distribute a Flier with an Offer They Can't Refuse

Fliers are one-sheet printed pieces whose goal is to get readers to take action. Since it's only one page, you can't present a lot of information about your company, but you can create an enticement that makes prospects want to contact you.

For example, you might send out a flier that offers a free CPT code analysis as a way to encourage prospects to call you. Once you have them on the line, you can provide them with more detailed information about your company and use your additional marketing techniques to move them closer towards a sale.

Fliers can be effective because they are inexpensive and can be distributed by hand in areas where you can have access to leave multiple sheets for doctors and office managers to see. For example, if you know someone who works in the hospital, you might be able to get your fliers into the doctor's or nurse's lounge. If you can get to the property manager of a medical building, he or she might let you put them in the property management office or even let you enclose your flier along with their management company's monthly rent invoices to doctors.

Be careful not to distribute your fliers in buildings that have signs prohibiting solicitation. It's best not to alienate a property manager whose friendship you might need for higher purposes.

Impress with a Brochure

A high quality brochure is one of the best print pieces you can invest in. The advantage of a brochure is that it can transmit a lot of information to your prospective customers, and not just from the text you write for the pages. Many elements of the brochure – the visuals, typography, your company logo, layout – all these factors play a role in transmitting information in the sense that a great brochure can make your company seem like a major player in the field, even if you are just a small home-based business.

Since three-fold brochures have six surfaces, you can squeeze in a lot of text and segment it into six clearly defined messages. You have your front cover which must attract the reader, followed by the first open fold page and the inside of the brochure, where you can create a story that leads the reader into wanting to know more about you, followed by the right hand fold where you can put your call to action and finally, the back side of the middle which is usually reserved for addressing.

Given how effective and important a brochure can be to you, you have to make sure it is professionally done and reinforces your branding message. Keep in mind that when someone in a doctor's office reads your brochures, they are receiving a statement about you and your company. Anything less than professional and perfect will be reviewed in a negative light. This means no typos, smudges, or incorrect information.

You can also find brochure stock with four panels that allow for a tear off reply card that recipients can send in for more information. A reply card is useful because it gives recipients a painless and immediate opportunity to get in touch with you after reading your brochure. They don't need to call you or find an envelope, write down your address and put a stamp on it. They simply tear off the card, check any boxes that you want them to check and stick it in that day's mail.

ClaimTek can offer you many of the print marketing materials discussed above, but one of the highest rated and most effective marketing assistance we can give you is in the form of the unbeatable brochures we have created for billing businesses that work with us. Our brochures have been carefully crafted to make doctors interested in your business, and we had them professionally designed and printed on the highest quality paper available. If you feel that you are not skilled at writing a great brochure, we certainly hope you will visit www.claimtek.com to see the amazing brochures we put at your disposal if you decide to work with us.

Write and Mail out Direct Mail Letters

Direct mail letters are simply longer versions of postcard marketing. A letter gives you a chance to say more to your potential clients to hook them into pursuing a course of action. The risk with a direct mail letter is that it will be tossed out quickly or end up in the wrong person's hands, i.e., someone with no authority. Of course, if you're sending direct mail letters, you really want them to be read by the person who counts – the doctors in charge. They are the ones who need to know what you can offer to improve their business.

If you are going to write direct mail letters, here are some ideas for what you might want to mention towards the top of the letter to get their attention:

- You can save the doctor money in billing costs because hiring an outside service is often less expensive than hiring a staff person.
- You can increase their cash flow because you bill insurers immediately and stay on top of reimbursements.
- You can increase their reimbursement rate by following up on rejected and downgraded claims, recouping money they would have lost.
- You can ensure HIPAA compliance.

These are the types of statements that will catch a doctor's eye because you are appealing to their bottom line.

Regarding the middle of the letter, consider that doctors are very busy people and don't have the time to read a long letter. If you write a long letter, you are just tempting doctors to throw it out. So keep your letter short and to the point.

However, it's ok to dress your letter up a bit, using different fonts, and bold or italic for easier reading that causes the doctors eye to flow. Bold any key word that you want to pop out like **cash flow, payment of claims, accounts receivable**, and words such as these. Aim to attract the doctor's eye and keep him or her reading to the bottom of the letter.

In terms of ending your letter, always ask your reader for a specific "call to action" you want them to take. This might be to phone you or to accept a call from you (such as "I will be calling your office in two days to talk to you about your billing needs."), or a request to fill out a form you've enclosed, or another specific action. Some medical billers offer an incentive with their direct mail letter, such as a "free" superbill code review as a way to entice doctors to invite you into their office. Once you are there, you can analyze their superbills to determine if they are using up-to-date coding, but also trying to market them further into signing on with your company for the full range of services you can offer.

If you send direct mail letters, here are additional guidelines about the timing and techniques of sending letters:

1. Mail your letters out on a Monday, so that they will be received on a Tuesday, Wednesday, or Thursday in the provider's office.

2. Don't mail the letters later in the week when they risk being received on a Monday because this is the heaviest mail day. Anything received on a Monday is usually thrown out.

3. Don't allow your direct mail letters to be received on a Friday because people are typically thinking about their weekend and getting ready to leave the office. They simply won't give your letter the thought it deserves.

4. Always handwrite the addresses on the envelopes or run them through your printer one by one. Don't use printed stick-on labels since these scream out to recipients, "Look out, this is an unsolicited direct mail piece!" In other words, if your letter looks like a mass-mailed direct mail piece, it is likely to not be read.

5. Use a real stamp on the letter to add to the impression that it is a personal letter. You can even write or type on the outside of the envelope a little note that says, "Personal and Confidential" at the bottom left hand corner.

6. In terms of how many direct mail pieces to send out, we recommend that when you first start doing direct mail, send only 25 to 50 per week, not hundreds. Given that you want to follow up on each letter with a personal phone call to the doctor the following week, it's best to send only as many letters as you have time for follow up. If you can't make all your calls, you are essentially wasting the value of the direct mail piece. It's better to decrease the number of letters you send out to just the number on which you can follow up.
7. In terms of finding addresses for doctors to whom you want to mail direct mail letters, you can obtain names and addresses in the same way as we indicated for your postcards lists – walking around to get them on your own or buying lists from direct mail vendors, from your state medical board, or from Medicare which maintains a list of doctors who do not file electronically. (Note: ClaimTek provides mailing lists with our packages.)

Don't Offer a Free Trial Period!

In the early days of medical billing, some new companies sent out direct mail pieces offering a free trial period as a way to get a healthcare provider to sign on with them. However, a free trial period is now a fairly bad idea because you will exert a large amount of time and attention on setting up the account while not making much money. Remember that when you first sign up a doctor, it can take time to set up the clearinghouse and obtain approval to file claims on behalf of that doctor. This means that you will incur a period of time during which you will need to "drop claims to paper," which will cost you more. As an alternative to a free trial period, you might instead offer a guarantee for the first six months of your service. If the provider is not happy with your work and how you are getting them paid, you will agree to step out and turn the billing back to the office.

Print up Rolodex Inserts to Pass Out

The usual method of reminding potential clients about your business is the business card. The problem is, business cards often get lost or tossed out. A better idea is to print up die cut Rolodex cards with your business name and logo on them. Whenever you send out a flier or direct mail piece, include one of these Rolodex cards. As a special bonus, you might even use the card to offer a free consulting phone call regarding superbills or CPT codes to ensure that people hold onto it.

Create a Fax Campaign

Some billers conduct a "fax" campaign whereby they create a survey asking doctors if they want to have their CPT codes analyzed for free or another free offer, such as a customized superbill design or a billing cost analysis. To save expenses on mailing this invitation out, and to increase the immediacy of the offer, they fax the letter to doctor's offices rather than mailing it.

The challenges with this marketing method are collecting the fax phone numbers and being certain that your faxes are read and not thrown away immediately. Concerning the former, you can obtain fax phone numbers by calling offices directly and asking the receptionist for their fax number or by walking into offices and getting a business card from the provider.

If you conduct a fax campaign, be sure you have a sentence at the bottom of your letter that informs offices how to be taken off your fax list if they so desire. If an office calls you to request removal, respect their request. One company we know received a $25,000 fine for not taking an office off their list that had requested removal.

Advertise Your Business in Chamber of Commerce Pieces

Many city Chambers of Commerce publish various advertising pieces that they give out to citizens and tourists. For example, a popular item in many cities is a "map of the city" on which are located various businesses that pay to sponsor the map. Some cities publish a "monopoly board" type game where the squares are various businesses in the city that have agreed to buy a space for purposes of advertising. While it may be a stretch for your medical billing and practice management business to sponsor one of these items, it is a form of thinking out of the box. You never know when a medical office might see the piece and contact you. You also might have the serendipity of a doctor from another city visiting yours and becoming interested in contacting you. There's no reason your business has to be restricted to local doctors.

Electronic Newsletters (e-newsletters)

Another form of marketing that is becoming increasingly popular among businesses is to write a monthly e-mail newsletter. The more knowledgeable you become about coding and medical billing, especially if you specialize in certain medical specialties, the more attractive your business will appear to anyone who receives your e-newsletter. It doesn't take much to create and write an e-newsletter. Two or three articles per month can be sufficient. You can create either a plain text e-newsletter using your ordinary email software and simply mailing it to your distribution list, or you can sign on with one of the email newsletter services such as Constant Contact (www.constantcontact.com) that allows you to create fancy HTML newsletters. (In fact, Constant Contact is free if you have less than 50 email addresses in your database.)

If you decide to write a monthly e-newsletter, the key is to remember the branding principle. You must constantly reinforce your brand by incorporating your company slogan and logo into your newsletter. And be sure your newsletter is well-written with no typos or grammatical errors. You will do your business a disservice if you send out newsletters that contain incorrect information, poor writing, or typographical errors.

Publish Articles on the Internet

The Internet has become a veritable publishing house with hundreds of opportunities for people to publish their own articles and have them distributed to millions of people around the world. There are dozens of "list servers" and article publishing web sites that allow you to upload an article that you've written and get it circulated to people who subscribe to that list. In some cases, the list servers are free and in other cases, you pay to upload your articles. Again, it is important that anything you write is accurate and well-written.

The value of publishing on the Internet is that it gets your name out into the world and can help you stand out from the crowd of other billing companies. In addition, your articles can often end up being cited by Google when potential customers do a search on your business or personal name.

Category 4 –Personally Visit Medical Offices and Make Friends

This category focuses on personal marketing methods that involve YOU personally going around and meeting potential clients. These methods can be very effective if you have an outgoing personality and don't take rejection personally. Here are some suggestions for how to get the most value from personal appearances to do your marketing.

Bringing Gifts into Medical Offices

Who doesn't like a gift? Practically no one will refuse a lovely little gift that you bring to them as you go from office to office introducing yourself and handing out brochures and a business or Rolodex card. Your gift can be personal and fun, such as a rose, packaged cookies, or a candy dish that you graciously present to the office manager. Flowers are great for cheering people up and putting a smile on their face. Alternatively, you can present a gift that is more like a promotional item, engraved with your company name, such as a calculator or other useful business item. There are hundreds of promotional items available that you can personalize with your company name on them to use as a free giveaway.

However, be sure any promotional item you give away is something that your potential clients will value and can use. Aim for something unique and new. Remember that doctors receive dozens of gifts from pharmaceutical salespeople who visit them week in and week out. Many medical offices already have plenty of refrigerator magnets, pens, and mugs.

A little tip about gift giving. Holidays are a great time to employ this marketing strategy. People are usually a little less on their guard at holiday time and thus more willing to accept small gifts on a warm sales call. As long as you are dressed well and have excellent manners, they will usually take some extra time to talk to you and accept your gift.

How to Get Past the Office Manager by Building a Relationship

In general, cold calling on medical offices is challenging. It's highly unlikely that you will be able to walk in and see the doctor in charge. You have to start with a more realistic goal—to befriend the office manager in order to get as much information as possible so that you can work towards getting a meeting with the doctor. In some instances, the office manager will be curt and perhaps even rude, and you will need to learn how to deal with someone who has a negative attitude towards cold callers. If you encounter such a person, continue to be personable and patient. Ask if you can leave your card and a brochure, and then walk out in a friendly way. Don't take it personally or make assumptions about why that person treated you rudely. You can never tell if someday, they might call you to invite you to come back to talk further about doing business with you.

Remember that all your marketing efforts must be aimed at getting a meeting with the doctor. Your goal is to get 15-20 minutes of his or her time to make an initial presentation about the value of outsourcing their billing and practice management needs to your company. This means that the office manager is extremely vital to helping you set up that meeting. Honor the office manager and let them invite you to stay. If you bring in a gift, make sure you present it to the office manager. He or she may take the time to talk to you if you bring in a gift.

Host a Lunch and Chat

Another good entree into medical offices is to offer to bring in lunch to the office or practice manager so you can present your company and find out if they have a need for your services. If you decide to try this, it works best in an office with which you are establishing a good relationship and have already warmed the person up through prior visits or phone calls. It's unlikely you can go into an office on a cold call and get someone to agree to have lunch with you. In addition, be sure that you go into your luncheon without any expectations of immediate results. It is best to think of your goal as being able to learn about the office's needs, such as how many claims they are doing per week or month, whether they are experiencing significant delays and downgrading in their payments from insurers, and whether their current billing person is on top of follow-throughs for unpaid claims. You want your luncheon to be personable, yet professional.

One more caveat: when you invite the office manager to lunch, make sure you clarify who is invited. You can ask the office manager to include one or two other staff, and even ask if one of the doctors in the practice might also be available. But be sure that your invitation is clear because otherwise, you can end up with the entire office thinking they were invited. In general, the more personable you are, the better chances you have to sign up an account, as business is most often based on building relationships.

Ask Offices for Referrals (and possibly offer to pay "Finder's Fees)

Referrals are clearly one of the best sources of business since you already have a foot in the door. The problem is, when you are first starting out and do not have a satisfied doctor yet who might refer you to one of his colleagues, it can be difficult to get a referral.

Given this situation, if you are personally visiting offices, you might as well get as much bang for your buck as you can from each visit. Don't leave a personal office visit without asking the person you are talking to if he or she might know another office manager or doctor in the building or in the community who might be interested in your services. After all, office managers often talk among themselves and it's completely within reason to think that one day, someone might actually give you a useful lead to a potential client.

Some billers offer to pay people a "finder's fee" such as $500 for any client who signs on with them based on their referral. It's probably best not to blurt this out blatantly, but after you've had some discussions with an office manager and you feel comfortable with the person, you might mention in passing that you offer a finder's fee. Then leave it at that unless the person asks you for more details, which allows you to open the door to a specific discussion of how much you are offering.

Category 5 – Big Ticket Marketing Options

This category involves marketing methods that tend to cost more than the methods above, but can pay off in big ways. You have to assess your own budget and risk-taking capability to use these methods, but many billing services have been successful with them, so don't write them off immediately.

Advertise in Your Local Yellow Pages

If you are ordering a phone line for your new business, you may have a choice between a residential line and a business line (if you are setting up your business from your home). While a residential phone line is perfectly sufficient for a home-based business (and it is less expensive), a business line typically has the advantage of getting you a free classified entry in your local Yellow Pages phone book. Many businesses use the Yellow Pages as the first place they search if they are looking for a service – and so having a listing in your Yellow Pages might bring you business. On the other hand, one medical biller who works with us told us that she just switched to a residential line, saving 50% of the cost of a business line, and then she simply buys a line in the Yellow Book.

Another option is to take out a large display advertisement in one of your local Yellow Page directories. The cost of display advertising can be hefty, depending on the size of your display ad, what city you live in, and the breadth of distribution of the directory. A good size to use is a one-inch column that gives you space for your business name, logo, and for listing your web site where readers can get more information about your company.

Remember that such ads are ongoing costs on a monthly basis for a year (or you must pay upfront before it's published). Think clearly about the value of Yellow Page advertising for your company. Notice whether other billing companies are listed in your Yellow Pages, and what their specialties are. If none specialize in the same field as you, the ad may be worthwhile.

Seek out Local and Community Print Advertising Opportunities

In every community, there are usually dozens of opportunities for medical billing companies to do print advertising. Most local medical societies and chiropractic associations have newsletters that accept advertising. There are probably many community publications in which you can advertise such as Little League magazines, school yearbooks, and others. Again, you never know when a doctor might see your ad because his or her children also participate in the community function that your ad is in. The other advantage of such publications is that they help you develop an image of being community-centered.

Appear at Trade Shows

Some of you may have big plans to grow your business statewide or even nationally. If this appeals to you, you may wish to look at having a booth at a medical trade show. Just about every medical specialty has a conference or trade show at which vendors have booths. Trade shows are valuable when you want to reach across state lines and expand your practice to other states or regions. They can also offer you a bit of vacation time surrounding the show.

But keep in mind that trade shows are high ticket items. A booth typically costs from $3,000 to $5,000, including booth rental, a banner, and some posters or artwork at your booth site. If you travel to the event, you also have to pay for shipping your booth and having it set up for you. You also have your own hotel lodging costs, transportation, meals, and any promotional advertising and materials you give out. You may need two people to manage your booth so you can leave once in a while to take a break.

When you put it all together, it could very well be that one large trade show costs you $7,000. However, it could also be that you land a contract with a major medical practice that makes up for the entire cost with the new revenues you will take in over the next year and beyond.

Go Big with a Billboard

In some small cities, it may actually be possible to rent an entire billboard to advertise your medical billing and practice management company. If you live in this type of area, why not splash your photo on a billboard and use a few catchy words to attract clients. A billboard is bold and gutsy. It shows the world you're a big player who is eager for business. If you try a billboard, be sure to create an ad that uses only a few words, perhaps no more than five. Don't forget that people must be able to read your advertisement as they are driving.

Category 6 – Phone Call Marketing

This category consists of the tried and true marketing method of phone calling to reach out to potential clients to let them know about your services. Phone calling is by far the least expensive way to market your business, but requires patience and commitment to get results.

Of course, you can begin a phone campaign to potential clients any time you want, but our advice is that it is better to send out some type of printed marketing piece in advance of making any phone calls. If the office has received your marketing piece, it effectively changes your cold call into a warm call. It allows you to introduce yourself and say something like, "Hi, I'm so and so and I'm calling to find out if the doctor received our letter." Just this one statement gives you a starting point for the phone call and helps you get the conversation going. But if you are quickly rejected, just move on to your next phone call. It's not about *you*, so don't take it personally.

If the party is helpful and stays on the phone with you, it's a good sign that you can initiate a longer conversation. But keep in mind that your phone marketing should have limited goals. Don't aim to tell the party on the line everything about your business. Focus on telling them just enough to pique their interest and then solicit their agreement to have you drop by the office for a face-to-face meeting during which you can present more details of your services. To do this, use language such as, "I'd like to take just 10 minutes of the doctor's time to see if my services can help your office." If the party says that the doctor is not free, then set up your appointment with the office administrator or office manager. He or she is the next best choice for a presentation. (To be sure there is no confusion, always double check by asking, "Will the doctor be attending the meeting?" (You don't want to show up expecting to talk just with office manager, and not be prepared to talk to the doctor.)

Another tip is that when you feel you are getting close to being able to set up an appointment on a phone call, always ask for the appointment by giving them specific choices of time rather than a general questions. For example, say, "Sure, I can come in this week to speak with you. What works best for the doctor, Tuesday or Thursday morning at 9:00 a.m.?" Don't say something like, "Is the doctor available on Tuesday?" In other words, if you ask a Yes / No question, you give the party a chance to simply say "no" rather than asking an open ended question where the party has to work with you to determine the best answer.

If you work with ClaimTek, we provide you with professional phone "scripts" that help you know what to say when you make calls. Our scripts give you confidence and supply you with specific wording to use when responding to objections. Our scripts were developed by professional sales people and are a tremendous asset if you have not done phone sales before. In addition, ClaimTek's programs that allow you to offer doctors free or discounted software along with many other unique services open a window to a whole new approach to effective telephone conversations. ClaimTek has developed specialized telephone scripts to help you with such dialogues.

Category 7 – Build Up Your Visibility

As a business person in your community, it is often very useful to spend some of your marketing efforts simply on becoming a known and well-respected figure in your area. Building your credibility and professionalism can go a long way towards getting clients who hear about you just because you are visible in your area. Doctors often want to do business with people whom they see involved with other professionals in your city. Your reputation precedes you. Here are various ideas to help you build your visibility.

Toastmasters

The organization called Toastmasters is one of the best venues to learn how to do public speaking so you can begin giving professional speeches to doctors' groups or when you have appointments in doctors' offices. Most people are deathly afraid of public speaking, but thousands learn how to tame their fears through training at Toastmasters. Learning how to speak in public can also make you more confident in one-on-one situations. There are thousands of Toastmaster groups across the US, and some large cities even have more than one. For assistance, contact your local Chamber of Commerce which can lead you in the right direction.

Joining a group like Toastmasters can also provide an informal networking organization for you. You are likely to meet other business people with whom you can network and share business leads. You may even find doctors attending Toastmasters, since some doctors want to become nationally known celebrities themselves.

Become a Speaker

Related to the above, an excellent way to market your business is to transform yourself into a public speaker of note in your community. There are dozens of opportunities to speak in front of the public, and even if doctors are not present, it can still serve your business purposes because other professional people who hear you may refer you to their doctors. Remember that each person you speak to is connected to at least 10 other people, so your name and reputation can get around quickly when you do public speaking. And one more time, you never know who might be in your audience. There may be a doctor or someone who works in a practice who can bring you in to meet the doctors.

Give Back to Your Community

Another route to becoming known in your community is to join a community service organization such as Kiwanis, Rotary, Lions Club or others. You can contribute your time or money to an organization and get your company name out there in exchange. In addition, many service clubs are always looking for speakers. Given that your specialty is healthcare, you might offer to speak about Medicare issues or insurance issues that the general public will appreciate. Or you can educate people about the healthcare system, by talking about changes in medical billing from paper to electronic, what a clearinghouse is, and other issues that some people might simply find fascinating. Always remember when you do public speaking that you don't have to be a perfect speaker. Audiences prefer someone who is honest, authentic, and is willing to just be real.

Join a Health Foundation

Finally, another way to gain visibility in your area is to become involved with a national health foundation. For example, you can join the Arthritis Foundation, American Cancer Society, or others. Getting on the board of one of these organizations often begins by volunteering to do some type of day to day activities. Once the people in the organization get to know you, they may ask you to join the board. There are often doctors on the boards who can turn into business for you. Most importantly, being involved in such organizations gives you a chance to hobnob with many of your local civic leaders and people involved in fundraising. The visibility you gain from such volunteering can go a long way towards getting your business up and running.

Are You Ready to Choose Your Marketing Mix?

We've now covered more than two dozen ways you can market your business. As you read through them, some hopefully appealed to you and you can see yourself comfortably doing them. Perhaps there were also some methods that you know you definitely will not approach now.

Here's a chance to mark off a shortlist of those techniques that you may want to try for yourself. Go through the list in the Marketing Checklist and place a check next to the ones that interest you. Keep this page marked as a reminder of all the methods you can explore when you are getting ready to begin strategizing your marketing.

Marketing Checklist

Option 1 –Tap into Your Own Resources

- Talk with Your Own Doctors
- Ask for Referrals from Friends

Option 2 - Network, Network, Network

- Join a Business Networking Group
- Join a Hospital Foundation
- Use Your Community's Master Calendar to Find Networking Opportunities
- Employer Advisory Council

- Hold Your Own Office Manager Meetings
- Tap Into Your Chamber of Commerce

Option 3 – Try the World of Direct Mail and Print-Based Marketing

- Conduct a Simple Postcard Campaign
- Distribute a Flier with an Offer They Can't Refuse
- Impress with a Brochure
- Write and Mail out Direct Mail Letters
- Print up Rolodex Inserts to Pass Out
- Create a Fax Campaign
- Advertise Your Business in Chamber of Commerce Pieces
- Electronic Newsletters (e-newsletters)
- Publish Articles on the Internet

Option 4 –Personally Visit Medical Offices and Make Friends

- Bringing Gifts into Medical Offices
- Host a Lunch and Chat
- Ask Offices for Referrals (and possibly offer to pay for them)

Option 5 – Big Ticket Marketing Options

- Advertise in Your Local Yellow Pages
- Seek out Local and Community Print Advertising Opportunities
- Appear at Trade Shows
- Go Big with a Billboard

Option 6 – Phone Call Marketing

- Phone calling

Option 7 – Build Up Your Visibility

- Toastmasters
- Become a Speaker
- Give back to Your community
- Join a Health Foundation

As you consider the above methods, always keep in mind that it is best to choose at least three to five methods and run them simultaneously. You cannot rest your hopes on just one method and expect to get business. For example, we know new billing companies that would buy an advertisement in the Yellow pages and then just wait for customers to come to them. That clearly doesn't cut it these days. You need to select a mix of "push" marketing and "pull" marketing so that you can be both pro-active and reactive.

In addition, you have to keep in mind that whichever methods you choose, you must maintain them for a period of time. As we said in the branding section of this chapter, it takes multiple repetitions of any type of marketing to get potential clients to recognize your business name and take action to contact you. You can't send a few dozen direct mail letters or make a few phone calls to doctors, and then think you've accomplished marketing. And you certainly cannot conclude that if you get some rejections when you first start out that it means you should give up.

You really need to work through your marketing efforts for one to three months in order to truly assess its effectiveness. You may get a client within your first month, or you may need to push through and continue marketing for another one or two months before you see a payoff.

This is yet another reason why working with ClaimTek can speed up your results. ClaimTek will train you to do marketing and has prepared an extensive selection of professionally designed and printed brochures, trifolds, fliers, and other printed materials that save you time and money over getting them written, designed, and printed yourself.

What to Do Once You Get an Appointment with the Doctor

The goal of all your marketing is to obtain a personal appointment in front of the decision maker, whether this is the doctor in a solo practice, the lead doctor in a multiple practice, or simply the office manager. Whoever you are meeting with, the stakes are high. This meeting is your chance to present your company and assess their needs in working with you. What should you do once you know you have an appointment scheduled? Here are some tips.

Scout Around Before the Appointment

One of the first things you want to do once you have set up an appointment is to do as much preliminary research as possible about your potential client. Don't walk into the office as if you are ignorant of their specialty or their needs. There is a huge amount of information you can learn about the practice even before you walk in the door so that you can seem informed, knowledgeable, and ready to meet their needs.

One element of this is to get a sense of the doctor's or manager's motivations in talking to you. For example, consider the following:

- Is there something happening in the doctor's specialty that might be affecting the office?
- Are there competitors to this doctor that might be causing them to want to beef up their practice management skills? Who are the other local players?
- Are there any HMOs who are going out of business that might be affecting this doctor's billing?
- Is the doctor part of an IPA that might be going out of business? (Note: One of the first clues of an IPA going under is that the payments start being held and extend beyond 30 or 60 days.)
- Are there any employers who are going out of business but whose employees tended to feed this doctor's practice? (Many large employers provide lots of patients to doctors in their area, so the loss of an employer can have a big impact on a practice.)
- Is there anything going on in your state regarding workers' comp that might influence this doctor?
- Has this doctor's office perhaps had a lot of staff turnover or lost its biller?
- Is the doctor difficult to work with and so any prior billing companies have left him or her?

These are all good questions to attempt to answer prior to your meeting.

You'd be amazed at how much information you can find out with a little judicious nosing around. Perhaps you can talk to someone in the doctor's office who can tell you some of these things. Or perhaps you can locate a patient of the doctor by just asking around among your own family and friends, and if so, perhaps the patient can give you a sense of what the doctor is like and whether there is anything going on in the office that is evident to patients.

As you do this research, always be professional. Do not give anyone the impression that you are being nosey or a rumor monger. Your goal is to build your ability to quickly understand the office's situation and to be able to empathize with whatever issues they may be facing. By being prepared in this way, you can also give a more targeted presentation about the services you can offer and the benefits of working with you.

This research also helps you figure out what questions you might want to ask the doctor, thus impressing him or her that you know about their business. You don't want it to seem that you snooped around beforehand, but if the doctor notices that you are asking good questions, it can be a point in your favor. For example, in today's "insurance-is-king" environment, you will probably often hear doctors tell you, when you ask about their aspirations and dreams, that they are being pushed to the wall by delays and downgrading in insurance payments and they are eager to preserve their independence and income security in the face of managed care. Many will also tell you that they want to practice medicine, not business. They are frustrated by Medicare, Medicaid, and private health insurance rules and regulations. Your ability to sell is strongest when you can address these issues persuasively and convincingly. You need to show your commitment to be a strong advocate for the doctor and to expertly handle his or her practice management problems.

How to Handle the Appointment

When going in to meet the doctor, make sure you are always about 10 minutes early to the meeting. If you arrive in advance by more than 15 minutes, it is considered invasive, so don't rush and be too early. Just wait in your car. Don't pressure them by being there too early. Ten minutes early is fine, but not more.

And, of course, **never be late.** No need to say why it's important not to be late.

Wear professional attire. For men, this would include a tie with a sports jacket. For women, it's a pant suit or dress with a jacket. But women, leave your jewelry at home so it doesn't seem like you are there on a social encounter and be sure long hair is pulled back or in appropriate business style. This is not the time to appear flirtatious.

And very important, **don't put on perfume or cologne**. Medical offices often request their personnel to avoid perfumes because some patients may be allergic.

Here are tips on how to conduct the conversation upon entering the office with the decision-maker:

1. Wait to be seated until they ask you to sit. To avoid awkwardness, initiate some small talk to get an easy and friendly conversation going. You can often find a good ice breaker by looking around the office and noticing something in the room that you like and then comment on it. A nice friendly opener helps set the stage for a relaxed conversation that follows. Avoid remarking on any photos though because you don't know who the people are. You might think it is fine to say "What a beautiful daughter you have!" only to find out that it's the doctor's wife. Maintain a professional, but personable appearance and don't shy away from being friendly or intelligent just because you are talking to a doctor. They are people, too, and despite being busy, they will enjoy the conversation much more if you exude a pleasant personality.
2. Once you sit down and begin talking business, this is when you can bring out any of the beautiful, impressive marketing pieces that you want to use during the meeting or to leave behind with the doctor to act on. But don't give anything to the doctor immediately, as it might encourage him or her to begin reading rather than listening intently to you and conversing.
3. Despite any research you've done and what you already know, begin by asking about what might be happening in the office and the reason for your meeting. This shows your interest in their business, and it also corrects any misinformation you may have erroneously discovered. Ask questions like, "How has your cash flow been? Are you having trouble collecting on claims? Do you have on-site personnel or an outside service doing your billing?" Let the doctor respond to your questions so you can further your understanding as to why you are there. Take notes as the doctor speaks, using a yellow pad. Not only does note-taking look professional, but it also helps you remember what issues you *must* address when it comes to your time to talk. Write down and number every issue that the doctor mentions so that when you later present, you can say something like, "Concerning your issue #1, here is what I propose ….. and for issue #2…., etc." In this way, you address one by one every concern the doctor has. This organized approach makes you seem highly professional, a trait doctors appreciate.
4. As you talk, try to find out what percentage of the doctor's patients are Medicare patients versus PPO patients, and what percentage are

within an HMO or IPA. Knowing these percentages is critical as it can reveal to you how much extra work it will take to process the claims. Medicare claims are far easier than commercial insurance claims because Medicare either makes clean payments or they simply don't pay. It's either black or it's white. But with commercial insurance, there are so many delays, downgraded payments, and rejected claims, you are going to have far more work with all the phone calls and follow ups. This information therefore factors directly into your decision about your fees, specifically the percentage you might ask for. (See pricing, covered below.)

5. Along with any research you've done and the conversation you have, you should be prepared at the close to clearly address how you can help the doctor with your services. Take each item the doctor may have mentioned one by one and tell him or her how you can resolve their problems and improve their bottom line. Focus on whatever main issues the doctor has mentioned. If he or she seemed sensitive to cash flow, emphasize how you will increase it. If the doctor talked about improving patient statements and making sure patient payments are completed on time, be sure to address this issue.

6. If you are just beginning your business and do not yet have any clients, it is a real Catch 22 if you are asked for references. It is best not to lie, but you don't want to lose the business. We recommend you say something like, "You would be my first doctor in this specialty. I have a whole team that I can tap into that can help me if there are any questions regarding this specialty." Some doctors will never even ask for references though. To strengthen your position as a start-up business, it is helpful to have cutting-edge technology and solutions to ensure that you can always make a compelling offer to potential clients. Doctors are busy, so you must be able to gain their attention with a compelling value proposition that gives them the motivation not only to listen to you but to take action.

7. While you cannot expect to nail a deal in a first meeting, be prepared for it just in case it happens. Have two copies of your standard contract printed out and ready to go, just leave your fees and pricing schedule blank since you need to know about the practice before you set this. (We'll address fees, pricing, and contracts in the sections below, but for now, keep reading to get a sense of what you need to do during this meeting.) If you are clear on what you want to charge

based on what you learned at this meeting, feel free to tell the doctor now. If you need to think about your pricing or ask more questions about the practice, tell the doctor that you will get back to him or her in 24 hours, but leave the contract for them to examine, along with a stamped return envelop in case they want to sign and mail it back to you.

8. Bring all the paperwork for your clearinghouse with you as well, in case the doctor signs up with you. Clearinghouses need to have official licensing information from each doctor for whom they process claims to ensure that the claims are not bogus and to track the information properly.

9. If the doctor does not immediately sign up with your company in this first meeting, always clarify what the next steps are. Don't walk out of the meeting being in limbo about what you are supposed to do next. Essentially, there are only two possible outcomes if the doctor does not agree to sign up with you at this meeting:

- The doctor communicates in one way or another that he or she is not ready to make a change now. Sometimes this communication is not evident, in which case it is helpful for you to clarify this directly. You might say something like, "I would like to do business with you and my company can solve the problems you are having with your claims and cash flow. Are you ready to sign a contract with us this month or in a month from now?" This type of question forces the doctor to answer you directly and to state a time period about when he or she might be ready, if at all. You can then know whether you should follow up with that doctor at a future time. You might even ask if the doctor would like you to get back to him or her or to the office manager at some later date. Whatever the answer, always express your thanks to the doctor for taking the time with you, and be positive and gracious when leaving. You never know why the doctor may be hesitating to contract with your company. It could very well turn out that you get a call from them in a few weeks or months. The fact that you had the meeting is usually a good sign that the practice has a sincere interest in making some type of change, and your personality, attitude, and professionalism can have a big impact on whether they select you.

- Alternatively, the doctor wants more information from you about your business or your pricing, in which case you should clearly commit to providing the information as soon as you can, preferably within 24 hours. Any expression of interest is a good sign that you are in the running for the contract, so it's important to take everything you learned in this meeting and put it to use as you pull together any follow-up documents required.

So, if the close of your meeting is unclear, always remember that your sales call must boil down to just one of these options: either a) you got the business, or b) the doctor is not quite ready or is not interested, or c) the doctor wants more information. All vague conversations must reflect one of these options. If you are unclear, ask the doctor to tell you specifically if they would like to work with you beginning this month or at another time. As we said, this will help ensure that you get a clear response. And if the doctor truly sounds like he or she is considering your business, be sure you know when the decision is going to be made and what you can do to follow up. You might even throw in a gentle push, such as, "Doctor, I take on just a few new clients at a time, and I'd like to be able to place you in the opening that I have this month, so I'll look forward to hearing from you."

Focusing on Service and Benefits for the Client

Whenever you meet with a healthcare provider, always remember the cardinal rule of sales – focus on meeting the customer's needs. In the case of doctors, those needs may be improving cash flow, increasing the reimbursement ratio, or stabilizing the physician's income security. Avoid touting your own credentials or background unless asked, and don't be longwinded about the technology of electronic claims. Your goal is assure the doctor's conscious or unconscious concern that your company can be trusted to fulfill his or her practice needs. You have to effectively answer the question, "How will this person help me operate my healthcare practice better?"

Be specific in stating how you will benefit the doctor. Let the doctor know that you can simplify the claims filing process, reduce office paperwork, accelerate the speed at which they are reimbursed, increase their collection efficiency, and improve their cash flow by thoroughly tracking and collecting on all accounts receivable, including secondary and tertiary insurers, as well as patients. Be specific in stating what your office does to help them. For example, you might say, "We follow up on all claims that have not been paid within 30 days. If we find that any information is missing, we will work with your office to get the data to ensure that the claims are paid immediately thereafter."

If you offer full practice management services, give the doctor a list of all the different reports that you can provide them to help them make better decisions in their day-to-day business. Show some sample reports so that the provider can see how effective having this information can be to their practice. Many providers are not even aware of the capabilities of medical billing software to organize and report on their practice. Reports can often reveal to doctors that they are overly billing only a few codes compared to the actual time and procedures they are truly performing. They may need to change their superbill to include more codes or to be more aggressive in using codes that have higher reimbursement rates.

One thing you can be sure about as a professional medical biller and practice manager – if a doctor is not outsourcing their billing to a professional company such as yours, it is very likely that they have a serious problem, even if the doctor is not aware of it. The fact is, the average in-house staff person does not know as much about medical billing and reimbursement as you will. This person doesn't have time to develop the expertise that you have or the time to be constantly learning. Given this, you have a leg up on any doctor who uses an in-house biller, and you should not hesitate to constantly reinforce that your company can benefit them in ways they cannot even imagine.

How to Price Your Services

There are essentially two tried and true pricing strategies in medical billing that have become standard. The first is pricing on a per claim / per statement basis, and the second is pricing according to a percentage of all income that you help collect for the doctor.

In general, medical billing companies today are increasingly aiming to price their services using the percentage method. But before we explain why this is so and why you too will likely want to use this method, here are the details about both methods so you can understand them.

Per Claim / Per Statement Method

The per claim / per statement pricing method is exactly as its name implies. You price your service literally according to each claim that you send out to an insurance company, whether it is electronic or on paper. It also doesn't matter if the claim goes to a primary, secondary, or tertiary insurance company. In short, every claim you submit counts.

Tallying claims submitted is easy enough to do these days. Most medical billing software programs will allow you to print out a list of all claims printed or sent electronically over a period of time, whether it's weekly or monthly. You can easily print such a list and invoice your doctor according to whatever payment schedule you set up.

In terms of how much to charge if you price on a per claim basis, it varies a great deal among billing companies. In areas where the cost of living is relatively low, a home-based biller may be able to charge only $3 or $4 per claim for the common types of claims filed by chiropractors, internists, podiatrists, pediatric physicians, dermatologists and other providers whose claims are straightforward. In areas where the cost of living is much higher, your billing company may be able to charge $5 or $6 per claim and sometimes more for complex claims that require backup documentation to be sent with the claims.

Billing companies that also print and mail patient statements price those separately. For example, your company might charge $1.50 to $2.00 per patient statement you mail out, plus reimbursement for the postage.

The advantages of the per claim / per statement pricing method are that it is simple and easy to calculate your fees. Each month, you tally how many claims and statements you've handled, multiply the counts times your pricing, and that is your total invoice for the doctor. For example, if in one month for one doctor, you submitted 600 claims and printed out 424 statements, and your fees are $3 / claim and $2 / statement, you would invoice your client (the doctor) $1,800 for claims and $848 for statements, totaling $2,648. It doesn't matter if the insurance companies have completed payment on those claims or not, or if the invoiced patients have sent in their checks – the doctor owes you $2,648 for your work that month.

Although it is simple and straightforward, there are numerous disadvantages of the per claim / per statement pricing method, which is why many medical billers have moved to the percentage method of pricing their services. One disadvantage is that claims are often not paid upon first submission. Insurers lose them, delay the payment, or the claim contains an error – and so many claims must get resubmitted a second and even a third time. This leaves a large gray area between you and the doctor. Do you charge your per claim fee for all those resubmissions? What if a resubmission was your fault for having mistyped the claim? What if the resubmission is the insurance company's problems, yet the doctor does not feel that he or she should pay you for their mistake?

Another disadvantage of the per claim / per statement method is that it doesn't pay you for any time you might spend on the phone with either insurers or patients. If you tell your clients that your service ensures that each and every claim gets paid, this means that you must follow up on unpaid claims, which takes your time. You may need to call insurers, file "tracers" (copies of claims marked tracer so that the insurer knows it's a duplicate claim that is being resubmitted), or go on the Internet to check the status of a claim. (Many insurers now have complete listings of claims and their status on a web site that authorized billers can check.) As for patients, you may get calls from them to inquire about their statement, or you may need to call patients to remind them about paying. These tasks can amount to a lot of unpaid time for you.

Doctors often don't like the per claim / per statement method either because it contains no built-in incentive for the biller to ensure that the claims get paid to the highest extent and as soon as possible. The biller can submit the claims to insurers and then bill the doctor the per claim fees, regardless of what happens to the claims. The same goes for patient statements. Although the biller may profess that he or she pursues unpaid patient balances, the motivation to make sure they get paid is not there.

In short, the per claim / per statement method is usually not in your best interests or the doctor. This pricing method may be fine if you have a smaller, part-time billing practice working with only a few providers, but if you are conducting a full-time medical practice management company, you are much better off pricing your services according to the percentage method, as described next.

Percentage Method

The percentage method essentially follows a single rule: you are paid according to a fixed percentage of any and every dollar that comes into the doctor's practice for which you do any processing. This means that you get a fixed percentage of all the reimbursements from insurance companies, all the patient payments, and even all the co-pays that are paid right at the doctor's office, since you have to record those payments and account for them, too.

The percentage method has the advantages we talked about above. You are compensated for the time you spend recording payments and pursuing unpaid claims because your efforts help get them paid. You are compensated for recording and tracking co-pays even though they were paid to the doctor. You are compensated for dealing with patients and questions they have on their statements.

Of course, the big question is, what percentage should you charge? What percentage is fair to compensate you for all the time you put into keeping patient records, typing and filing claims, pursuing unpaid claims, and helping patients with their statements? In general, the answer is that billing companies that perform full and advanced practice management usually charge between 4% and 15% of all collections. This is a large spread, but there are many factors involved that affect which percentage you should charge. Here are some guidelines:

- In general, the average fee is 6% to 10% for simple medical practices such as chiropractors, internists, podiatrists, dermatologists, and so on. This percentage is based on what you collect, not what you bill out. The determining factor in this range is the complexity of the claims. Does the doctor tend to use the same billing codes over and over, which makes your work easier? Do the claims tend to be paid without question, with few denials or downgrades, which means that you seldom have follow up to do? If the answer is Yes to these two questions, you will be able to charge 6% to 8%, but if the answer is No, you may want to make a case for 8% to 10%.

- The second rule of thumb in the percentage method is that the higher the dollar amount of the typical claim, the lower the percentage you can charge. For example, if you are billing for a surgeon who submits only 50 claims per month but those claims average $5,000 per claim, you can only ask for perhaps 4% to 7% as your percentage. However, if you are billing for a family practitioner who has 250 to 600 claims per month with average fees of $50 to $100 per claim, you might go ahead and ask for 7% to 10%.

- A third guideline to consider in determining your percentage is the amount of extra work you need to do for each client. For example, let's say you find out that a potential client's practice requires you to file many secondary and tertiary insurance claims. This adds a layer of additional work for you because you have to track the primary payment and then submit the claim to the secondary insurer, sometimes with backup paperwork that you have to print out and mail. Certain providers have many denied claims that require appeals and that too is extra work. As we said earlier in the chapter, this guideline suggests that it is critical for you to get as much detailed information as you can from prospective clients, so you can assess the degree of extra work you may need to do. Extensive extra work might mean you increase your usual fee of 7% or 8% to 9% or 10%.

- Finally, a last guideline to consider is that if you sign on a new doctor who wants you to review unpaid claims more than several months old, you don't want to include these in your standard rate. Many doctors come to hire an outside billing service precisely because they discover that they have lots of old outstanding claims (remaining from prior poor collection techniques) and so now they expect you to pursue them to get them paid. Such claims can be very lucrative for you and impress your client if you can get them paid, but they always take extra time. It is therefore very appropriate to ask the doctor for 12% to 15% of these claims. Considering that any money you bring in is a windfall for the doctor (since he or she expected never to be paid on them anyway), it is likely that the provider will happily agree to your higher percentage. You might even remind them that if they didn't have you to follow up on these claims, they may need to send them to a collection agency that charges 35% to 55%, so your fee is still a bargain.

Note that when you charge on the percentage basis, all your services are included in your fee. After all, you are doing full practice management for that fee. Your work includes inputting patient records, getting the superbills from the doctor's office (by fax or in person), entering claims, filing claims either electronically or on paper, printing patient statements, appealing denied or downgraded claims, posting receivables (payments) from insurers and patients, printing and mailing patient statements, and possibly answering phone calls from patients and/or doing "soft" collections where you call patients who are delinquent in their payments. Your percentage fee should also include preparing weekly, monthly, and year-end reports for your client.

Choosing Between the Two Methods of Pricing Your Services

As we indicated above, if you are coming into medical billing and intend to begin a professional, full-time, full practice management company, you are probably better off selecting the percentage method rather than the per claim / per statement method. In general, this method pays off better. For this reason, we recommend that anytime you meet with a prospective client, always think in terms of starting out with the percentage method and use the per claim method only as a fallback.

Many billing companies are generating handsome incomes themselves because they receive a percentage of every dollar that their clients take in. Think of it this way: if you have a doctor who generates $450,000 each year in total collections from insurers and patients, and your contract stipulates that you receive 7% of this amount, that's $31,500 income to you from one doctor alone. If you have five doctors generating between $400,000 and

$600,000 per year, and you charge 7% for each of them, you have the potential to earn between $140,000 and $210,000.

Nevertheless, as we also said, the per claim / per statement is fine if you run a small practice and the claims are simple. Let's say you have only three clients who each bill out an average of 325 claims per month, and you charge $4 per claim. That's $1,300 per doctor times three doctors, which equals $3,900 income per month for yourself.

Note that you can use a different pricing method for each client you have. There is no rule against charging one client with the percentage method and another with the per claim / per statement method. The only problem is that if one of the doctors refers you to another doctor, your new client may expect you to charge the exact same rate as the referring colleague receives. That could cause problems if the two practices are quite different.

One conclusion to draw from this discussion is that you need to be analytical about your pricing and try to evaluate each practice on its own terms. Anytime you meet with a prospective client, assess as accurately as you can how many claims per month, the average dollar value of the claims, and, if possible, the total billable amount from the office per month. Of course, many doctors will not want to divulge their personal financial information to you, especially in a first meeting. However, if you can focus the doctor on how well you will increase his or her collection efficiency, you may be able to obtain a ballpark figure that allows you to estimate the doctor's annual income. You can then do your own comparison between the per claim / per statement and percentage methods to see which way you come out ahead.

If you are stuck evaluating the percentage you might charge, see if you can ask the doctor how much they are currently paying their billing company, or how much they are paying an office staff person to do the billing. This may help you get a ballpark of the amount of money the doctor is already willing to pay for billing and/or practice management services. Next, ask the questions we discussed, such as:

- What is the number of patients in the practice on Medicare versus commercial insurance? Medicare tends to be easier to bill than commercial insurers who often deny or downgrade payments, so you have much more work to do with patients on commercial insurance.
- What is the number of patients, if known, who have multiple insurances (secondary and tertiary)? The more patients who have multiple insurances, the more billing you will have to do.

- What is their current reimbursement ratio (how much is billed versus how much is collected on average)? The lower the ratio, the more problems the office has, since it means that they are billing out far more than they are collecting.
- What is the aging of the collectibles? How much is 30 days old? 60 days old? 90 days old? The greater the dollar amounts that are due by 60 or 90 days, the worse the situation and the more work you may need to do to pursue the unpaid claims.
- How many patient statements are typically mailed out per month? Is the doctor having problems collecting from patients?
- Does the practice have claims older than three or six months that they want you to pursue and collect on?

This information will be critical to your decision on whether to increase your standard percentage fees. Consider the following rationale for upping your fees. Let's say that a single doctor's billing and practice management takes you an extra five hours of work per week and you'd like to get compensated for your work at $50 / hour. That means you'd like to have an extra $250 per week in fees from that doctor, thus $1,000 per month. Meanwhile, let's say the doctor generates $35,000 per month. Your usual 7% fee would provide you with $2,450 per month. But since you'd now believe you need to receive an additional $1,000 per month for the extra work, hence $3,450 for the month, you may decide to ask the doctor for 10% which would net your $3,500.

As this example shows, it's important to be able to calculate how much extra work you may have to do and what impact each extra 1% fee will earn you. If a doctor generates $25,000 per month on average, each extra 1% more in your fees earns you just $250 more, barely enough to cover five hours extra work over the entire month. But if the doctor generates $50,000 per month, each extra 1% you charge earns an additional $500, enough to cover perhaps 10 hours of extra work per month.

With experience and time, you will learn how to make these types of assessments quickly whenever you meet with a doctor so that you can quote your fees on the fly during the meeting when the question comes up. Or alternatively, bring a calculator with you and ask the doctor to excuse you for a few minutes while you go to the men's or ladies room where you can privately make some calculations about the fee you think you might ask for. Of course, you can also tell the doctor that you need to analyze the situation following your meeting and that you will get back to him or her with a specific pricing proposal within 24 hours.

Finally, if you decide to work with ClaimTek, we will help you determine the best pricing for you on a case-by-case basis. Anytime you have an appointment with a provider, we will help you analyze the situation and determine your pricing strategy. This feature is part of ClaimTek's *Consulting Support Services*. ClaimTek also offers you unique software that allows you to do an automated billing cost analysis for doctor's offices, comparing the doctor's costs in doing the billing in-house versus how much it would cost if they use your services. The software generates side-by-side comparison tables and graphics to support a compelling argument, usually in your favor.

Tips on Negotiating Strategies

Negotiating your fee with a prospective client can be stressful, so here are some tips to consider:

- Based on the analysis you conduct for the doctor's office, start out as high as you think you can get when you begin negotiating fees. Consider that the doctor will probably make a counter offer, so don't begin at the lowest percentage you are willing to settle for, because you may need to give in a little to maintain the diplomacy of the negotiations. Start high and expect the doctor to ask you to cut something off. Or offer to reduce your fee upon hearing any objections, as that makes it seem like you are already giving them a reduction.
- You may want to offer a low rate to your very first client just to get the business and give yourself a referral. However, don't make it your policy to price yourself too low just to win business, because you may actually be doing yourself a disservice by trying to lowball contracts. When you work for too little, you can end up with no time available to find better paying clients on whom you can make a better profit. It's wiser to think about your long-term survivability because you won't stay in the business unless you make a profit at it.
- Think in terms that your pricing reflects the quality of your service. If you consider yourself a professional and you intend to give your doctor premium service, be confident about asking for premium pricing. Point out to the doctor that while you may cost an extra $500

per month, you can help bring in an extra $5,000 per month through your attention to timely claims filing and your dedicated pursuit of all unreimbursed claims and unpaid patient statements.

- Keep in mind that you may not want to increase your fee for at least a few years. Most doctors won't appreciate a billing service that tries to increase its fees every year, as it gives the feeling that you have done a "bait and switch" job on them. Doctors are under the gun from insurers themselves, and their own incomes are often stretched. Some doctors are paying off huge medical school loans, and most have very high liability insurance and office rent. Therefore, it is likely that whatever percentage or per claim fee you agree to, you will need to stick to it for perhaps two or more years.
- If the doctor has resistance to the fee you would like to charge, reassure them that your fees are comprehensive and include all the services you have. Reinforce that you don't nickel and dime your clients. For example, you don't charge for long distance phone calls to patients or trips to their office to pick up the superbills, and so on.
- Finally, recognize that all people negotiate. Be ready for some give and take. Don't take the negotiation personally as an accusation about your character, work ethic, or reliability. It's common for people to ask for a special deal or a reduced price. Be prepared to yield some ground, but don't throw yourself at the customer's feet in order to get the business. Good negotiations should convey that you respect yourself and expect others to pay you fairly and treat you appropriately. Just remember when you are negotiating your fees, the best deal is a win / win deal.

Creating Contracts

Whenever you sign up a doctor, you can't rely on a handshake for your deal. It's critical to have a legal contract between your company and the medical practice that spells out the terms of your agreement and adds protections for you. This agreement doesn't need to be long. It can be as little as one page or as many as five. You can hire a lawyer to help you hammer it out, you can write your own and have a lawyer review it, or you can work with ClaimTek and we will supply you with templates for several legal contracts.

Medical billing and practice management contracts typically cover the following:

1. ***Services provided.*** The contract must state what services you will provide to the medical practice. If you are doing full medical practice management, list precisely as many services as you can account for, such as maintaining and updating patient records, keying medical claims, submitting claims to a clearinghouse, posting receivables from insurers and patients, preparing and mailing patient statements, fielding phone calls from patients, appealing denied or underpaid claims by making phone calls and writing letters to insurers, preparing monthly reports for your client, keeping ICD-9 and CPT codes up to date, and so on. Be as specific as possible so there is no misunderstanding of your responsibilities.

2. ***Fees.*** The contract must indicate the fees you will charge your client so that there is never any dispute or lack of clarity. Indicate also how frequent you will invoice your client.

3. ***Authorized Agency.*** It is important that your contract state that you are an authorized agent for the doctor to call on their behalf to insurance carriers and patients. You need this in writing for HIPAA purposes and to ensure that anyone you speak to is aware of the fact that you have been authorized to speak to them about their medical account with your client.

4. ***Confidentiality and Non-Disclosure.*** The contract must state that you and your staff will maintain the confidentiality of all medical records in your keeping, and that you will not disclose to any party who is not authorized to receive information about patients. Meanwhile, on the other side, you want your contract to also state that the provider will keep your billing company information confidential, such as your procedures and fees.

5. ***Waiver of Damages.*** It is useful that you include in your contract a "waiver of damages" that indicates that your billing service is not responsible for any damages caused by your client's billing insurers. This statement is intended to protect you against errors that your client may unintentionally or intentionally make in coding and billing medical procedures. You must protect yourself from such errors, and remember, you are not allowed to do any coding yourself. You are simply a pass-through for the coding the provider has given you –

and thus, you are effectively not a party to any errors the doctor may make.

6. ***Duration of the Agreement.*** Include a clause in your contract indicating the amount of time the agreement lasts. In general, it is best to write your contracts for at least six months, if not a full year. Remember that it may take you a lot of time to set up a new practice, because you need to key in or import all the past patient, provider, and insurance records. It is simply not worthwhile to create a contract for just one, two, or three months. You won't make back your investment in time. We recommend that you aim to write your contracts for a year, and step back to six months if the doctor insists. By the way, here are two additional tips about the duration of your contract:

- If your contract is going to be for at least a year, but you are unsure if you priced the account correctly, consider adding a statement indicating that your fees can be reviewed after six months. This gives you a chance to try out the account and determine if you have properly priced your services. You can indicate in the contract that the fees can be modified after six months, and if any new fees are not acceptable to the provider, he or she can terminate the agreement. This is a low-risk statement to add to your contract, because most providers don't really want to keep changing billing services, especially if you are doing the excellent job you intend to do.

- A rule of thumb in billing contracts is that the larger your client, the longer you want your contract. In fact, some billing services write their contracts for as much as two years for large clients. For example, if you sign a contract with a clinic, aim to make it for two or even three years. It simply takes a lot of work to set up and handle a large client, and you want to protect your investment of time and effort for as long as you can. If you write a contract for longer than one year, definitely add a rider, as suggested above, that allows you to add an increase of perhaps ½ percentage point each year to the first year's fees to account for inflation and as a salary raise for yourself.

7. ***Termination Process.*** Your contract should also specify the basis on which it may be terminated. You might, for instance, have a termination clause indicating that the agreement can be cancelled only for just cause, such as delinquency in filing claims on your part or delinquency in paying your fees on your client's part. But frankly,

keep in mind that, as in any business, it is counterproductive to have clients with whom you are not happy or who are dissatisfied with you. We recommend here that if you are not getting along with a client, it's far easier to part ways than to litigate. Just have a friendly conversation with the client and make it clear that he or she needs to get a new biller. However, it is best to write any termination clause so that it gives you and your client 30-day notice, rather than having termination become effective immediately.

Overcoming Common Startup Marketing Problems

You're coming close to the end of this chapter, but we have a few more things to discuss about marketing. Many people get into business without realizing that marketing must consume perhaps 80% or more of your time when you first begin your business. You are going to need commitment and persistence in your marketing efforts. It takes time and repetition to land that first client, and then the second one, the third one, and so on.

Here are some tips on a few common start-up problems that often prevent people from succeeding in medical billing and practice management. These suggestions are based on comments and experiences we've heard about from people who were not prepared for these types of start-up issues, so it's important that you read these over and remember them as you work through your first few months in business.

Difficulty Getting a Response from Potential Clients

Many people go into medical billing with high expectations about how quickly they are going to land their first doctor. But medical billing is just like any business. As we said before, the rule in marketing is that it takes as many as six to eight impressions before people respond to advertising or marketing. This is not to say that you have to mail seven brochures to your list of doctors before anything happens, but we are suggesting that you will generally need persistence and repetition to get their attention. Just mailing out one brochure is usually not enough. That's why in this chapter, we gave you more than two dozen methods to reach doctors.

Think of it this way. If you employ three to five techniques discussed, you have a good chance of crossing paths with several potential clients more than a few times. For example, you might send out a direct mail letter, followed up by a phone call, followed by a warm sales call with a gift basket to the doctor's office, followed by seeing that doctor at a fundraiser you attend because you volunteered at a hospital foundation, followed by a postcard offering a free superbill code analysis – and finally, you get a call from the doctor's office manager that they would be interested in talking to you.

It is these sorts of consistent, professional marketing efforts that turn into landing a client. You never know where that first client is going to come from, so you need to keep working at it. Mix your marketing methods up until you find the right combination that fits your personality and your skill set.

Nevertheless, if you believe your response rate is far too low for your efforts, you might also want to re-evaluate what you are doing. Perhaps your direct mail letter needs revising? Perhaps your gift item when you walk around medical offices is not the eye-catcher that you really want. Perhaps your offer for a free code analysis is not being sent to the right audience. There might be numerous reasons that you need to re-evaluate your marketing. Perhaps you simply need to try some other marketing methods.

Financial and emotional barriers are some of the reasons that prevent many doctors from wanting to hand over their cash flow to anyone. (Imagine a doctor who is already losing income from insurance companies and feeling frightened about his or her future. Will this be a trusting person?)

Slow Decision Making from Potential Clients

One truth you should be aware of in this business is that doctors can be very slow in making up their minds about outsourcing their billing or changing from one billing service to another. In some cases, there may also be office politics involved, such as an office manager who insists on maintaining control over each and every decision, even though you have met with a doctor and received a tentative go-ahead to take over the practice management.

The way to counteract slow decision-making when you are very close to landing a client is to be absolutely firm in letting the doctor know that you would like to take over the billing immediately. By communicating your confidence to the doctor, you can often reassure him or her that you are the right person for the job. As we pointed out earlier, use precise language when you talk to a doctor about starting the job. Don't say, "When would you like me to begin?" but instead use wording like, "I only add one new client at a time. I have an opening right now. Would you like me to put you in the opening?" This type of phrasing comes from a position of strength and adds value to your time.

Resistance to Outsourcing Practice Management

Some doctors are so ingrained in their traditional ways that they may not understand the value of the services you offer. They may ask you questions out of curiosity to find out about how you can help them, but they constantly revert back to thinking they can continue to handle all their billing in-house.

You're actually fortunate if you encounter a client like this, because they can be persuaded to change. Here are some ideas to show them how you can help their practice:

- Ask the client if their office billing person keeps up with code changes in their field each and every year.
- Does this person understand how to determine if the codes being used are clearly the only choices available to their practice?
- Does this person use modifiers?
- Does this person present the doctor with reports that analyze which codes are most often billed to indicate if the practice is maximizing its potential?
- Does the in-house billing person track the reimbursement ratio and report that to the doctor?
- Has the reimbursement ratio been going up?

As you can see, tough questions like these are aimed at showing the doctor that their in-house person, while a loyal employee, may not have the depth of skills and expertise that you can bring to the billing and practice management. By appealing to the doctor's bottom line, you are very likely to help bring about a shift in his or her thinking – and then you simply need to make a strong closing argument that your company is the right candidate to help the doctor maximize the practice's profits.

If the Client Does Not Want to Outsource, You Can Still Build a Relationship

One of the advantages of working with ClaimTek is that if you have a doctor who still insists on doing the billing in-house after your presentation, you have the option of selling them the MedOffice software and other viable services. You can also sell them complete training and support, so that you can walk away from the appointment still a big winner.

In our experience, out of 10 presentations, you might get one or two situations like this and we encourage you to capitalize on them. The advantage of having this opportunity is that it allows you to build a relationship and stay connected to the doctor's office, even if you don't get the billing and practice management business right now. You never know if sometime down the line, the doctor may change his or her mind and decide that they do indeed want to outsource their billing to you. For example, if they experience instability in their office, such as staff who come and go quickly, they'll remember you as being dependable. You can then grow your relationship with from a software or service client to becoming a full practice management client.

The goal is to plant the seeds in as many places and ways as possible. For this reason, the ClaimTek business opportunity program allows you to offer several ways to prove your credibility, either by winning the billing contract yourself or selling the software and services. With both our *Principal* and *Preferred* programs, you get a significant discount on software. This discounts allow you to resell the software, making either a profit on each unit sold to a medical provider. In addition, you can typically charge between $50 and $100 per hour for training the office staff to use the software, which usually takes at least a day! You can also charge a fee, such as $995, for annual support, which is still lower than average in the industry.

Again, the idea here is to leave the presentation with some type of connection if they choose to wait on outsourcing the billing. We help you cover as many bases as possible. Contact ClaimTek to learn more about becoming a vendor of our software and reseller of many services along with starting your medical billing or practice management business.

The Final Step: Write a Brief Business Plan to Chart Your Path

In this chapter, you've learned about dozens of marketing techniques to get your business off the ground, detailed information on two ways to price your services, an explanation of how to write a contract between your company and your clients, and suggestions for how to handle common startup problems. Now, as we come to the close of the chapter, we want to help you with one final issue that can be of great value to you, especially if you are a new entrepreneur – writing a business plan.

If you've never written a business plan, don't worry about doing this. It's not all that difficult and it's not even an absolute requirement that you do this. But it can be very useful to you as a business person. It's something you do for yourself to improve your thinking and help you make clear plans for growing your business. It also doesn't matter if you're not a great writer; no one has to read this. It's a document just for you, in which you make estimated projections about your income and growth rates, and you answer for yourself important questions such as these:

- Will I do just claims or full practice management?
- Will I offer additional services? If so, which services? (See Chapter 8.)
- Do I want to submit claims while sitting in my home office in my pajamas or do I want to get dressed up and go to an office that I rent?
- Do I want to have employees?
- Do I want to keep growing each and every year?
- Do I want to have lots of phone calls all day long or keep to myself and just run my business?
- Do I want to bill for doctors who are located throughout my state, or in other states, or do I want to have my clients only in my own town or city?
- Do I want to be marketing constantly or hire someone to market for me?

Even with all these questions, your business plan doesn't need to be very long. You can write your plan on your own computer using just your word-processor, or you can purchase specialized business plan software, such as *Business Plan Pro*, from Palo Alto Software. That software program actually has a pre-written business plan for starting a medical billing business that guides you along as you write. You simply change the names to your own and plug in your own details and numbers. If you write your own business plan, here is a list of topics that are commonly included:

I. Executive Summary

This section is just a summary of the contents found in the rest of the business plan. You don't need to write a summary if you are the only one viewing the business plan.

II. Company Presentation

This section of the plan focuses on what your company is about. It usually contains sub-sections such as the following:

- *Mission Statement* – This is a terse statement of the essential goals you are trying to fulfill for your clients. It helps you find a quick way to characterize your business.
- *Description of your business goals and financial requirements* – this sub-section lists your business goals in terms of how many clients you want to have and how much money you need to get the business off the ground.
- *Product and service offerings* – this sub-section discusses the products and services you want to offer. You may wish to expand this section after you read Chapter 8 in this book which lists many additional services you can offer outside of all the services we've covered so far in discussing full practice management.
- *Technology and resources* – This section lists the technology you may need, such as computer, phone equipment, fax machine, car, postage meter, etc.
- *Factors determining success* – This section summarizes your own thinking about the factors that you believe are critical to fulfill in order to achieve the success level you want. For example, you might give some thought and write about the timeline you would like to follow to land your first client, followed by the time to get the second one, as those are factors that you want to aim to achieve for your success. Or you might write about the specialty medical market you want to focus on learning.

III. Competitive Analysis

- *Major competitors and competitive positioning* – this section discusses everything you know about your competitors and how you need or want to position yourself so that your services are better than theirs. Perhaps you plan to offer more personalized service, or you aim to become a better expert in billing and practice management in a specific field than any competitor.

IV. Market Analysis

- *Market barriers* – this section discusses any challenges you face to getting into the market in your area. For example, one barrier might be that you don't have full time to begin your business if you are going to be working at your regular job until you land your first client. This is a barrier that you need to take into account, as it will impact your time to do marketing and follow-through.

- *Market demand* – This section discusses what you know about the market demand for your services. You might, for example, research how many doctors are in your immediate area or make some projections about the size of the medical specialty market you are going after.

- *Marketing plans (advertising, public relations, direct selling*) – This section is where you select and summarize for yourself all the marketing methods covered in this chapter (and any others you know about or learn about) that you are going to undertake. Develop your list of methods into a full marketing plan that covers one year; for example, think through how much you are going to spend on each method and when you are going to implement each method.

V. Income Analysis

- *Budget projection (income and expenses, gross profit / net profit)* -- Most entrepreneurs like to do a one-year income projection on a month-by-month basis when they write their first business plan. In the first few months, it is best to estimate realistically how much your startup expenses will be and allow for a period in which you may have no clients or perhaps only one or two. Then project your income over the next few months according to the assumptions you would like to make for adding more clients to your roster. If you want, you can also do a three-year budget projection, and always keep it updated, year after year.

This is the basic outline for writing a business plan. Try to write up the above sections and sub-sections in as much detail as you can now (or after you finish reading this book). Again, you don't need to be Donald Trump in your strategizing. This plan is just for you to help you solidify your thinking. Flesh out as much of the detail as you want, but the more you do, the better. If your plan is very rough, go back to it in a month or two and revise it once you know more about what you might want.

You'd be surprised at how useful it can be to have a business plan. For many people, the very act of writing down their goals often makes the future seem real and more easily achievable. It fuels them to reach for their goals rather than making them feel pessimistic. So, be upbeat about writing your business plan – and use it to your best advantage.

How to Get a Fast-Start in Medical Billing and Practice Management

We hope you've learned a lot from this chapter chock full of information about how to go about marketing your business and pricing your services. You are now in a good position to get down to work, selecting the marketing methods that are best suited to your personality and skills. You may even be ready to begin writing your direct mail letters, brochures, fliers, and other print materials, as well as determining what type of networking you might initiate, and other ideas for your marketing.

Before you move on to the next chapter, let us repeat that the *key* to marketing is *to make sure you put in the time and effort every day.* No matter what business you are in, it takes time to build your clientele to the point where the business supports you. Medical billing has been touted for years as a top business for people to get into, but unfortunately, there are people who believe they can jump into business or buy a pre-made business opportunity program and begin making money within days or weeks.

The truth is, being successful in medical billing and practice management doesn't happen like magic. It takes commitment, dedication, persistence, and professionalism to put together a high quality marketing program that introduces your company to the healthcare profession. Then when you meet with doctors to sell your services, you have to prove to them that you are responsible, professional, and knowledgeable enough that they can trust you with their claims filing and their patient collections.

We can't emphasize enough that if you decide to go into medical billing on your own or by purchasing a business opportunity that does not provide you with superior training and excellent support with your marketing, you must allow yourself plenty of time to learn the business and develop a successful marketing program that lands you clients.

This is why ClaimTek has spent years developing the best business startup opportunity you can find. We know that the challenges of getting into medical billing are real and that most of you need extensive professional support. We have positioned ourselves as truly the only company that provides you with the highest levels of support and assistance. We provide you with far more than any other software or business opportunity company around.

We provide you with over 2,000 pieces of professional startup marketing materials, including many types of brochures, fliers, a business presentation, and more. All of our marketing support materials are professionally written, designed, and printed on high quality paper stock in order to help you get into business much faster than doing it on your own or by working with any other business opportunity.

Please be sure to look stop by our web site (www.claimtek.com) for details about how we can help you get into business faster than any other program.

7

What to Do Immediately Before and Once You Have Clients

Once you get your first client, you're in business! You're on your way to a new career and an opportunity to earn an excellent income in a challenging, exciting, and interesting job.

But do you know what to do? Have you been trained precisely in how to set up your client with your clearinghouse? Do you know how to use your practice management and billing software? Are you clear on how to get the patient files from your provider into your software system so you can begin keying in the claims? Do you have an arrangement to get the superbills from the doctor on a regular basis? Do you know how to transmit claims and fix any errors that are returned? Do you know which reports to provide your client on a weekly or monthly basis? Do you know how to do accurate accounting for your business?

Many books about medical billing and practice management are available, but frankly, most of them fail to give you this detailed information. That's why we've devoted this chapter to helping you understand what to do both before you get your first client and once you get that client. We'll explain here all the details of the daily process of getting your billing service up and running.

We've divided the work you will need to do into two phases:

- **Phase I** – Before you get your first client, and
- **Phase II** – Upon signing up your first client

Let's begin with the Phase I activities that you'll need to get working on soon.

PHASE I: BEFORE YOU SIGN UP YOUR FIRST CLIENT

Step I-1: Set Up a Paper Filing System to Maintain Your Records

Even though medical billing itself is done almost entirely using electronic claims, there are still an extensive amount of paper documents involved in the business. Even as we write this book, efforts are being made to reduce the paperwork, but for the moment, you will need to file away various types of records that you receive from doctors and insurers.

For example, many of your clients are going to give you paper encounter forms (superbills) or mail, fax, e-mail or download them to you so you can key in the claims. Then, each time your doctors receive a payment from an insurance company or Medicare, they get a paper document called the Explanation of Benefits (EOB) – or in the case of Medicare, it's called the Explanation of Medicare Benefits (EOMB) – which displays which patients are included in the payment and a summary of all the services (claims) billed, the fees charged, and the fees paid for each, along with a total check for the entire amount. If a commercial insurance company or Medicare processes, say, five patients all at once for your client, you would receive one EOB or EOMB, with all five listed and all their services – and that paper document must be filed away and kept for seven years. Finally, if you ever file an appeal for a denied claim, you will need to keep a copy of the EOB that shows the denial as well as your own form or letter appealing the denial.

In short, you must have a well-organized paper filing or digital storage system to store all the documents you receive and generate yourself.

Here is a filing system that I (Nancie) created over my 15 years in medical billing. My system is based on helping you get organized quickly and stay organized. This means you won't risk keyboarding and sending claims twice because you accidentally mixed up some folders or get claims for one doctor mixed in with those of another doctor. The system works as follows:

Setup of the System

1. The first element in my system is to use color coding for your files. Go to your office supply store and buy color-coded file folders, giving each doctor you manage a single color. If you are billing for a larger

practice that has multiple doctors, you still give the entire practice one color to make sure it remains quickly identifiable. However, if your client or an entire practice has multiple locations, you can use a different color for each location. That makes it easier to identify immediately, just by color, which practice you are working with and you will have less confusion and errors in filing.

Of course, you may eventually end up with more doctors than file folder colors. If that happens, you can double up on the colors and then use labels on the files to distinguish between two doctors or groups who have the same color. Regardless, you can find a large assortment of colors available in many office supply stores.

2. Back in Chapter 5, we talked about having a rollaway cart among your furniture. The purpose of this cart is to keep all the files that are currently "active," versus the "passive" files you can put away for permanent storage in your filing cabinets. Active files are those documents you need to take out or use consistently, while passive files are those that you will most likely not need on a daily or weekly basis. (Reminder: if you are using a rollaway cart, these typically do not have tops that lock the folders inside. Therefore, you must be sure to have an office that you can lock to protect the data privacy as HIPAA requires.)
3. Each doctor whose practice you manage has three active file folders stored in a hanging folder (like a Pendaflex hanging folder) in your rollaway cart. For example, assume Dr. Smith is your client and you've decided to color code him with blue folders. In your rolling cart, you have the following reusable blue folders that stay positioned in the rollaway cart at all times:

- One folder labeled **Incoming Superbills** where you store superbills (encounter slips) to be keyboarded and processed
- One folder labeled **EOBs** where you store the Explanation of Benefits that come in for that doctor
- One folder labeled **Follow-Up** where you store any documents on which you need to do some type of follow up, such as claims that were denied or which you are appealing.

Note that if you bill for a large practice of, say, four or more doctors or one of your doctors sends you superbills to process more than once per week, you may want to have multiple incoming claims folders that you organize in some logical way for yourself. For a very large practice you might even have a courier service bring you the encounter forms every single working day of the month, and you can then have one incoming file dated for each day of the month. That is, you would have 31 folders dated 1-31.

Filing Superbills / Encounter Slips

Here's what to do when you get superbills from your providers:

1. As soon as you receive new superbills from your client, put them into the folder for incoming claims in your rollaway cart.
2. Process the claims in the folder at any time you are ready. (Processing the claims means that you keyboard the information from the superbills in the folder into your medical billing software and send them in batches to your clearinghouse or, in some cases, directly to insurance companies.)
3. Once you have processed the claims, move the completed encounter slips (superbills) into your permanent storage filing cabinet that you set up for each doctor. Use the same color folders as you use in the rollaway cart for each provider to maintain your color coding. You can simplify your file storage by using end-tab color folders which are slightly larger than regular file folders and have one edge sticking out that you can label. (These are the same types of sideways folders that you can see in doctor's offices).

As you process the completed superbills and go to store them, it is easiest to just gather them with an entire week's worth of superbills into one storage folder and label it using the last date of the week. Don't bother sorting them by date of service. That takes too much time given that you seldom need to go back and check them. Storing them according to a full week of service is sufficient. (Note: if you are billing for a practice that sends you more than 50 claims per week, you may need to set up daily or bi-weekly folders in your permanent file cabinet. For larger accounts, you may even need daily folders by location.)

In this way, for each doctor, your permanent storage will eventually end up with 52 weekly folders (or possibly for large practices, with as many as 200 or so daily folders) storing the completed superbills per year for that practice. This system makes it easy to pull out a paper copy of a superbill if you ever need to verify a claim already processed.

At the end of the year, it is also useful to move all the files for each doctor to another location to make room in your file cabinet for the coming year's paper files. As we noted in a previous chapter, you might even consider scanning the paper files, transferring them to CD, and then destroying the paper copies. Or if your agreement with the doctor's office allows it, you can return the paper copies to them after one year.

Filing EOBs

As you receive EOMBs and EOBs from Medicare and insurance companies, you will need to process them in your software by recording the receivables (payments) and posting each payment to its corresponding claim. We will explain how this is done later in the chapter. (Note: recent advancements in technology are increasingly allowing insurance payments to be posted electronically in your system, eliminating the need to key in payments from some insurers.) For now, in terms of filing paper EOBs, you can handle your smaller accounts in the same way you manage the superbills, using one file folder per week for filing the posted EOBs for that account.

If you have large accounts that receive many EOBs per day, you might want to use one folder per deposit group the doctor makes. For example, assume that one of your medical practices receives 10 EOBs per day from different insurance companies and Medicare. At the end of each day, they take the checks from the EOBs and deposit them all at once, and send or fax you copies of the 10 EOBs. You then process the EOBs and file all 10 of them in one folder that you date using the deposit date. That way, you can look up an EOB by knowing its deposit date. This system also helps because some doctors may ask you to balance out your daily posting of receivables by comparing the total amount you posted with the deposit slip. If they match, it indicates that you have posted all the receivables correctly.

Using the Follow-Up Folder for Pending Claims

In the beginning of this section, we recommended that you keep a file called **Follow Up** in your rollaway cart. This folder is your "tickler system" to remind you about work that needs follow-up.

For example, if you have a superbill for a patient whose record in your software says they require an authorization from the insurance company before the claim can be processed, you would pull the encounter form out of the **Incoming** folder and put it into this **Follow Up** file, then communicate to the provider that you cannot process the claim until you get the authorization information. Although you could send the claim back to the provider, it is easier to just email the provider and ask for the information you need. This avoids delaying the claim for a week or two. Once you receive the authorization, you can then process the claim and put it back into the folder with the other claims you received in that batch.

Special Worker's Comp Folders

If you are working with doctors who handle worker's comp or personal injury (PI) claims, you may also want to have additional file folders that are labeled by the patient's last name. The reason for this is that you must access these files frequently because worker's comp and PI claims can be paper-intensive, often requiring you to resubmit records several times. You can find a patient's file more easily when you make one folder per name, containing all the superbills and reports for that patient.

Step I-2: Get to Know Your Medical Practice Management Software

Even though you do not yet have clients, be sure you know how to use the software you bought for your medical billing and practice management business. For some strange reason, people tend to buy medical billing software, but then keep it in the box while they develop their business plans and marketing campaigns. Of course, the problem then is that you never know when you might land that first client, and you end up scurrying to install the software and learn how to use it. By this time, you have too much pressure on you to figure out the software and you can easily make mistakes.

To ensure that this does not happen to you, we recommend that you become completely familiar with your software well in advance of having clients. Make sure you know how to input patients and claims, and how to submit claims electronically. Read through the manuals you get with your software. Test out any sample data you get.

If you purchase ClaimTek's MedOffice software, you will receive the 450-page *Complete User's Manual* that explains every menu command in the software in complete details with screen illustrations, plus our 110-page *Guide to Medical Billing Using MedOffice* which focuses on billing details and functionality. These two training manuals will quickly get you up to speed and prepare you for managing your medical billing business from the day you get your first client. MedOffice also contains a sample hypothetical doctor's practice to which you can add patients, enter claims, and practice doing billing and paying receivables. As indicated, this chapter also teaches you some of the major steps in billing and practice management using MedOffice as an example of how to perform these tasks. So, you will get to learn about MedOffice as you go through this chapter.

Be aware that most software companies do not provide the extensive personal training and user-friendly, illustrated software manuals that ClaimTek provides, so be sure to consider your training when you purchase software. ClaimTek supports you throughout the process so that you will never feel that you don't know what you are doing.

Step I-3: Research Clearinghouses and Be Ready to Select One

As explained earlier, clearinghouses are intermediary businesses that receive claims from medical billers and funnel them to the different insurance companies. The advantages of clearinghouses are that they allow you to send all your claims to one central location rather than having to transmit them to dozens of different insurance companies one by one. Clearinghouses also perform critical verification checking on claims, ensuring that data is not missing or incorrect before forwarding claims to their appropriate insurance companies. This process can save you a great deal of money and effort because if a claim is missing information, the clearinghouse notifies you immediately or within a few hours of submitting the claim, allowing you to fix a data entry error or contact your client to collect any missing information from the original superbill that may have caused the error. Correcting errors immediately means that the claims can be resubmitted quickly and your client will not experience a delay of several weeks as would have happened if you mailed in paper claims or did not use a clearinghouse to check your claims.

There are numerous clearinghouses used by medical billing services and the choice of which one to use is yours. If you work with ClaimTek and use our MedOffice software, we help you get set up with one of several clearinghouses and arrange discounted fees for your business, so you can actually skip the step of researching all the various clearinghouses available because we have done that for you. MedOffice is already set up to automatically connect to a few clearinghouses once you have your account information.

However, if you are going to start a medical billing company on your own or purchase software from another company, be sure to spend some time before you get your first client, researching clearinghouses to learn about their fees and select one that is right for you. Each clearinghouse has its own fee structure and you will want to compare prices and fees. In general, you cannot arrange a clearinghouse at this time because they usually require you to have clients for whom you are billing before you can sign up an account with them. But once you obtain your first client, you need to be ready to sign up with a clearinghouse, so do your research now.

Note that some medical billing software is preformatted to connect to only one clearinghouse, which is not a good idea. What if you don't like the customer service there? What if the clearinghouse increases their fees? What if they go out of business? So, keep in mind that you must have medical billing software that offers you the ability to connect to several clearinghouses.

Using ET&T, Gateway EDI or ENS, as your Clearinghouse

ClaimTek recommends several clearinghouses, each of which offers you very special competitive rates. Here are profiles of three clearinghouses that ClaimTek works closely with:

- **ET&T** offers outstanding customer service and charges on a per-claim basis. At the time of this writing, they have a one-time $140 setup fee, with no annual or per doctor fees. However, there is a per claim fee of 35 cents, but no charge for rejected claims. You can submit both medical and dental claims through ET&T. These prices are effective at the time of this writing and may change in time.
- **Gateway EDI** is a flat monthly fee clearinghouse and offers outstanding customer service and online training. At the time of this writing, they do not charge a setup fee and have no annual or per claim fees. Gateway EDI offers several levels of service, currently all based on a flat monthly fee, currently ranging from $75 to $120 per month, depending on which services you choose. For example, you can select either 1) all the electronic claims that you need to send per doctor per month, or 2) all the claims you need to send *plus* online eligibility verification and real-time claims status inquiry.
- **ENS-Health** is a flat monthly fee clearinghouse and also has good customer service and online training. At the time of this writing, they charge a one-time setup fee, with no annual or per claim fees and several levels of service. ENS-Health offers two levels of service, both based on a flat monthly fee: either 1) all the electronic claims that you need to send for only $49 per doctor per month, or 2) for $69 per doctor per month, all the claims you need to send *plus* online eligibility verification and real-time claims sta-

tus inquiry. Remember, either monthly fee includes all the electronic claims you need to send! Note that these fees may have changed since the printing of this book.

- **Other Clearinghouses** – ClaimTek also makes available to you several other clearinghouses. Any clearinghouse that accepts the HIPAA ANSI standard EDI format is compatible with MedOffice.

Choosing the right clearinghouse is an important step that can save you headaches down the road. To help you determine which clearinghouse is your best deal, do some calculations to determine if you are better off working on a per claim method or a flat monthly fee method. Don't forget to take into account any setup fees you may need to pay when determining your best option. For example, if your cost is a flat fee of $49 per month per doctor, it translates into 140 claims at 35 cents per claim. So, if you expect to file more than 140 claims for one of your providers per month, you will be better off working with a flat fee clearinghouse. However, each clearinghouse has its benefits, so do research or contact ClaimTek to help you make the decision.

PHASE II: ONCE YOU HAVE YOUR FIRST CLIENT

Beginning with this step, assume you now have signed up a client and are ready to begin working with your first provider. He or she has signed your contract and you will now perform all their billing and practice management. What should you do first? What are the steps you need to take?

We are going to present 10 steps you must follow to get going in your new career. These steps will show you how to set up your client in the software and how to begin filing and submitting claims, as well as doing patient statements and reports for your doctors.

We are going to demonstrate the entire process using ClaimTek's leading-edge practice management software, *MedOffice*. If you have not yet purchased any software for your medical billing and practice management business, please visit www.claimtek.com to learn about the advanced features and ease-of-use of MedOffice. This is the software you will receive if you work with ClaimTek by purchasing any of our business opportunity programs – or you can purchase MedOffice separately.

MedOffice was developed over a period of nearly four years after significant research into medical billing software. Every effort was made to design MedOffice as the easiest-to-use, more reliable, and most screen attractive software for practice management on the market. As we go through the rest of this chapter, you will see various screen shots taken from MedOffice that show how easy it is to use the software, while at the same time teaching you the many skills you will need to operate a medical billing and practice management business.

Keep in mind that a major advantage of using MedOffice is that it can handle all types of medical claims, whereas many other medical software programs charge you for the extra modules to process claims other than those processed on the standard CMS 1500 claim forms. MedOffice handles all of the following:

- CMS 1500
- CMS 1450 (also known as the UB)
- DME – (durable medical equipment)
- Ambulance
- Chiropractic
- In addition, ClaimTek also offers DentOffice, a dental software program.

PLEASE NOTE THAT MEDOFFICE SOFTWARE IS IN FULL COLOR ON YOUR COMPUTER SCREEN.
THE SCREEN SHOTS IN THIS BOOK ARE SHOWN IN BLACK AND WHITE.
PLEASE GET YOUR FREE SAMPLE DEMO OF MEDOFFICE TO VIEW THE ACTUAL COLOR SCREEN SHOTS.
DOWNLOAD YOUR DEMO COPY OF MEDOFFICE AT www.claimtek.com.

Step II-1: Create Your Clearinghouse Account and Set Up Your Doctor

Literally, the VERY first thing you should do now is sign up with your clearinghouse immediately and give your client their forms to fill out and sign. As we just presented, doctors must provide the clearinghouse with legal identifying information to authorize insurance carriers to pay them for their services. In addition, you need to sign up with the clearinghouse and sign a contract with them to process claims through them. As stated above, if you work with ClaimTek, we help you through this entire process and make it easier for you to get this step done. If you work alone, you should proceed at this time to contact your selected clearinghouse to sign up with them.

The importance of doing this immediately is that it can take from one to four weeks to be approved by a clearinghouse to send claims through them. The clearinghouse must take the legal information from your doctor and obtain authorization from insurance companies to send claims to them. Some insurance carriers confirm their approval quickly and let you begin processing claims within 48 hours of sending in your provider's information to the clearinghouse. But other insurance companies may take as much as four weeks to approve your provider. This is why you need to get the ball rolling right away after signing your client.

Note also that some clearinghouses may ask you to submit twenty or thirty test claims as soon as you can to confirm that you know what you are doing and to ensure that your software setup has been done correctly. Even when your test cases have been approved, if you are awaiting authorization to bill from various insurance companies, the clearinghouse will instruct you to print your claims on paper and mail them in during the wait period, or the clearinghouse may even print them out for you and mail them in. See the Sidebar for more information about what to do during this lag period before you can submit electronic claims to your clearinghouse.

Delay Periods from Insurers Before Being Able to Submit Claims

In general, clearinghouses will tell you that it takes two to four weeks to get approved by various insurance companies and Medicare to authorize your providers to submit electronic claims through the clearinghouse. This is pretty standard. Even if your physician has already been submitting electronic claims through their prior billing agency, they must go through a new insurance authorization process when they change to your billing company.

Due to this delay in getting your client authorized to submit electronically to various insurers, you may wonder if you should start out by filing claims on paper until the authorization comes through. Our advice is, talk to your clearinghouse and see what they predict for the delay. In certain cases, some clearinghouses will let you begin submitting commercial insurance claims through the clearinghouse within one week, knowing that the insurance company authorizations will soon come through.

Step II-2: Enter Your Client's Practice Data into Your Software

In this step, you begin getting your software ready to begin billing for your client. The first item on the agenda is to set up your doctor's practice, which must be done before you begin entering any claims data. This task involves entering information about the practice you are billing for such as the practice's name, address, tax ID, data about the individual provider(s) who you will be billing for, the insurance companies that his or her practice usually bills, the CPT and ICD-9 codes you usually deal with, and the Facility codes.

To demonstrate how this data is entered, we are going to show you the process using ClaimTek's MedOffice software.

Enter Practice Setup Data

You must always begin by creating the provider's practice in your software. This means keyboarding basic data such as the practice's name, address,

Figure 7-1

Practice Setup screen from MedOffice.

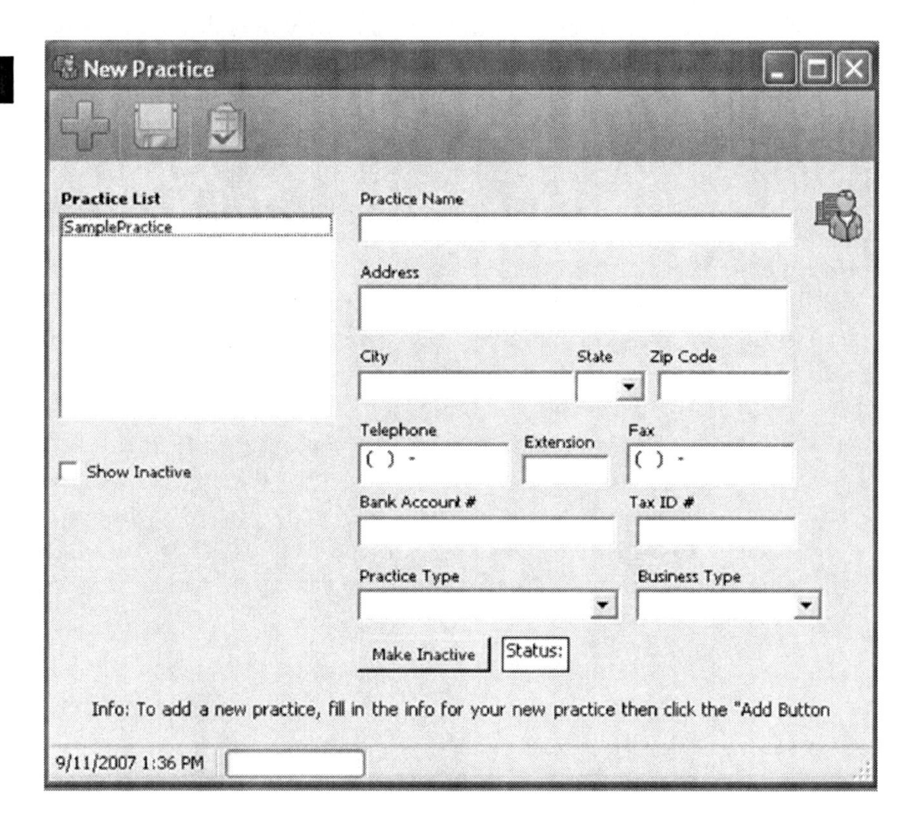

city, and so on. The screen shot in Figure 7-1 gives you a sense of the type of data you will need and how easy MedOffice makes it to fill out this information. You simply tab from one data field to another as you type. (Note: if you use different software, your screen will be different. This is true for all the screen shots you see in this chapter.)

Enter Provider Data

Next, you enter data into your software about each provider in the practice for whom you will do billing. If your client is a solo practitioner, you need to enter data only for him or her. If your client is a larger, multi-doctor practice, you need to fill out the screens for each provider. Here are some sample screen shots to show you the type of information you will need.

In Figure 7-2, for example, you enter basic information about the provider:

In the screen shown in Figure 7-3, you enter information about the

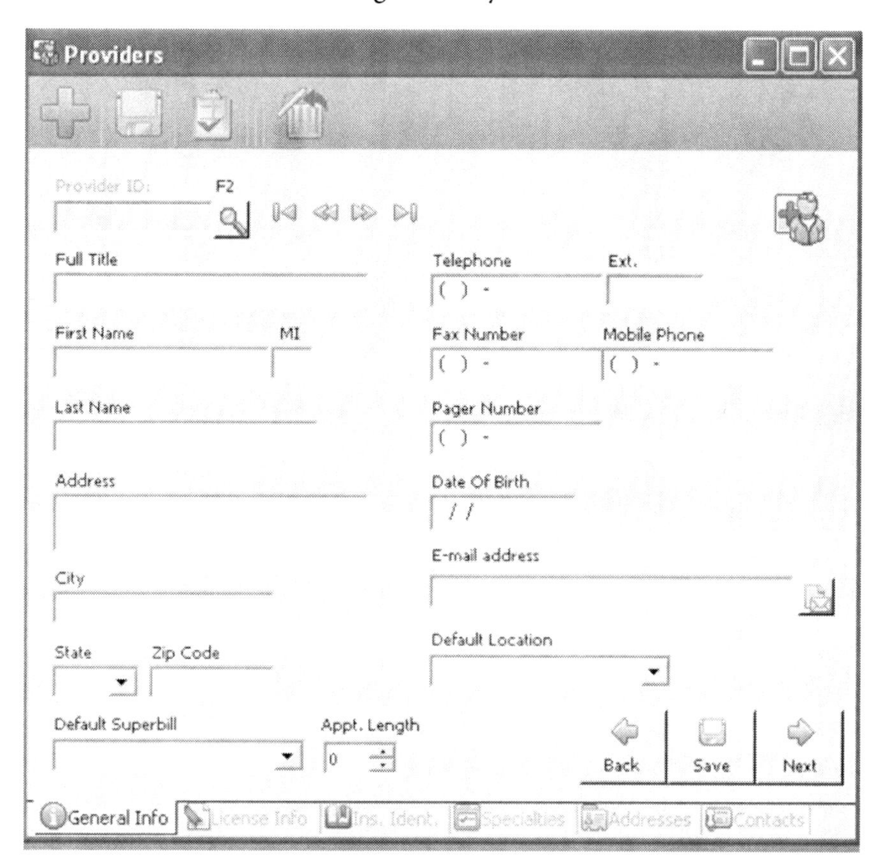

Figure 7-2

Provider setup screen from MedOffice.

provider you are billing for, such as the provider's Federal Tax ID, State medical license number, specialty number, Drug Enforcement Agency (DEA) ID, Unique Provider ID (UPIN), and so on. The UPIN is assigned by Medicare. Note that as of 2006, doctors are receiving a new National provider identification number called the NPI to eventually replace the many ID numbers providers now have. (MedOffice is fully compliant with the use of the NPI.)

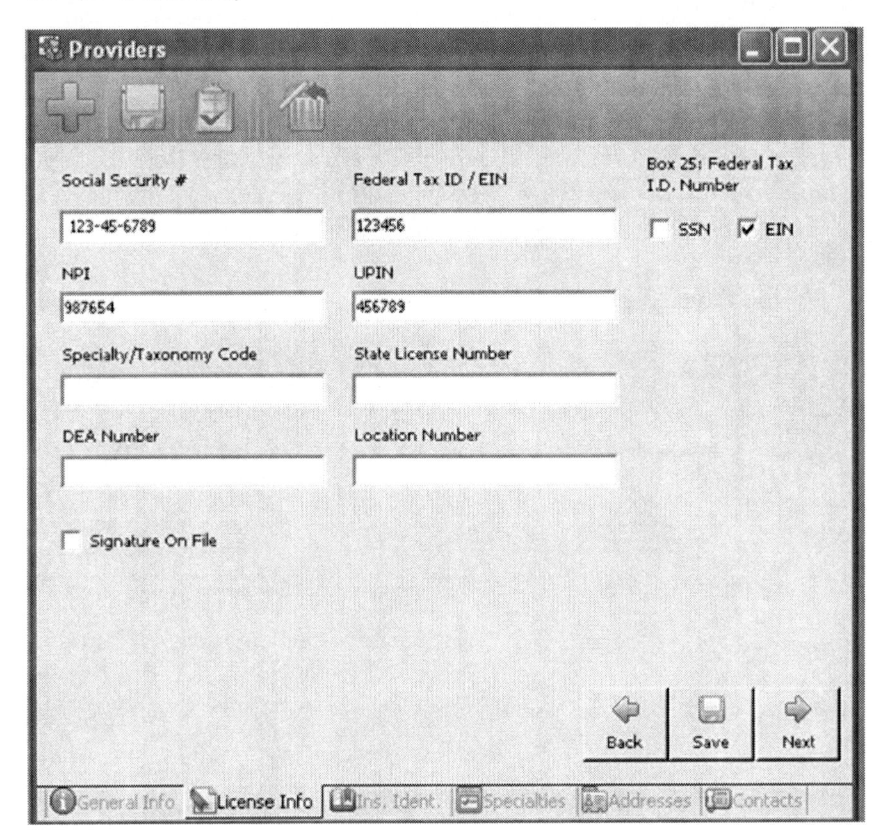

Figure 7-3

License information screen for providers from MedOffice.

Enter Insurance Company Data

After you enter in information about each provider you bill for, the next item to enter is as much of the data as you can about all of the insurance companies used by your provider's patients. Doctors typically have many patients who use the same insurance companies because the doctor belongs to various Preferred Provider Organizations (PPOs) organized by those insurers. Of course, doctors constantly get new patients and so, obviously, you need to keep adding insurance companies into your software as time goes on. But, in initially setting up your doctor, you can usually keyboard in at least a few insurers to whom your doctor typically bills. These common insurers may include your local Medicare office, BlueCross, Blue Shield, Tricare (CHAMPUS), Railroad Medicare, Aetna, Cigna, United Healthcare, and so on. Figure 7-4 shows a screen shot of the type of data you typically input for insurance companies.

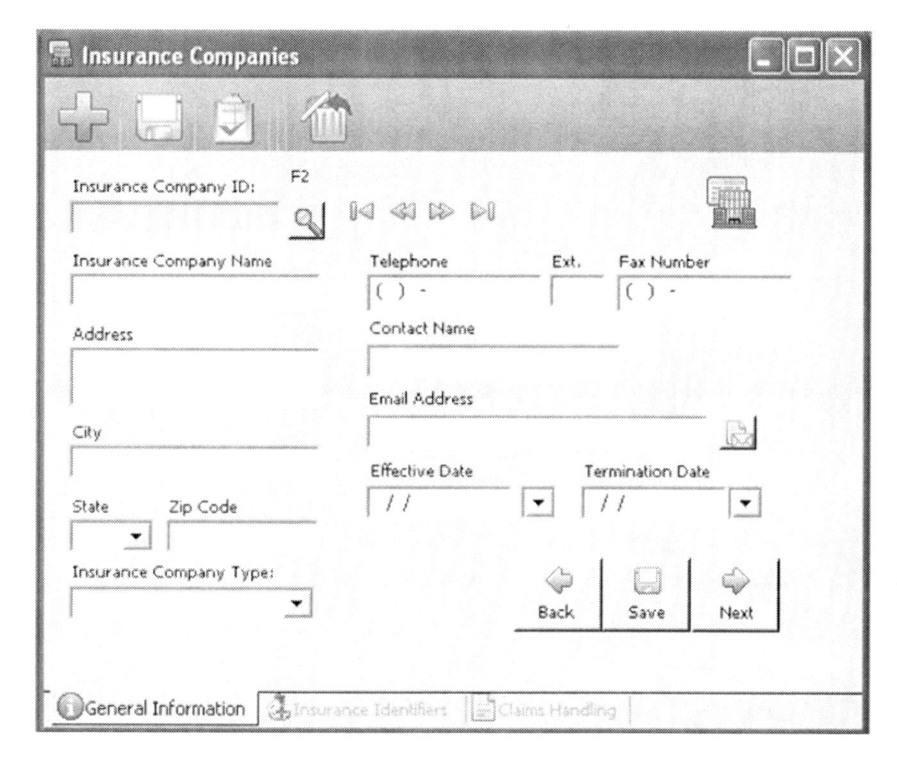

Figure 7-4

Insurance company setup screen from MedOffice.

The next two figures show additional data you enter for each insurance company. In Figure 7-5, you key in the insurer's identification information for that doctor, such as his or her Payer ID, Carrier ID, Group name and ID, and so on. In Figure 7-6, you enter information about how the claims are to be filed for this provider. For example, if the provider is part of a group practice, he or she may still bill claims as a non-group provider or as part of the group, and this must be indicated.

Figure 7-5

Insurance identifier screen shot from MedOffice.

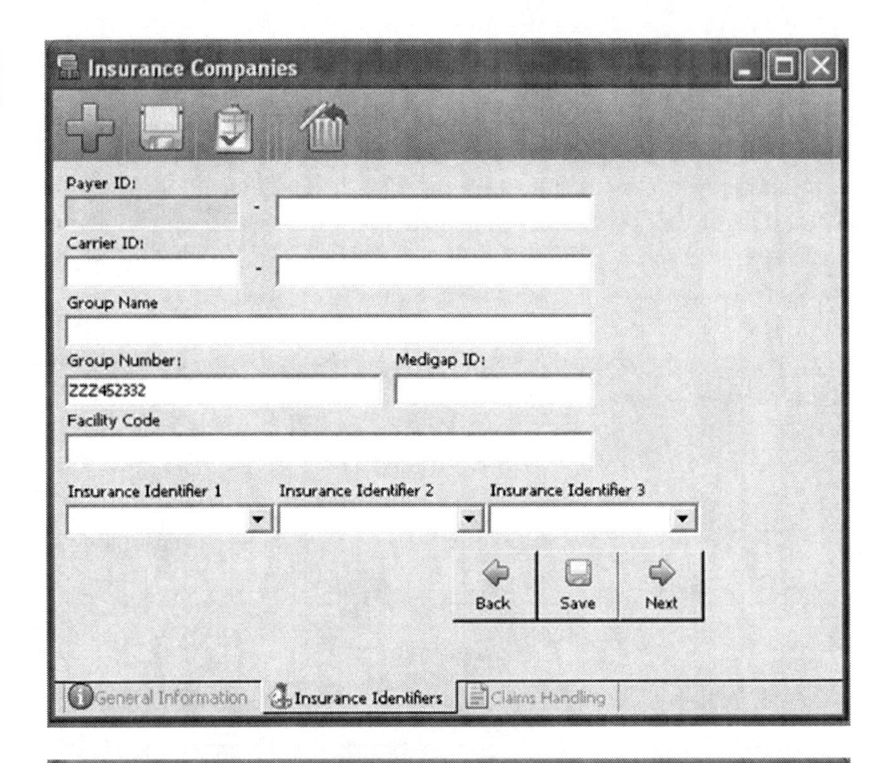

Figure 7-6

Claims handling screen shot from MedOffice.

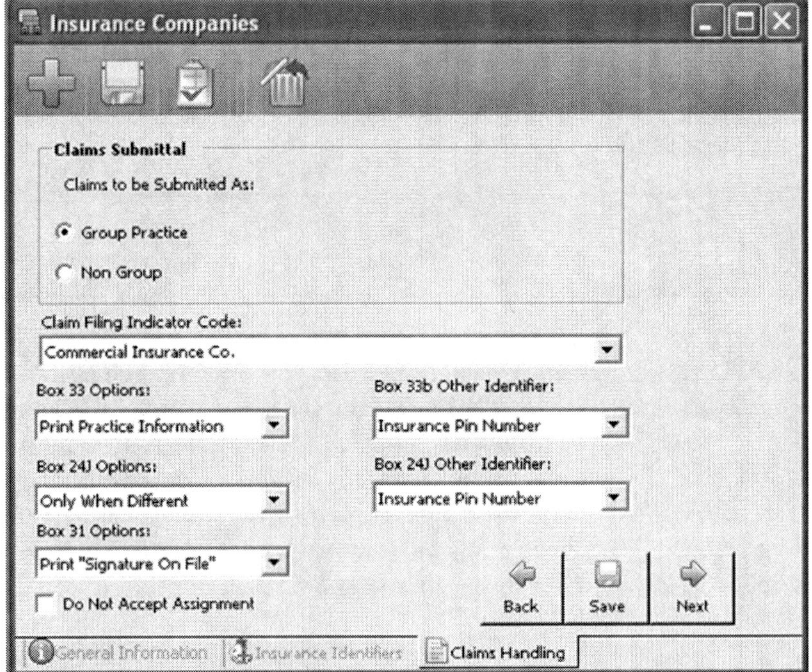

Enter Diagnosis and CPT Codes

Next, you load into your software the diagnosis (ICD) and procedure (CPT) codes that your provider typically uses. As we discussed in the chapter on codes, there are thousands of diagnosis and procedure codes, but most doctors use only a few dozen or perhaps a few hundred on a day-to-day basis. So, rather than importing or keying in thousands of codes, it is much easier just to keyboard in the common codes your provider uses. ClaimTek's MedOffice software allows you to import any number of medical codes if desired.

MedOffice also allows you to create shortcuts to those codes so that when you do billing, you can use fewer keyboard strokes. Using what is called "code linking," you can save a lot of time when you enter claims. For example, let's say that your doctor commonly sees patients and performs CPT 97110 (therapeutic exercises), but each time he or she performs this procedure, a cold pack therapy (CPT code 97010) is also done for that diagnosis. Thus, as you are setting up your practice's procedure codes, now is a good time to link those codes and give them a combined shortcut. You might thus assign the shortcut "5" to mean CPT code 97110, and then whenever you code this on a claim, it automatically also brings up CPT code 97010 at the same time. This linking saves you keystrokes and time.

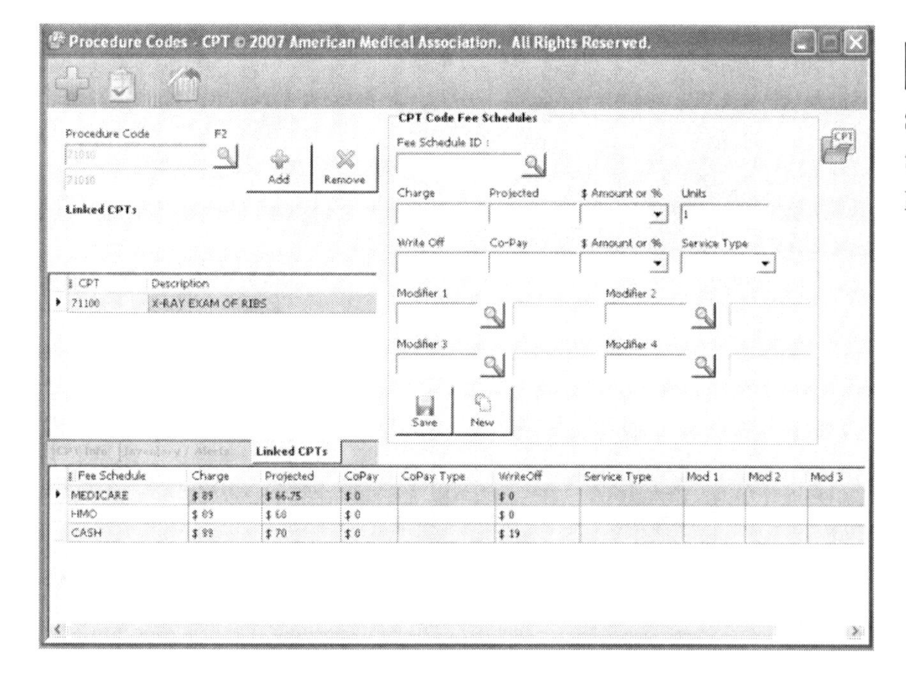

Figure 7-7

Screen showing how to link CPT codes in MedOffice.

Figure 7-7 shows you the screen shot from MedOffice where you can link codes.

Enter Place of Service Codes

The next items to key in while setting up your practice are the codes commonly used to indicate where the medical service was performed, called the place of service code. If your provider sees patients in an office as well as at a hospital or other types of locations, you need to enter these codes because claims require the place of service to be listed. There are dozens of these codes, so it is a time-saver to pre-enter only those codes that your provider commonly uses to avoid mistakenly typing codes that your provider never uses.

For example, some standard codes are:

11 – at the provider's office
12 – at the patient's home
21 – in an inpatient facility
22 – in an outpatient facility
24 – in an ambulatory surgery center
31 – at a skilled nursing facility.

Step II-3: Enter Your Provider's Fee Schedules

Providers often use what are called "fee schedules," which are based on contracts they have with insurers to accept limited payments for their services in exchange for being part of the insurer's PPO. When the doctor bills that insurer, they must therefore file the claim according to the agreed-upon fee schedule for each procedure (or they may bill above this amount and write off the difference).

Fees schedules can vary from insurer to insurer. For example, Dr. Jones may be a member of the local Blue Cross PPO and the Cigna PPO, as well as a Medicare provider. These three insurers have different payments for each procedure that Dr. Jones commonly performs. Even though Dr. Jones charges $135 for a certain procedure for cash patients, he or she may only be allowed to charge $105 to Blue Cross, $97.50 to Cigna, and $82.25 to Medicare. Note: this doesn't mean that Dr. Jones receives this amount from each insurer. The "allowed" fee is the amount the doctor can charge, and then the insurer pays only a portion of the allowed amount (usually 60-90% depending on the patient's contract, or whatever amount is left after the patient pays a flat co-pay of $10 or $20). Depending on the insurance plans, the patient is usually responsible for any unpaid balances that remain after insurance payments.

As the billing person, you must get each fee schedule that your provider has agreed to, and key it into your software for each commonly used procedure code. MedOffice allows you to have unlimited fee schedules per provider, although you usually don't need more than a few, including a "cash" fee schedule which might be how much the doctor charges patients who have no insurance or with whose insurance company the doctor has not agreed to a fee schedule.

Figure 7-8 shows a screen demonstrating one method of entering fee schedules with MedOffice. (Note: MedOffice actually has several methods of creating fee schedules, but for simplicity, we show just one method here.)

In this screen, you first create a new fee schedule on the left-side of the screen, giving it a name and indicating the dates of its validity. The conversion factor is a percentage used for advanced fee schedule work that is not relevant for most practices.

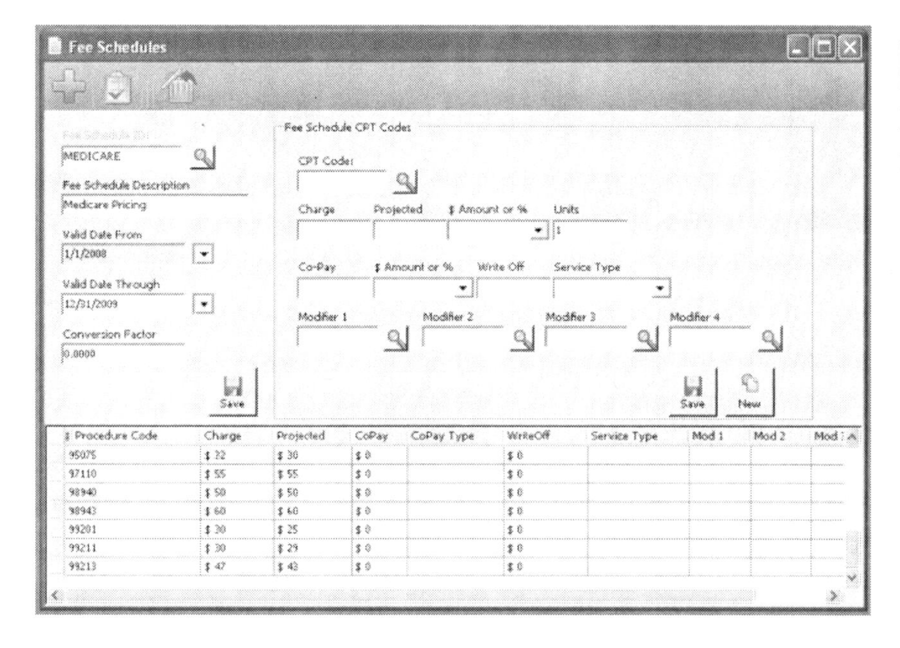

Procedure Code	Charge	Projected	CoPay	CoPay Type	WriteOff	Service Type	Mod 1	Mod 2	Mod :
95075	$ 22	$ 30	$ 0		$ 0				
97110	$ 55	$ 55	$ 0		$ 0				
98940	$ 50	$ 50	$ 0		$ 0				
98943	$ 60	$ 60	$ 0		$ 0				
99201	$ 30	$ 25	$ 0		$ 0				
99211	$ 30	$ 29	$ 0		$ 0				
99213	$ 47	$ 43	$ 0		$ 0				

Figure 7-8

Fee schedule screen from MedOffice.

Once you define the fee schedule on the left-hand side of the screen, you move to the right hand side and, one-by-one, in the CPT Code field, you pull up each procedure code that your provider uses (which you already keyboarded in the software in Step II – 2 above) and type in the following:

- ***Charge.*** How much the provider wants to charge for that service
- ***Projected.*** The amount, often called the Allowed Amount, is how much the insurer has agreed to pay under the terms of the contract that your doctor has with the insurer. In MedOffice, you can express this amount as a dollar figure or a percentage, such as 80%.
- ***Co-Pay.*** The patient's co-pay amount for this procedure (Note: patients often pay a one-time co-pay per visit to the doctor's office, so the co-pay might be listed for the CPT code that relates to the visit charge).
- ***Write Off.*** The amount the doctor will need to write off, representing the difference between the charge (the usual amount the provider wants to charge) and the projected (the allowed fee the insurer will pay).
- ***Modifiers.*** Enter any modifiers that are commonly used with this procedure code.

Those are the basic steps to creating a fee schedule. If your provider has multiple fee schedules, you would repeat the above process for each one.

There are many advantages to creating fee schedules, at least in our MedOffice software (however, these advantages may not be true in other software). First, pre-entering fee schedules allows you to correlate a patient with the corresponding fee schedule maintained by his or her insurer. This allows you to reduce keyboard strokes when you key in claims for that patient because as soon as you type in the CPT code in the claim form (as will be shown below), the fee for *that* service for *that* patient will automatically populate the fee field in the claim form.

Secondly, if you have linked CPT codes together, the claim will automatically fill in several CPT codes and their fees all at once. This saves even more keystrokes when you type up claims.

Third, by entering the "projected" (allowed) amount along with the usual charge for each procedure, you can prepare reports that show your client more precisely how much money is estimated to be received in insurance payments from unpaid claims. For instance, even though your doctor may appear to have $3,450 in outstanding claims for services from insurers, you are able to prepare a report that indicates that only $2,739 is actually expected to come in allowed fees, accounting for write-offs under contract. Your client therefore has a much more realistic picture of his or her cash flow than assuming that $3,450 is the outstanding balance.

Step II-4: Enter Each Patient's Data by Importing Files or as You Receive Encounter Forms

You've now essentially set up the medical practice for which you are billing and you're almost ready to begin filing claims. However, before doing any claims, you must input the patient's information for each claim, and you have several methods of doing this.

First, if your client is using billing software, you may be able to ask them to export their patient files for you to import into your software. MedOffice, for example, allows you to import patient files from several other software programs. The benefit of importing the files is that you can obtain your doctor's entire list of patients all at once and thus avoid keyboarding them in one-by-one.

However, importing files can be risky, as you may import bad data or even viruses. For this reason, it may be wiser to simply key in each patient as he or she comes in to see your provider. In addition, you won't waste time keying in patients who are inactive, that is, patients who no longer see your provider or who only come once every few years. There is no point wasting your time keying in patients who may never require any billing.

Thus, if you decide not to import the provider's existing patient fields, the other alternative is to type in each patient's data as the patient comes in to see the doctor, which generates an encounter form. Inputting patient data is not difficult. In general, you need to enter only a few bits of information since your purpose is billing, rather than to maintain the patient's complete medical record. Filing claims requires only a few mandatory items, whereas a complete medical record such as the doctor's office maintains has much more information in it.

Getting Patient Data from Your Provider

Note that whenever you first enter data for a patient, you need to obtain all the patient information from your provider. As you review these screens from MedOffice in this chapter, take note of what you need to ask your providers to forward to you each and every time you are preparing a patient's claims. For example, as the billing company, you must have a photocopy of the patient's official Insurance Card showing his or her group number and personal ID number. You also need copies of the various forms the patient filled out in the doctor's office, including the Patient Registration Form, the Release & Assignment of Benefits form, the Pre-Authorization form, and the HIPAA Privacy Form. If the patient paid a co-payment at the provider's office, you need a copy of the receipt, since you need to key the co-pay amount in.

These paper forms provide you with the data you need to key in before you can file claims for that patient. You can get all this information from your provider either in person when you go to pick up the encounter forms, or by asking them to include it when they fax you the day's encounter forms, or by having them mail or overnight a package to you containing the day's encounter forms and backup materials.

Figures 7-9 through 7-13 show the screens in MedOffice as examples of what you need to complete when you are entering a patient in order to file claims for that patient.

In Figure 7-9, you enter "general" patient information and the only fields necessary for claims on this screen are First Name, Last Name, Birth Date, Sex, Address, City, State, Zip, and Home Phone. The other fields can be skipped for now.

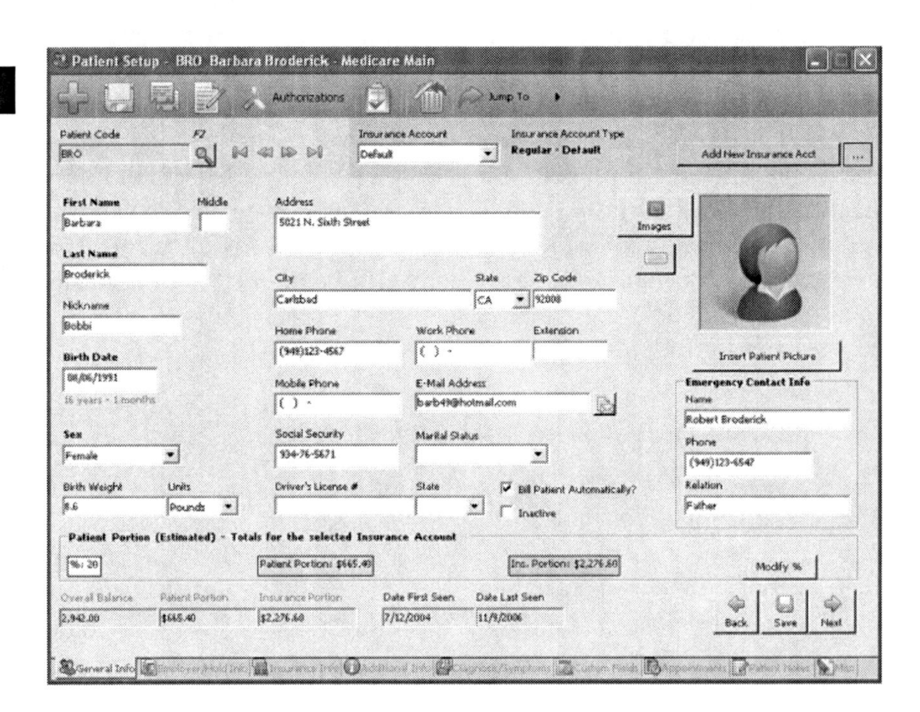

Figure 7- 9

General Patient Information screen in MedOffice

Figure 7-10 shows the next screen in MedOffice that would require you to fill out information for purposes of filing a claim on behalf of a patient. This screen collects data about the patient's insurance coverages, including the primary insurance and any secondary and tertiary insurance the person may have. For each insurer, you must identify the insurance company name, the insured's ID number, the group plan number, the type of insurance (e.g., commercial, Medicare, Tricare, etc.), who the insured person is relative to the patient (e.g., is the insured person the same as the patient (Self), or is the insured person a Guarantor of the patient), and so on. Also included on this screen is a listing of the patient's authorizations, which we will explain below.

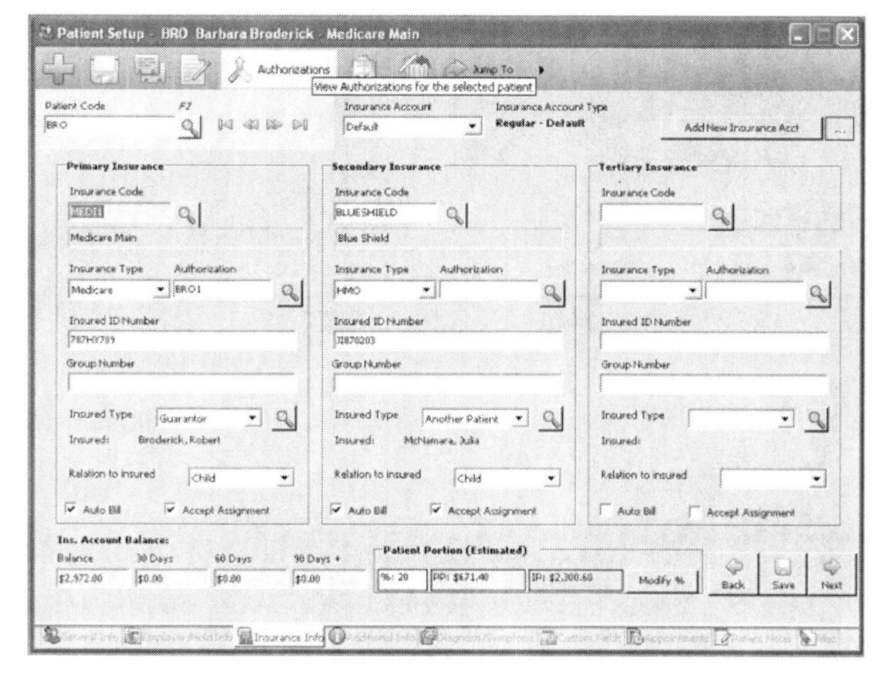

Figure 7-10

Patient's insurance screen in MedOffice.

Figure 7-11 shows the additional screen in MedOffice concerning authorizations that you must fill out for patient's whose insurance requires them to have prior-authorizations for services. On this screen, you can fill out the authorization number, the start and end dates of the authorization, and how many appointments or the dollar value the patient has been authorized for. Note that MedOffice helps doctors and billers count the use of authorized visits for each patient so that he or she does not exceed the number or dollar value that has been authorized.

Figure 7-11

Authorization tracking screen in MedOffice.

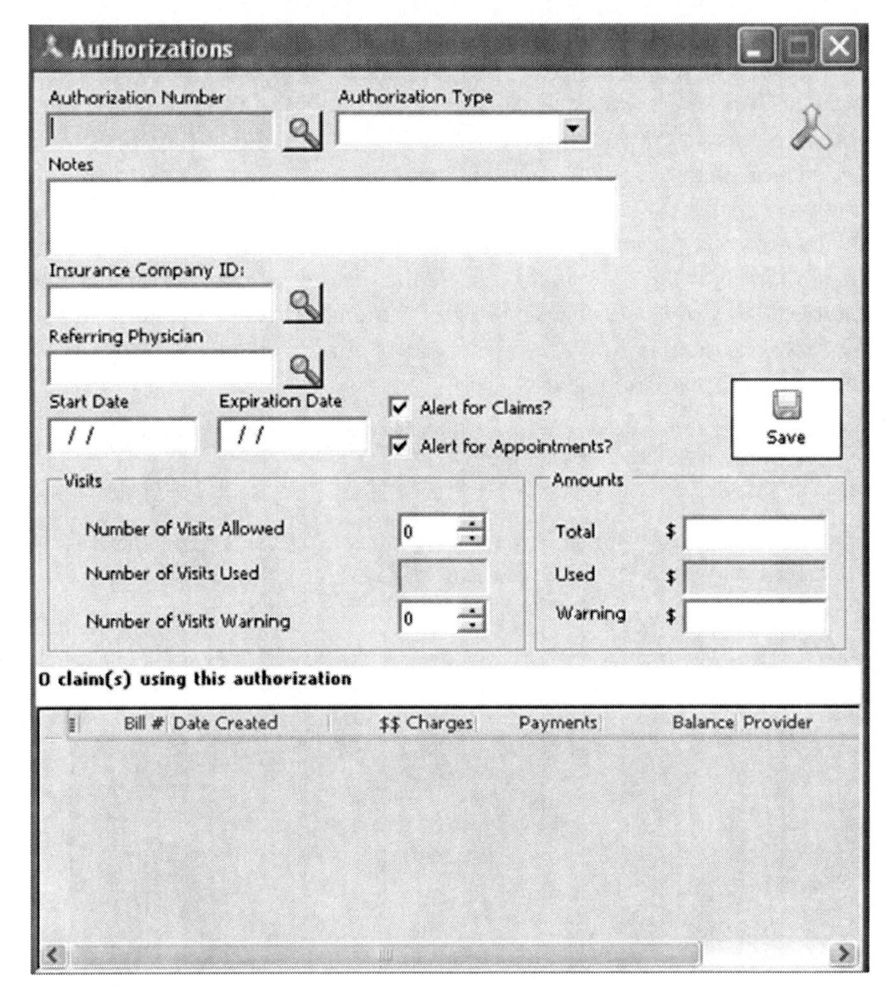

Figure 7-12 is an optional screen in MedOffice that may be worth keying in for patients because entering data in this screen now saves you keystrokes each and every time that you file claims for this patient in the future. On this screen, you can enter the patient's usual provider, facility where seen, co-pay amount, and fee schedule. These fields show up on the CMS 1500 claim form, so by entering here, you won't need to key them in whenever you file a claim on behalf of this patient.

Figure 7-13 displays another screen from MedOffice containing various fields that are useful to fill out now to save keystrokes every time you file claims for a patient. On this screen, you enter up to four default diagnosis codes for the patient (i.e., if the patient commonly sees the provider for the same diagnosis over and over again, they can become the *default*

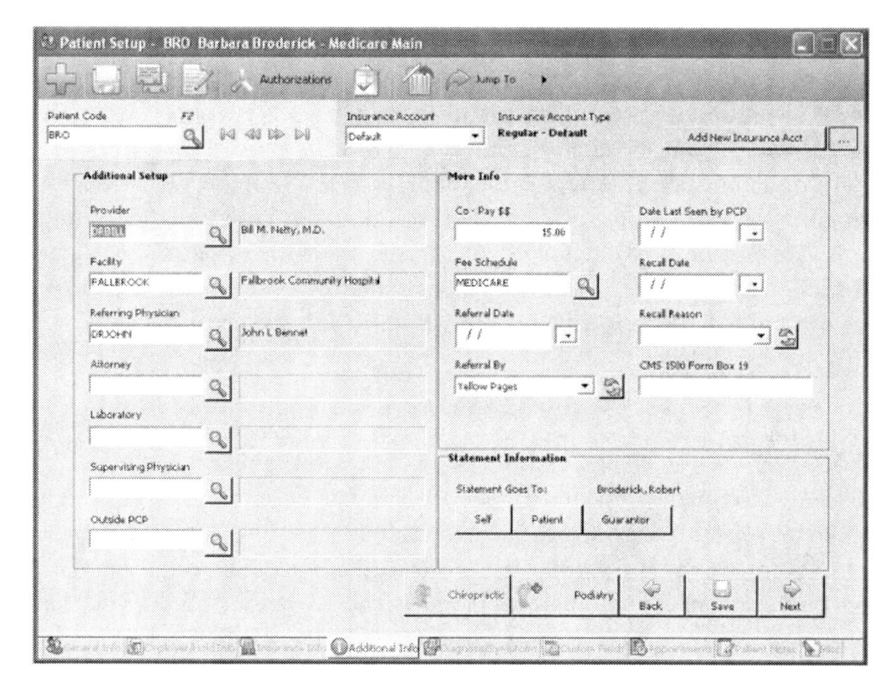

Figure 7-12

Additional Information screen in MedOffice for common defaulted patient information.

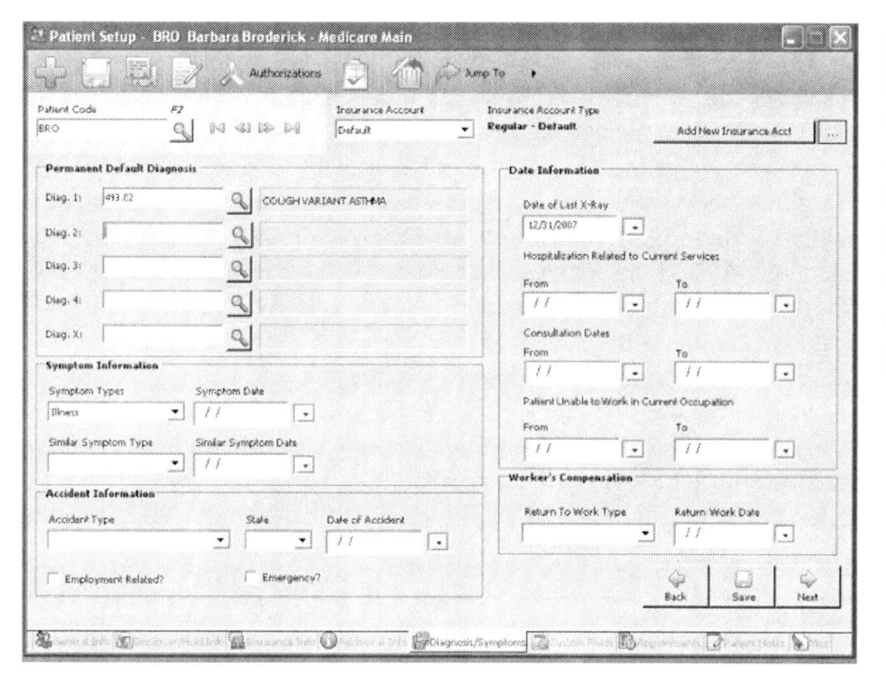

Figure 7-13

Optional diagnosis and accident information screen in MedOffice for certain types of defaulted data for a patient.

diagnosis). You can also enter information on symptom type and date, as well as an accident date because these fields may also get automatically transferred to the CMS 1500 claim form for certain types of patients if the claim relates to an accident.

The above screen shots from MedOffice are examples of what you might need to do to begin filing claims for patients. Other medical billing software may be different, but as you can see, MedOffice makes it very easy to jump from patient screen to patient screen to enter new patient data before you begin entering claims, which we will cover next.

Step II-5: Get the Encounter Forms and Begin Keying in Claims

You are now ready to begin the process of entering claims and submitting them to insurance companies for your client.

Of course, the first thing you need to do is arrange to get the daily encounter forms (superbills) from your client. As we said above, you may already have arranged to receive these and backup documentation in order to enter each patient's data before you arrived at this step. But once you do that for each patient who is "new" to your record keeping, the only documents you will need from your provider in the future are the daily encounter forms. If your provider's office takes note of which patients you've already input into your system, they will need to update you on backup material for a patient only if that individual changes addresses, insurance plans, or other important status updates.

In terms of getting the encounter forms, some billing companies literally go to their clients' offices every day or a few times per week to physically pick them up. Other billers have the provider's office fax them the encounter forms (and sometimes the backup materials for "new" patients). You can also set up a special fax number where faxes come into your email address as scanned attachments.

One biller asks her providers to use a simple paper grid sheet on which they write the name of the patient, the diagnosis code(s), the CPT codes, and any pertinent notes. This simplifies how much paperwork must be faxed to your office. The grid looks something like this:

Date of service	Patient Name	ICD codes	CPT	Notes

This simple grid saves the provider from faxing you pages and pages of encounter forms, since they can simply hand write in the names and codes. Be sure, however, that the person in the office writes clearly so that you won't mistake any characters or numbers.

Once you have the encounter forms, you can now enter claims data for your client. Before we continue though, let's clarify some language about claims. A "claim" actually means two things. Some billers use the word "claim" to mean each CPT code that a doctor bills for. If a patient sees the provider and has three procedures codes affiliated with the visit, then the provider bills 3 claims. However, most billers use the word "claim" to refer to the entire CMS 1500 form, on which you can bill up to four diagnosis codes and six CPT codes per form. In this sense, a claim is the entire bill and the individual CPT codes are considered "line items" belonging to the same claim. Both uses of the word "claim" are fine, but it can be confusing if you use the term one way and another person uses the term the other way, so just be sure you clarify your own use of the word when you speak with other people.

For purposes of this book, we use the word "claim" to mean the **entire** CMS 1500 form on which you can key in up to six CPT line items. However, be aware that the CMS 1500 claim form has spaces for only four diagnosis codes and all the CPT codes you use must relate to those diagnosis codes. (Some types of medicine such as chiropractors may actually use more than four diagnosis codes, and the CMS 1500 has an extra box where extra diagnosis codes can be placed, but in general, only four diagnosis codes are accepted for most claims and all the procedure codes listed must coordinate with the diagnosis codes.)

Figure 7-14 shows the Master Claim screen in MedOffice that is used to input claims.

In this screen shot, the circled fields are the only ones you need to fill in if you are filing a standard CMS 1500 claims for most medical services. As you can see, only nine fields need to be keyed in:

- ***Patient Code.*** Select which patient you are filing for (in MedOffice, you can easily select from the list of patients you have already keyboarded into the system)

- ***Provider.*** Select which provider in the practice is the patient's usual provider (this is not necessarily the one who provided the service, which will be entered further down on the screen). In MedOffice, if you entered a default provider for a patient when you did the patient setup, this field will automatically populate, saving you keystrokes.

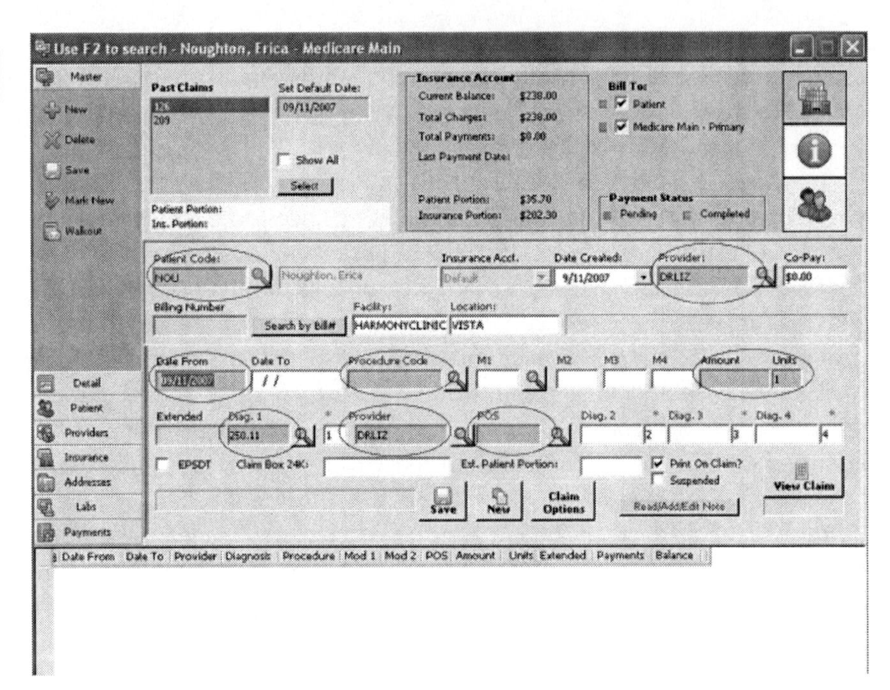

Figure 7-14

Claims Master entry screen in MedOffice. Only the fields circled above (which are actually colored yellow in the full-color software) need to be keyed in to enter standard claims.

- ***Date From / To.*** This is the actual date(s) when the medical service was provided.
- ***Procedure Code.*** You input *one* procedure code here, one at a time. Once you complete one line item and SAVE it, you can then input additional CPT codes. As we said, a single CMS paper claim form allows you to have only 6 CPT codes, but MedOffice allows you to input more CPT codes per claim because doctors are allowed to print more than one page per claim. So, for example, if you keyed in 11 CPT codes for a single form and then printed the claim, you would end up with two printed CMS 1500 pages considered as a single claim with the same bill number, with the first page having six line items and the second page having five line items. Get it?
- ***Amount.*** You must key in the dollar amount of the fee for the medical service here. However, if you have keyed in fee schedules and attached this patient to one of the fee schedules, MedOffice will automatically populate this field with the correct fee for this patient.
- ***Units.*** Enter how many units of service were provided. Some medical services are delivered in single units, but some are delivered in multiple units. So this field tells the claim how many times to multiply

the fee by. If the fee is $42 and there are two units of service, the item actually totals $84.

- ***Diag1.*** Enter the first diagnosis code here, which must be the primary diagnosis for this patient. There is room for additional diagnosis codes if needed on the screen, as you can see in spaces labeled Diag2, Diag3, and Diag4.
- **Provider.** Enter the provider who actually provided the service for the patient here.
- ***POS.*** You select here the place of service code (from those you already entered) for this claim. This can be set to automatically default to the same code for all claims if most claims typically use the exact same code.

Once you have keyed in the data for these nine fields, you click SAVE and that completes one line item for this claim. In MedOffice, the line items that you enter appear at the bottom of the screen, once you click the SAVE button, as shown in Figure 7-15:

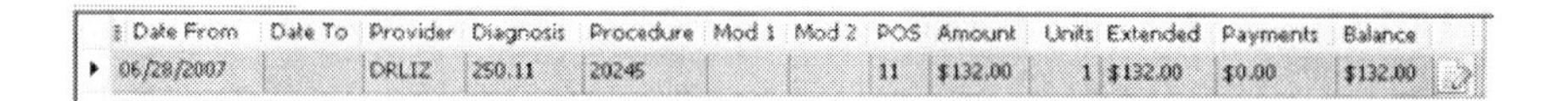

Figure 7-15

Work space at bottom of Claims Master screen showing how line items are added to workspace when keying in claims.

Next, if you have more than one line item (i.e., several CPT codes for this same patient encounter), you key them in one at a time, just like the first one. However, you now have less keying in to do because most of the fields maintain their same data, so the only fields you have to enter for the second, third, fourth, etc line items are the additional CPT codes and their associated fees and number of units. The patient's name, provider, diagnosis codes, date of service, and place of service all remain populated since those cannot change within a single claim form.

For example, assume you receive an encounter slip (superbill) for John Smith and the form indicates two diagnosis codes and four CPT codes. As just described, you would enter all the data necessary for the first CPT code and its fee and number of units, then click SAVE. You then follow this by entering the second CPT code and its fee, and click SAVE. Then enter the third CPT code and its fee, and click SAVE. And finally enter the fourth CPT code and its fee, then click SAVE.

When you are done with a single claim, you click NEW, and that clears the screen entirely while recording the claim for John Smith. That's it! You are done with entering this claim.

Note that certain types of claims may require you to enter additional information, for which MedOffice has the Claim Options button on the Claims Master screen. (Don't forget also that other software may do this differently.) In MedOffice, you simply click on the Claim Options button for claims that require you to list a referring physician, accident information, Medicaid information, lab services that were billed to the provider who now is billing the insurer for the lab fees, claims for early pregnancy tests, and claims for podiatry, chiropractic, or Tricare / CHAMPUS. The Claim Options button shown here leads to additional screens in MedOffice that we will not display in this book.

How long does it take to complete a claim? Initially, a few minutes for a new patient because you need to enter patient demographics and insurance information, etc. However, once the patient information is in, it takes only seconds to enter a claim. Once you are comfortable with the system, you can enter 80 to 100 claims per hour.

Step II-6: Batch and Submit claims

Once you have keyed in all the claims for the group of encounter forms that you received from your client, you must prepare them for transmittal to your clearinghouse or directly to insurers. This process is often referred to as "batching" claims, because you can select a limited "batch" of claims for transmittal from among those you keyed in.

For example, assume you keyed in claims for 150 patients from one provider over the course of three days. You now want to get them ready to transmit, but you realize that you can batch 37 of the claims electronically to Medicare, and 107 claims electronically to your clearinghouse, and six claims that must be printed on paper because they are going to a secondary insurer which sometimes requires backup materials to be mailed along with the paper claims.

In MedOffice, you batch claims using the screen shown in Figure 7-16.

In Figure 7-16, you begin by naming the batch you are creating, and selecting the type of claims (Primary, Secondary, Tertiary) and the Submission Type (paper or electronic). Next, if you want to filter the claims to

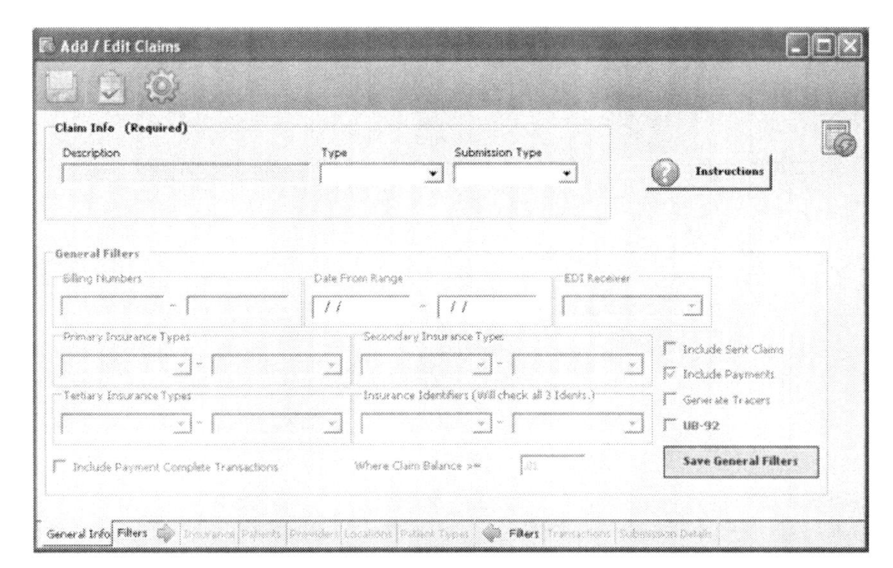

Figure 7-16

Screen from MedOffice illustrating how claims are batched.

create a limited batch from all claims that you have not yet processed, you can use any of the dozens of filters that MedOffice offers you. In the screen shot in Figure 7-16, you can filter by billing #, dates, primary insurance type (Medicare, commercial, CHAMPUS, etc.), secondary insurance type, tertiary insurance type, and insurance identifiers (codes you enter into the system for each insurance company that you might want to identify using your own system). In addition, MedOffice has additional screens (accessed using the tabs you can see at the bottom of the screen in Figure 7-16) where you can add further filters, such as limiting the batch to only certain insurance companies, certain patients, or only certain locations (such as a client of yours who has multiple locations and you prefer to batch the claims by specific location). As you can see, you can create as many batches of claims to file as you want in MedOffice (and again, other software may be different or not as versatile as MedOffice).

Once you've entered the filters as shown in Figure 7-16, your next step is to generate the batch. In MedOffice, this is done using the screen shown in Figure 7-17.

On this screen, you simply click on the *Find matching transactions* button and MedOffice searches all new claims that have been entered but not yet submitted to insurers using your criteria in the filters.

Figure 7-18 shows a sample screen shot of what MedOffice returns after searching for matching claims. In this sample, MedOffice found 14 claims that matched the criteria input with the claims filters.

Figure 7-17

Find matching claims to create a batch screen shot from MedOffice.

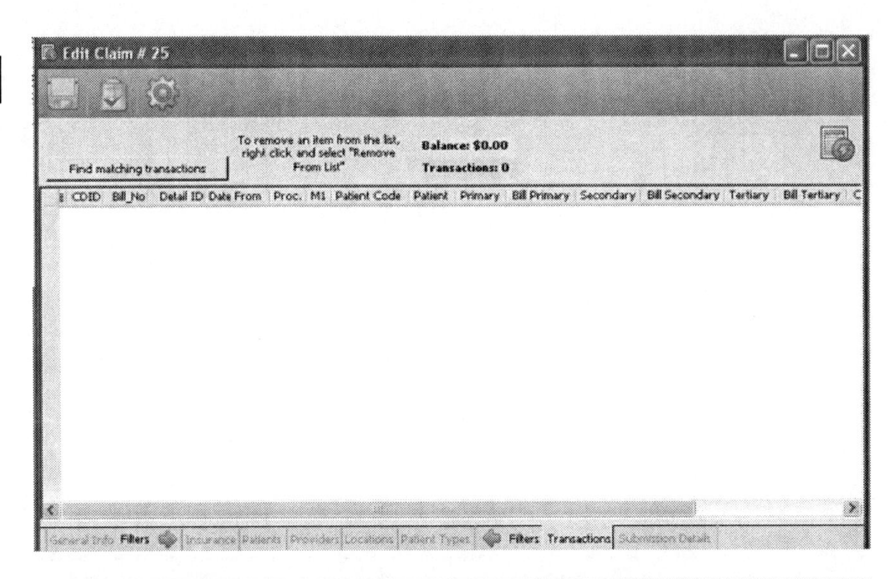

Figure 7-18

Screen illustrating how MedOffice finds all claims that match the filters applied to batching a set of claims.

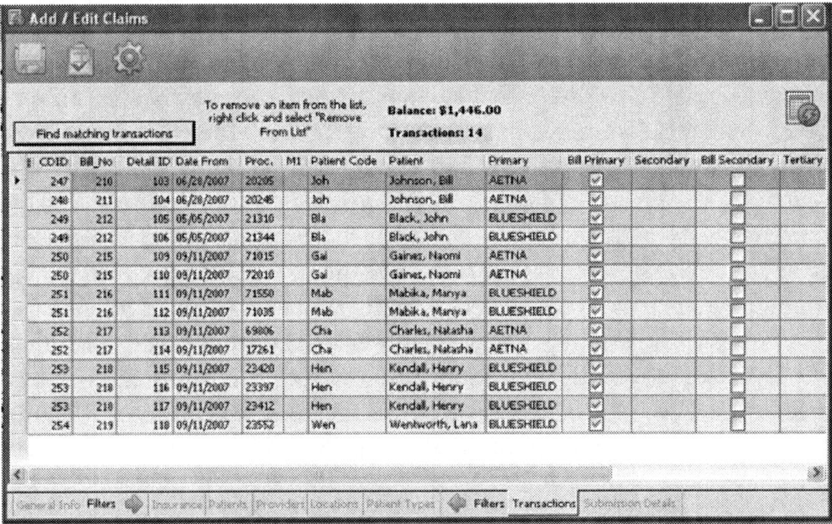

Now that you have batched a set of claims, your next step is to get them ready to transmit to your clearinghouse or to insurance companies directly.

In MedOffice, you simply click the icon at the top of the screen shown in Figure 7-18 to bring up a window where you decide how you want to send the claims, as shown in Figure 7-19.

Notice in the screenshot in Figure 7-19, there are three radio buttons from which to choose how to prepare your claims:

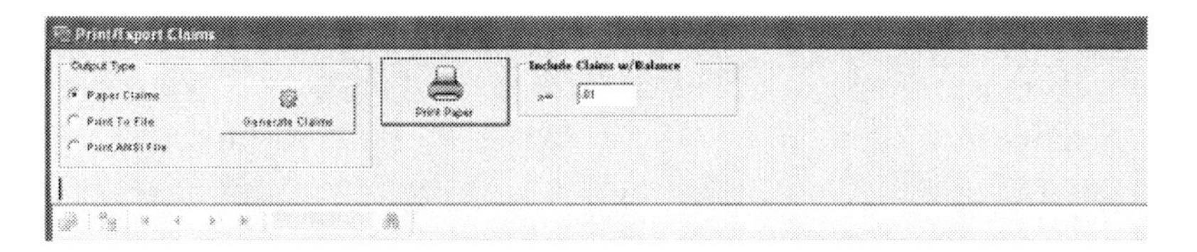

Figure 7-19

Preparing claims to be printed or transmitted screen in MedOffice.

- **Paper** – Select this option if you want to generate paper claims.
- **Print to File** – Also known as "print image," this option is used if you want to generate an image of a paper claim. This format was formerly used for electronic claims whereby the data was sent to a clearinghouse where it was processed as if it were a paper claim. Today, clearinghouses convert print image claims to ANSI, as explained below. ANSI has essentially become the new standard for transmitting electronic claims.
- **Print ANSI file** – Select this option if you plan to transmit electronic claims. ANSI is the official format mandated by Medicare for electronic claims whereby the data is specially formatted for electronic data interchange. (Note: the data is not encrypted, but simply just formatted a specific way that the government set up for when data is exchanged electronically.)

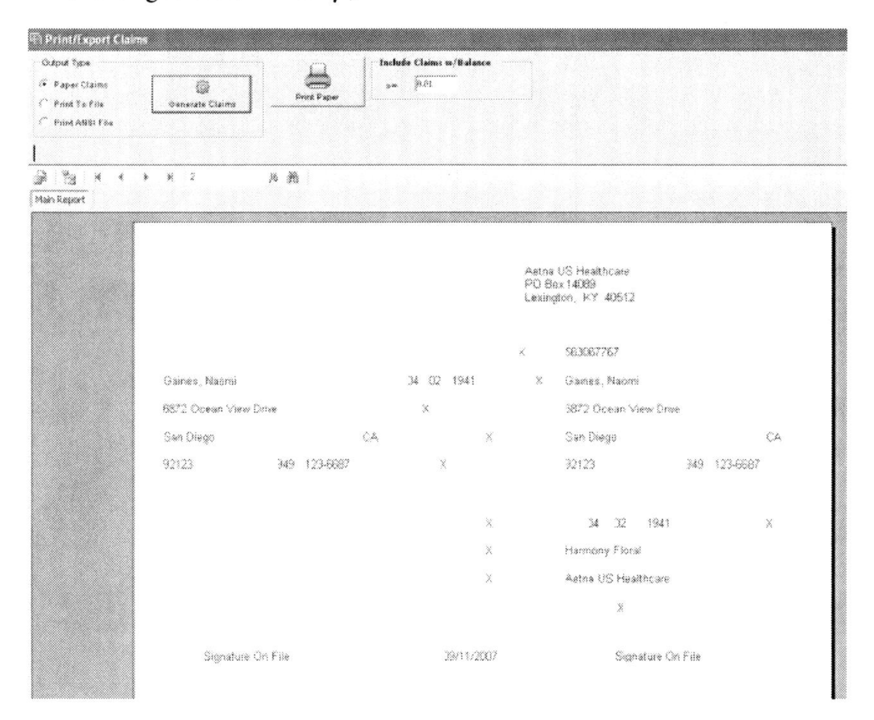

Figure 7-20

Layout for a Paper claim before it is printed on the CMS 1500 red form.

Here are examples of what the claims look like on screen. Both the Paper claim and the Print to File claim look like Figure 7-20. Note that the Paper claim is printed on the official CMS 1500 claim form, so the layout you see in Figure 7-20 displays how the claim appears without seeing the red grid lines pre-printed on the CMS 1500.

Figure 7-21 displays what an ANSI claim looks like on the screen. As you can see, the claim is formatted a specific way which still allows you to read some of the data. However, the ANSI format is a standardized format that is applicable for all electronic claims.

Figure 7-21

Sample ANSI claim printout before transmission.

ISA*00* *00* *20*55221 *ZZ*22332 *050217*1930*U*00401*0000
00001*0*T*!|GS*HC*MED*MED*20050217*1930*1*X*004010X098A
1|ST*837*0001|BHT*0019*00*13*20050217*1930*CH|REF*87*00401
0X098D|NM1*41*2*Sample Practice*****46*S-ETIN|PER*IC*Chester
Cubingsworth*TE*6199821289*EX*123|NM1*40*2*ETT*****46*R-
ETIN|HL*1**20*1|NM1*85*2*Sample Practice*****24*12349876|N3*555
Main Street|N4*San Diego*CA*92012|NM1*87*2*Sample
Practice*****24*12349876|N3*555 Main Street|N4*San Diego*CA*9201
2|HL*2*1*22*1|SBR*P********13|NM1*IL*1*Broderick*Robert****MI*7
87HY789|NM1*PR*2*Medicare Main*****PI*67678HJ|N3*32464 Main
Blvd.|N4*Twin Peaks*CA*92391|HL*3*2*23*0|PAT*19|NM1*QC*1*Brod
erick*Barbara****MI*787HY789|N3*5021 N. Sixth Street|N4*Carlsbad*C
A*92008|DMG*D8*19910806*F|REF*SY*934765671|CLM*Bro*153***02
!!1*Y*A*Y*Y*S|AMT*F5*100|HI*BK!84200|NM1*DN*1*Bennet*John*L
XX*7869018|NM1*82*1*Netty*Bill*M24*786540099|PRV*PE*ZZ*
|NM1*FA*2*Fallbrook Community Hospital|N3*8978 Dove Road|N4*Fa
llbrook*CA*92028|HL*4*1*22*0|SBR*P*18*******13|NM1*IL*1

Step II-7: Print Claims or Transmit Them Electronically to Clearinghouse

Once you have generated a batch of claims, either in paper form or ANSI form, your next step is to either print the batch on paper CMS 1500 forms or transmit the ANSI file to your clearinghouse or directly to insurers.

Paper Claims

Printing paper claims is easy. Simply load your printer with a supply of CMS 1500 forms and select the [button] button from the screen. Figure 7-22 shows what a printed paper claim looks like.

1500

HEALTH INSURANCE CLAIM FORM

APPROVED BY NATIONAL UNIFORM CLAIM COMMITTEE 08/05

Medicare Main
32464 Main Blvd.
Twin Peaks, CA 92391

1. MEDICARE [X]
1a. INSURED'S I.D. NUMBER: 787HY789
2. PATIENT'S NAME: Broderick, Barbara
3. PATIENT'S BIRTH DATE: 08 06 1991 — SEX: F [X]
5. PATIENT'S ADDRESS: 5021 N. Sixth Street
6. PATIENT RELATIONSHIP TO INSURED: Child [X]
CITY: Carlsbad — STATE: CA
8. PATIENT STATUS: Other [X]
ZIP CODE: 92008 — TELEPHONE: (949) 123-4567
9. OTHER INSURED'S NAME: McNamara, Julia
11. INSURED'S POLICY GROUP OR FECA NUMBER: NONE
10a. EMPLOYMENT? NO [X]
b. OTHER INSURED'S DATE OF BIRTH: 09 07 1964 — SEX: F [X]
10b. AUTO ACCIDENT? NO [X]
c. EMPLOYER'S NAME OR SCHOOL NAME: Toys For Fun
10c. OTHER ACCIDENT? NO [X]
c. INSURANCE PLAN NAME OR PROGRAM NAME: Medicare Main
d. INSURANCE PLAN NAME OR PROGRAM NAME: MG 675471

READ BACK OF FORM BEFORE COMPLETING & SIGNING THIS FORM.

12. PATIENT'S OR AUTHORIZED PERSON'S SIGNATURE — SIGNED: Signature On File — DATE: 09/17/2007
13. INSURED'S OR AUTHORIZED PERSON'S SIGNATURE — SIGNED: Signature On File

17. NAME OF REFERRING PROVIDER OR OTHER SOURCE: John L Bennet — 17b. NPI: 7869018
20. OUTSIDE LAB? NO [X] — $ CHARGES: $0.00
21. DIAGNOSIS OR NATURE OF ILLNESS OR INJURY: 1. 493.82

	24. A. DATE(S) OF SERVICE	B. PLACE OF SERVICE	D. CPT/HCPCS	E. DIAGNOSIS POINTER	F. $ CHARGES	G. DAYS OR UNITS	I. ID. QUAL.	J. RENDERING PROVIDER ID. #
1	09 06 07	11	97110	1	55 00	1	1C / NPI	78667656 / 12345
2	09 04 07	11	97110	1	55 00	1	1C / NPI	78667656 / 12345
3	09 06 07	11	98940	1	50 00	1	1C / NPI	78667656 / 12345
4	09 06 07	11	97110	1	55 00	1	1C / NPI	78667656 / 12345
5	09 06 07	11	98943	1	60 00	1	1C / NPI	78667656 / 12345
6							NPI	

25. FEDERAL TAX I.D. NUMBER: 789456 — EIN [X]
26. PATIENT'S ACCOUNT NO.: Bro
27. ACCEPT ASSIGNMENT? YES [X]
28. TOTAL CHARGE: $ 275 00 — 29. AMOUNT PAID: $ 15 00 — 30. BALANCE DUE: $ 260 00
31. SIGNATURE OF PHYSICIAN OR SUPPLIER: Bill M. Netty, M.D. — DATE: 09/17/2007
32. SERVICE FACILITY LOCATION INFORMATION: Fallbrook Community Hospital, 8978 Dove Road, Fallbrook, CA 92028 — a. 89078754
33. BILLING PROVIDER INFO & PH #: (619)982-1289 — Sample Practice, 555 Main Street, San Diego, CA 92012 — a. 12345 — b. 1C78667656

NUCC Instruction Manual available at: www.nucc.org — PLEASE PRINT OR TYPE — APPROVED OMB-0938-0999 FORM CMS-1500 (08/05)

Printed on Recycled Paper

Figure 7-22

An example of a paper claim printed on a CMS 1500 form.

Of course, once you print a batch of paper claims, you need to put them into an envelope and mail them to the insurer. As this book has pointed out, while paper claims are easy to do, the problem is they take a longer time to process at clearinghouses and insurers. Earlier in this book, we told you how paper claims no longer have priority in processing, and go through a long process at insurance companies that can take from 60 to 90 days before your client is paid. In general, you want to avoid paper claims unless:

- You are either just beginning billing for a doctor and the practice has not yet been authorized to submit electronic claims to a clearinghouse.
- You are sending secondary claims, tertiary claims, or worker's comp claims that often require backup paperwork.
- You have claims for an insurer that is not in the clearinghouse's payor list.
- You have a corrected form for a claim that is already in the insurer's adjudication system.
- You are printing an appeals claim.

Electronic Claims

Transmitting electronic claims using MedOffice is also easy. MedOffice has a menu command Transmit Claims, which brings up a window in which you select the clearinghouse to which you want to send your batch of claims, as shown in Figure 7-23.

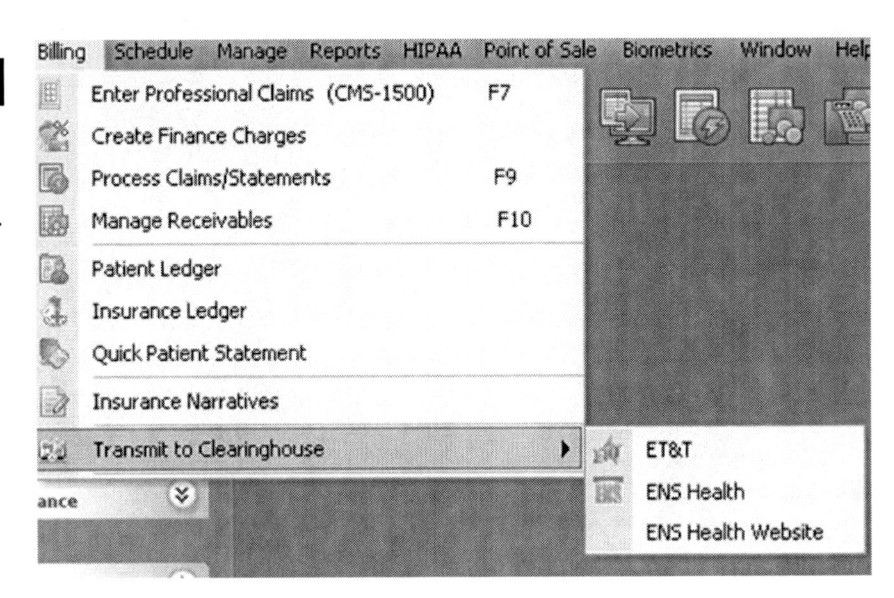

Figure 7-23

Transmit claims to a clearinghouse screen in MedOffice.

Note that MedOffice is already set up to allow you to transmit claims to several clearinghouses (but you must sign a contract and obtain authorization to transmit). If you want to work with any other clearinghouse, you can easily set up the operations for that using the MedOffice clearinghouse set-up screens. Your clearinghouse will inform you about the settings you need to put into the set up fields to ensure the modem transmissions work properly. Some clearinghouses also let you submit claims to them over the Internet by logging onto their secure web site and transmitting through that.

Now, let's talk about what happens when you transmit claims to a clearinghouse. Each clearinghouse works a little differently, but in general, this is what you will experience and why electronic claims offer so many advantages over paper claims.

First, you log onto the clearinghouse and click on the command to Send Claims. Within minutes after transmission, while you are still logged on, you will probably receive back a reply that says in writing "Claims file was received successfully." This report may also include claims that were rejected and need to be fixed. Some clearinghouses allow you to correct claims with minor errors immediately and even return those claims to you in a "fix it" file. Once you make the corrections, you can resend the claims during the same transmission.

In addition to the immediate report for claims you just transmitted, many clearinghouses will provide you with an updated report on previously filed claims (such as claims you filed last week). This other report contains information back from the various insurance companies to which those prior claims had been sent. For example, it might have a listing of all claims received and adjudicated for payment at each insurance company. It might also indicate claims where the patient did not have eligibility for payment, in which case it would show next to the claim "no eligibility." Or the report from an insurer may come back requesting reports or backup documentation for a claim.

As you can see, the combined benefits of electronic claims and using a clearinghouse are significant. If a claim has minor errors in it, you save an enormous amount of time because you have the opportunity to fix them immediately. If the claim is missing information or needs backup documentation or the patient is not eligible for the payment, you find out within a week so you can discuss the claim with your client and determine what to do next. If the claim is "clean," you also find out typically within a week, so you can count on your provider being paid usually within another few days (since insurers typically send out EOBs and checks within 10 days of receiving electronic claims).

Step II-8: Process Receivables from Insurers and Patients

As a full service medical practice management company, your job is not only to key in and submit claims to insurance companies, but also to handle the other side of the billing – *recording the payments that come in!* Don't forget that doctors receive payments from both insurance companies and from patients, so we're going to review how both of these procedures are handled, again using the MedOffice software as an example of how you perform this type of recording. In addition, we'll also cover in this step the recording of capitation payments from insurance companies which are treated a little differently than regular fee-for-service receivables. Capitation receivables will be discussed last, so let's begin by talking about regular insurance payments.

Recording Insurance Receivables

After you've submitted your claims, your client will begin receiving payments from the insurers. If you filed electronic claims, many insurers issue checks and Explanation of Benefits documents within 7-10 days. Note also that if an insurer receives batches of claims for several patients of the same provider, they usually return to the provider just one EOB document summarizing the payments for all those patients involved in that set of claims. These EOB documents give the provider a complete listing of how much was allowed for each line item CPT code, how much was paid, how much was denied (and must therefore be written off as a write-off or adjustment), and how much is the patient's responsibility to pay.

Your next step is therefore to make an arrangement with your client to get copies of the EOBs (or EOMBs) and payment checks. Many providers simply make photocopies of the EOBs and a copy of the deposit slip for the checks and fax or mail them to the billing company. Insurance companies are increasingly allowing EOBs to be viewed online, and so doctors are giving their billers permission to view and download the EOBs.

Once you receive the copies of the EOBs, your job is to go into your software and record the payments. Note that recording receivables is perhaps the most precise work you must do as a biller, requiring a keen eye and attention to detail. The reason for this is that you cannot record a lump sum payment for a claim if there is more than one line item. You must actually key in the line item details, so that you can accurately track the payments and write-offs for *each* CPT code you billed.

For example, assume you billed a single patient's claim for four CPT codes, and the charges were $78, $97, $103, and $37. However, let's say that the insurer paid two of the codes fully, but paid the other two codes at only partial rates, requiring your client to write off a portion of the fees. You thus need to record all this in detail so that you can accurately balance out the claim and keep track of which CPT codes caused write-offs. Patients need to know this information when you bill them, and it helps your client to know exactly how much has been paid for each and every CPT code billed.

Here's how MedOffice handles the recording of receivables to show you how the details are done. Figure 7-24 shows how you begin the process.

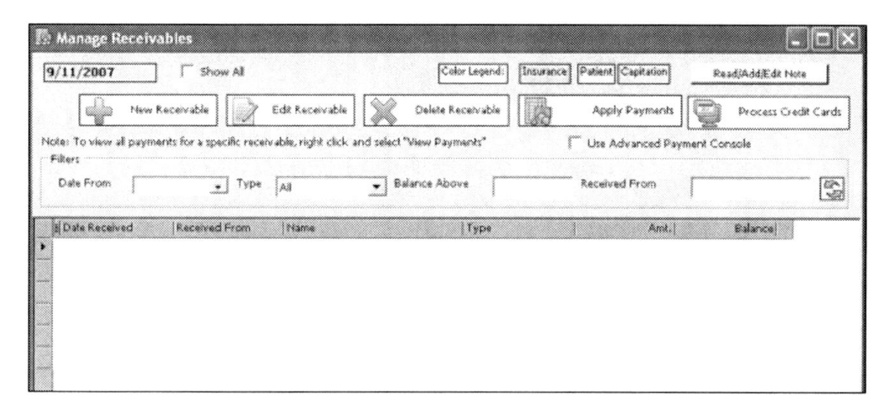

Figure 7-24

The Manage Receivables screen in MedOffice.

You begin by clicking on the New Receivable button shown at the top of the screen to bring up the New Receivable screen, as shown in Figure 7-25, where you record the type of receivable (insurance, patient, or capitation) and the amount of the entire check. At this time, you are not yet indicating which patients the check covers. This only records the entire receivable amount.

Figure 7-25

Recording a new insurance Receivable screen in MedOffice.

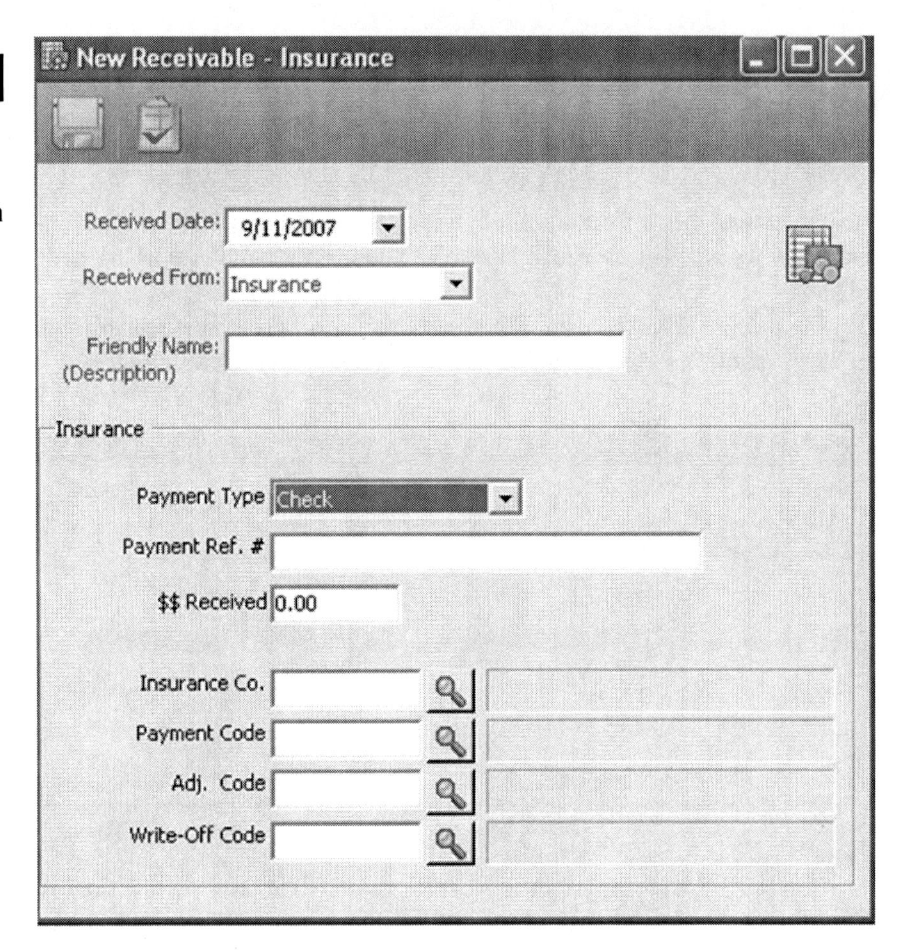

Your next step is to apply the receivable to specific patients and their claims. To do this, MedOffice uses a single window that allows you to select patients and enter the dollar amounts to each outstanding line item they have open. Figure 7-26 shows the Payment Console window where this is done.

Figure 7-26

Payment Console window for applying receivables in MedOffice.

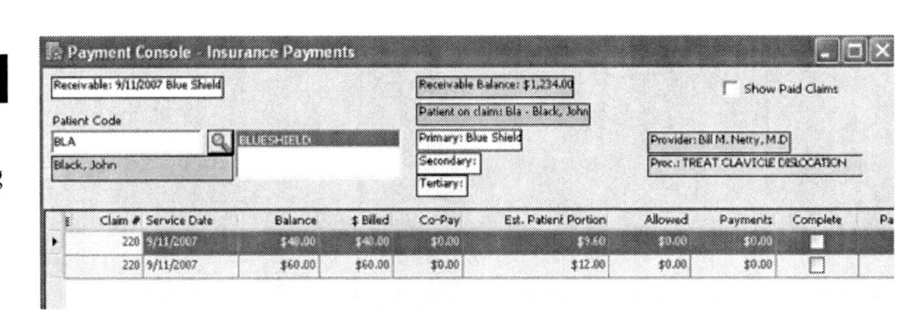

Using the Payment console is easy. You begin by selecting, in the Patient Code box, the first patient named in the EOB for whom you received a payment. Once you select that patient, all his or her outstanding charges will be displayed in the work space on the screen. In Figure 7-26, you can see two outstanding claims for patient John Black, one line item for $48 and one for $60. While looking at your EOB and its breakdown of the payments for John Black, you simply highlight in the Payment Console workspace which line item you want to pay and click the ADD PAYMENT button to bring up the payment screen shown in Figure 7-27.

In this window, MedOffice automatically defaults to the amount of the line item, because most insurance companies pay this amount of the claim if it was billed according to the fee schedule. For example, for the $48 line

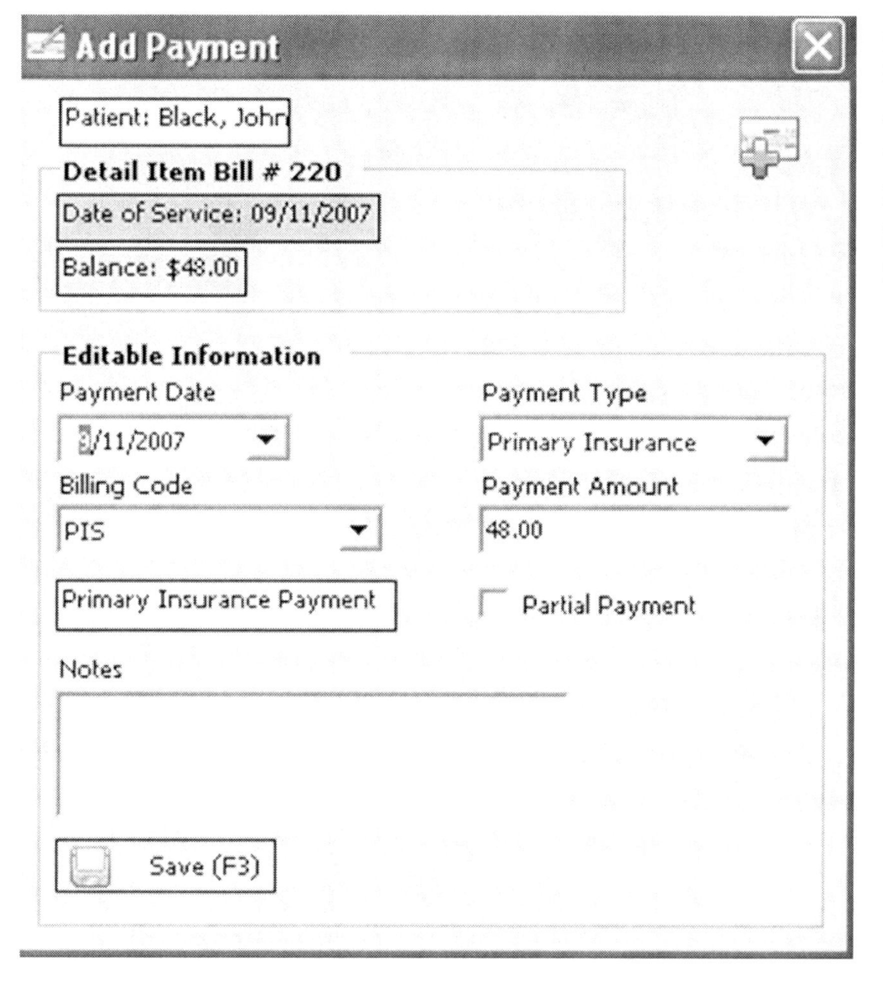

Figure 7-27

Add Payment window to apply an insurance payment to a patient's line item.

item, this screen defaults to show a payment of $48 with the automatic billing code of PIS (Primary Insurance Payment). Simply click SAVE and you have just recorded the payment of $48 for this line item.

However, let's say that the insurance company paid only $42 on the $48 line item and expects you to adjust (write off) $6. In this case, you enter $42 into the Payment Amount field in Figure 7-27 and then return to the Payment Console where MedOffice allows you to automatically write off the missing amount by clicking on the Mark Complete button to bring up the screen shown in Figure 7-28.

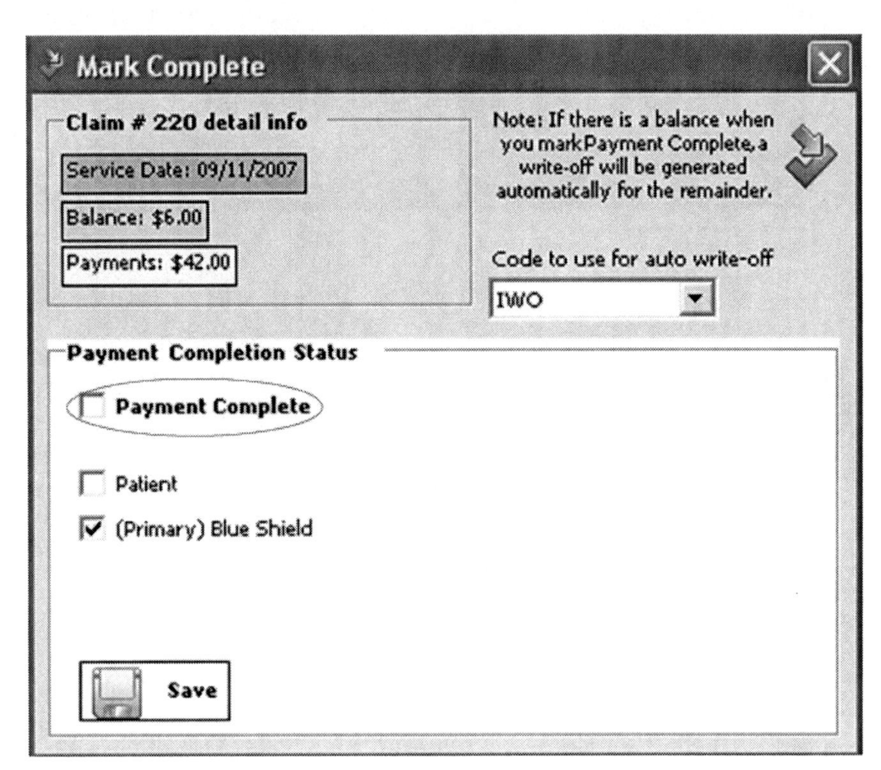

Figure 7-28

Mark Complete window that automatically writes off any missing amount from an insurance payment.

Using the Mark Complete screen, you can check the box for Payment Complete, and MedOffice automatically writes off the $6 difference between the $48 billed amount and the $42 paid amount. This automatic process simplifies your need to do any calculations for write-offs, one of the features of MedOffice. In this way, when you eventually send a monthly statement to your patient, he or she will see exactly how much the insurance company paid, how much was written off according to the contract, and how much he or she might now owe as patient responsibility.

Note that MedOffice also has an "Advanced Payment Console" where, once you become skilled at applying insurance receivables, you can quickly select patients and type in the dollar amounts yourself for payments. Figure 7-29 shows the Advanced Console, though we won't explain its use in great detail here. Remember that other software may not offer the features that MedOffice does, so if you are using different software, you may not find this type of functionality. The Advanced Console is useful when you are processing a large EOB from an insurer that covers many patients because you can code all the line item payments in the exact same way. Therefore, in Figure 7-29, you select which codes you want to apply to all the keyboarding you are about to do, e.g., all payments will be PIS, all write-offs will be IWO, and all adjustments will be chargebacks. You can also check a box to have MedOffice auto-populate the fee schedule writes offs.

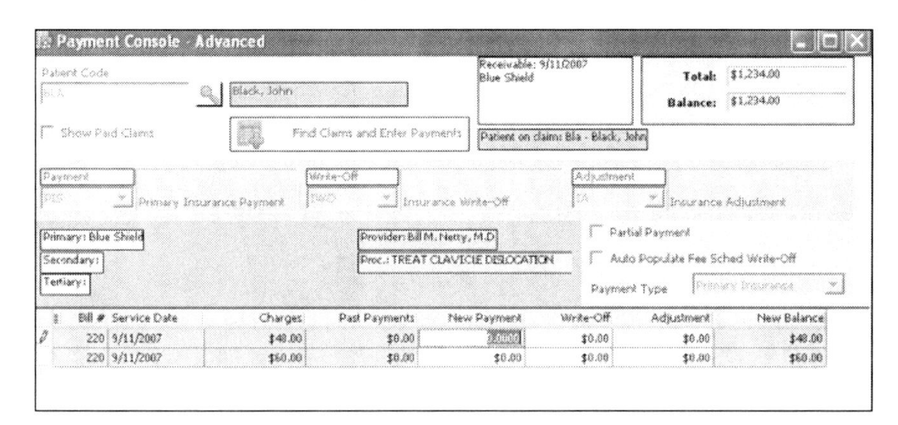

Figure 7-29

Advanced payment console in MedOffice.

Once you set the parameters for coding on the Advanced Console, you select a patient and then type in the payment amounts directly into the console workspace as shown in figure 7-30.

Bill #	Service ...	Charges	Past Payments	New Payment	Write-Off	Adjustment	New Balance
108	7/27/2...	$43.00	$0.00	[illegible]	$0.00	$0.00	$43.00
108	7/27/2...	$89.00	$0.00	$0.00	$0.00	$0.00	$89.00
138	10/11/...	$30.00	$0.00	$0.00	$0.00	$0.00	$30.00
138	10/11/...	$25.00	$0.00	$0.00	$0.00	$0.00	$25.00
138	10/11/...	$10.00	$0.00	$0.00	$0.00	$0.00	$10.00
218	9/11/2...	$145.00	$0.00	$0.00	$0.00	$0.00	$145.00
218	9/11/2...	$58.00	$0.00	$0.00	$0.00	$0.00	$58.00
218	9/11/2...	$120.00	$0.00	$0.00	$0.00	$0.00	$120.00

Figure 7-30

Advanced Console workspace showing patient line items.

For example, assume you are processing an insurance payment that covers 10 patients. You select the first patient, John Doe, and the workspace immediately shows all his outstanding claims, such as shown in Figure 7-30. Now simply key in the insurance amount paid, the write-off, and any adjustment. If you checked the box for Auto Populate Fee Schedule Write-off on the Advanced Console, you don't even need to type in the Write-Off in the workspace. MedOffice does it for you. If you are recording insurance payments for six of the outstanding line items shown in Figure 7-30, all payments would be considered Primary Insurance Payment and you don't need to code each one. Once you finish recording the line item payments for John Doe, you click SAVE, and then select the second patient covered in the EOB. And so on. In this way, the Advanced Console saves you several steps when you are processing large insurance EOBs that contain payments and adjustments for many patients at a time.

MedOffice makes it easy to record these types of large insurance payments. Figure 7-31 shows a window that MedOffice provides where you can view the sum total of an insurance payment and all the patients to whom it has been applied. For example, in this window, you can see that the insurance payment was for $1,234, out of which $712.70 remains to be applied. You can also see to which accounts the balance of $521.30 has been applied (to patient codes Bla and Hen).

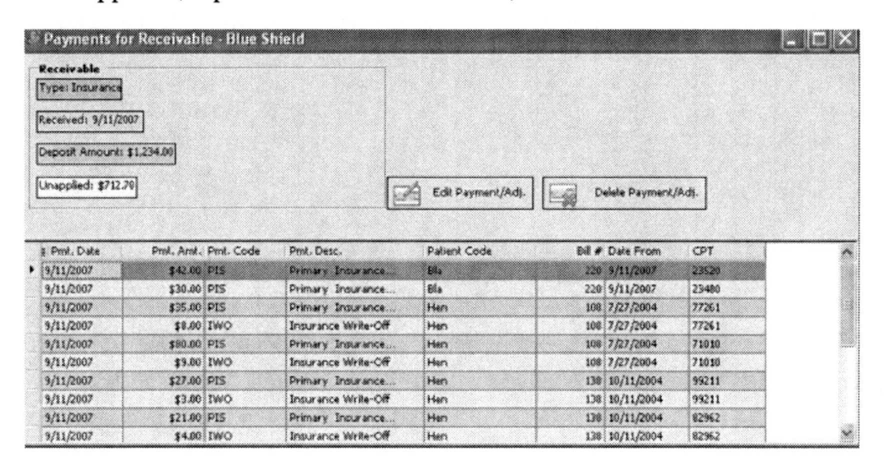

Pmt. Date	Pmt. Amt.	Pmt. Code	Pmt. Desc.	Patient Code	Bill #	Date From	CPT
9/11/2007	$42.00	PIS	Primary Insurance...	Bla	220	9/11/2007	23520
9/11/2007	$30.00	PIS	Primary Insurance...	Bla	220	9/11/2007	23480
9/11/2007	$35.00	PIS	Primary Insurance...	Hen	108	7/27/2004	77261
9/11/2007	$8.00	IWO	Insurance Write-Off	Hen	108	7/27/2004	77261
9/11/2007	$80.00	PIS	Primary Insurance...	Hen	108	7/27/2004	71010
9/11/2007	$9.00	IWO	Insurance Write-Off	Hen	108	7/27/2004	71010
9/11/2007	$27.00	PIS	Primary Insurance...	Hen	138	10/11/2004	99211
9/11/2007	$3.00	IWO	Insurance Write-Off	Hen	138	10/11/2004	99211
9/11/2007	$21.00	PIS	Primary Insurance...	Hen	138	10/11/2004	82962
9/11/2007	$4.00	IWO	Insurance Write-Off	Hen	138	10/11/2004	82962

Figure 7-31

Payments window in MedOffice that shows how you can view to which line items payments have been applied for a large insurance receivable.

Recording Patient Receivables

Doctors also receive payments from patients. If you are running a full practice management billing business, you need to record these patient payments in order to perform a full accounting for all claims that you have billed. How do you find out about patient payments?

In general, most doctors ask their patients to mail the payments directly to them. Then they either photocopy the checks or make a simple list of the individual patient payments and send or fax the documents to their billing company to use in recording the patient payments. Some doctors open up what's called a "lock box" bank account. With this type of account, patients mail their payments to the lock box post office box. The bank opens the mail and deposits any checks into the doctor's account, and the doctor is the only one who has access to the account. However, the bank gives the payment stubs that came with the patient payments to the authorized billing company. This type of account makes it easy for the checks to get deposited while you receive the documents that allow you to enter in the data.

In fact, you should be aware that Medicare requires that billing companies do NOT have direct access to a doctor's Medicare payments. As you can imagine, this is a security measure that prevents fraudulent billing. Imagine if a billing company could, on its own, submit claims to Medicare without the doctor even knowing that this was being done, and then have the Medicare reimbursement check sent directly to the biller. This would be a closed loop controlled by the biller and it would be possible for a doctor to never find out about it. This is why Medicare implemented this policy, insisting that medical billers cannot have control of a doctor's bank account or even direct access to pulling their fees from the doctor's account. For this reason, when you fill out a Provider Participation Agreement with Medicare, there is a page in the agreement that specifically asks who receives the money and if the billing company has access.

Whatever way you set up with your client to receive data about patient payments, keep in mind that this must be an ongoing, consistent process so you can ensure correct bookkeeping for all outstanding claims. Your doctor's cash flow depends entirely on making sure that insurance companies pay their portion of the claims, and that patients pay their responsibility as well.

Recording patient payments is done almost the exact same way as the basic method of recording insurance payments. You begin at the Manage Receivables screen shown in Figure 7-24 and click on New Receivable. Then in Figure 7-25, instead of selecting Insurance in the type of receivable, use the pull-down menu to select Patient Receivable and record the amount and the name of the patient from whom it was received. You will then see the receivable you recorded in a screen such as shown in Figure 7-32 below, where a hypothetical receivable for $140 for patient Bill Johnson has been recorded.

Figure 7-32

Recording a patient receivable in MedOffice.

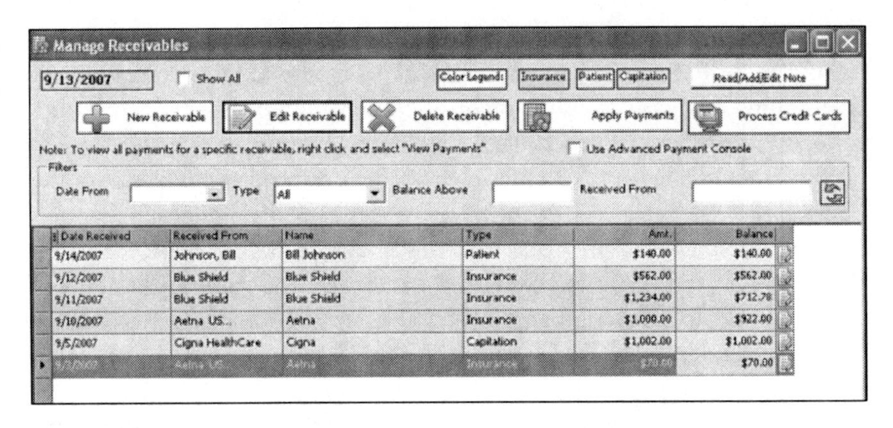

As with insurance payments, you next need to apply the patient receivable you recorded to his or her individual claims and line items. Simply click the Apply Payments button in the screen in Figure 7-32 and all of the patient's outstanding claims appear in the workspace, as shown in Figure 7-33.

Figure 7-33

Patient payment console and workspace in MedOffice.

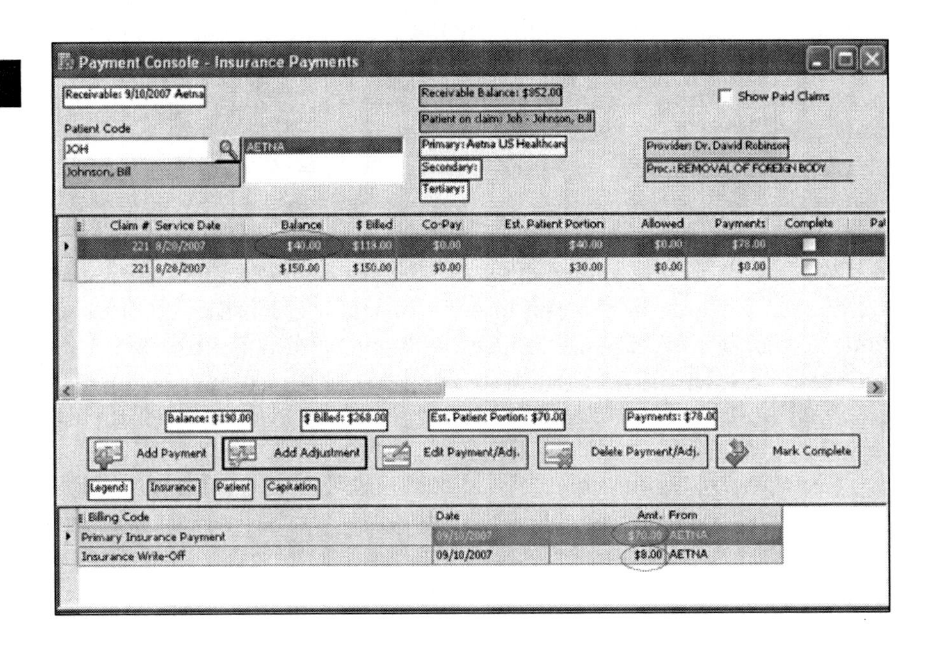

Just as with insurance payments, highlight the line item you want to pay (in the screen in Figure 7-33, the patient has two line items). Notice that the insurance has already paid $70 on this item and wrote off $8.00. This leaves the patient's balance at $40.

Click the Add Payment button on the bottom of the screen to bring up the Apply Payment Patient window, as shown in Figure 7-34, where you can enter the amount of the patient payment to apply to this line item. Notice that the payment is coded PP (Patient Payment), because you need to distinguish insurance payments from patient payments in your records. Notice that the remaining amount on the line item, $40.00, automatically displays in the Balance area and in the Amount Paid area.

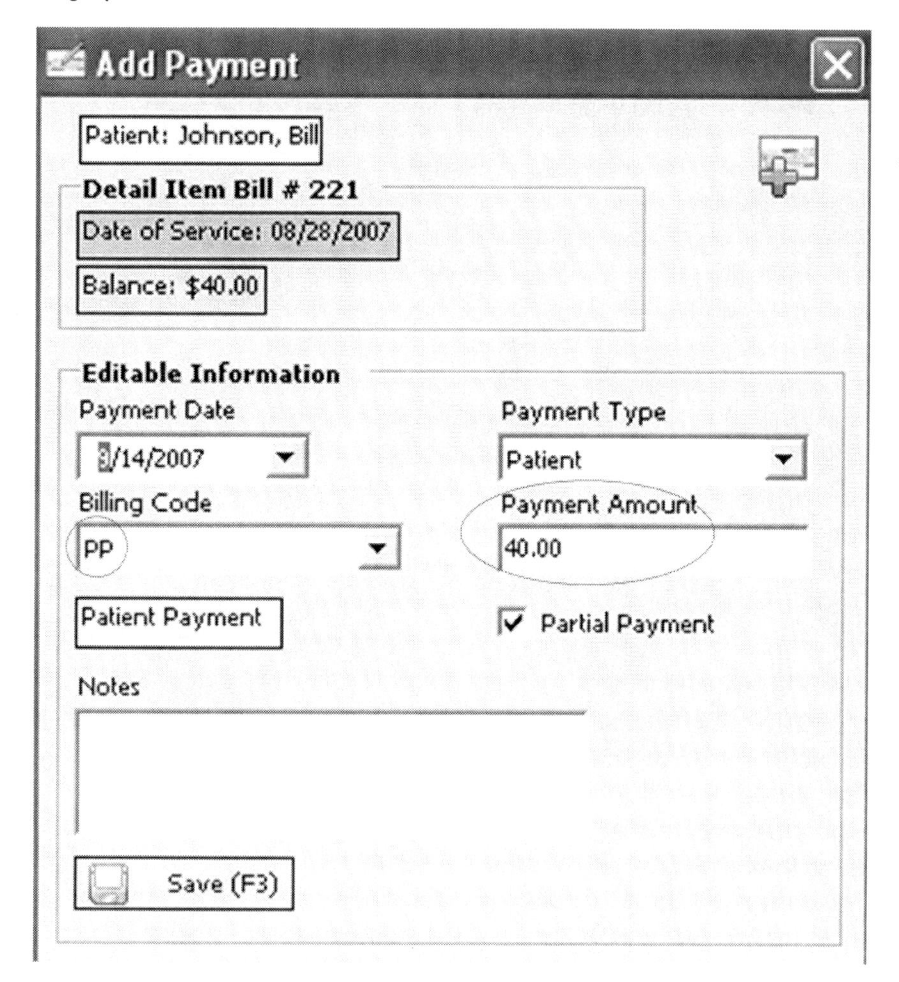

Figure 7-34

Patient payment window for applying a patient payment.

After recording this patient payment, the claim is now fully paid. You can return to the Payment Console and, by checking Show Paid Claims, the console will display all insurance and patient payments for Item #221, as shown in Figure 7-35.

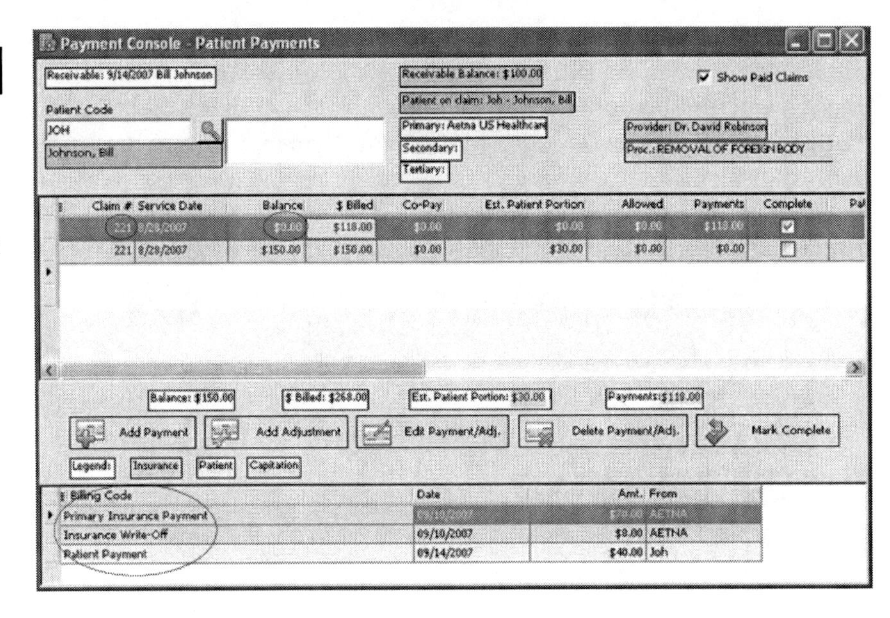

Figure 7-35

Payment Console showing both insurance and patient payments on one line item.

In this sample screen, we can see that the total amount billed was $118 for this line item, and insurance paid $70.00, wrote-off $8.00, and the patient paid $40.

Recording Capitation Receivables

Capitation refers to the process of insurance companies and HMOs paying doctors "per head" rather than based on the standard fee-for-service rates. When a provider belongs to a capitation type of insurance plan, he or she receives a fixed dollar amount to see patients each and every month, regardless of how many patients actually come in for office visits or what medical services are provided. The advantage of a capitation plan is that the doctor can count on a fixed income each and every month. However, the risk is that the provider may lose money compared to charging for his or her time based on fee-for-services.

The way billers account for capitation payments is only partially similar to the way you account for fee-for-service payments. First, even though your client will not collect fees for individual claims, you still process claims to any insurance company that pays your provider based on capitation. The claims will be denied (because the provider receives capitation payments, not fee for service payments), but you still receive EOBs back that allow you to track which patients services have been provided and a tally of their fee for services, even though you are not going to get paid based on that.

Next, each month, you record the capitation payment checks that your client receives as follows. At the Management Receivables screen shown in Figure 7-24, begin by clicking New Receivable. Then, as shown in Figure 7-36 below, select Capitation in the "Received From" field and record the amount received.

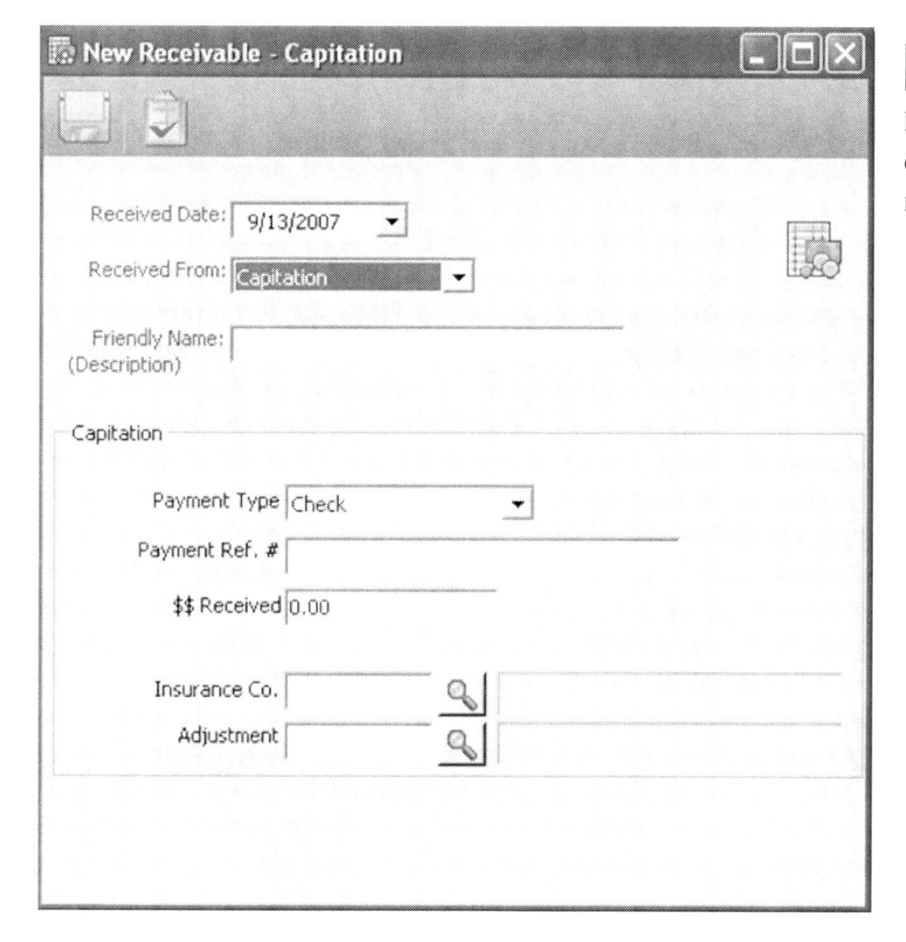

Figure 7-36

Recording a capitation receivable.

Next, using the Manage Receivables screen (exactly as shown in Figure 7-25), select one of the patients to whom the capitation payment applies. Just as with insurance and patient payments, this will bring up the list of outstanding line items for this patient, if any, as shown in Figure 7-37 below.

Figure 7-37

Applying a capitation payment to a patient in MedOffice.

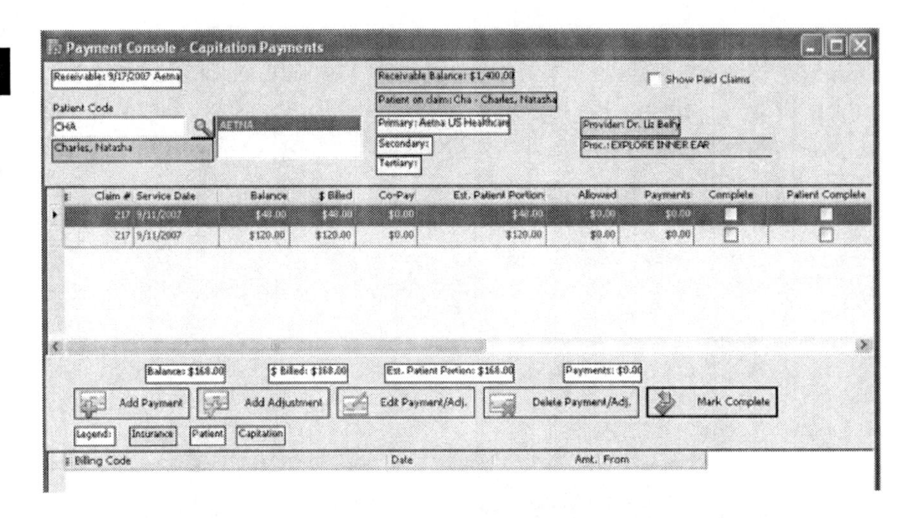

Figure 7-38

The Add Capitation Adjustment window in MedOffice.

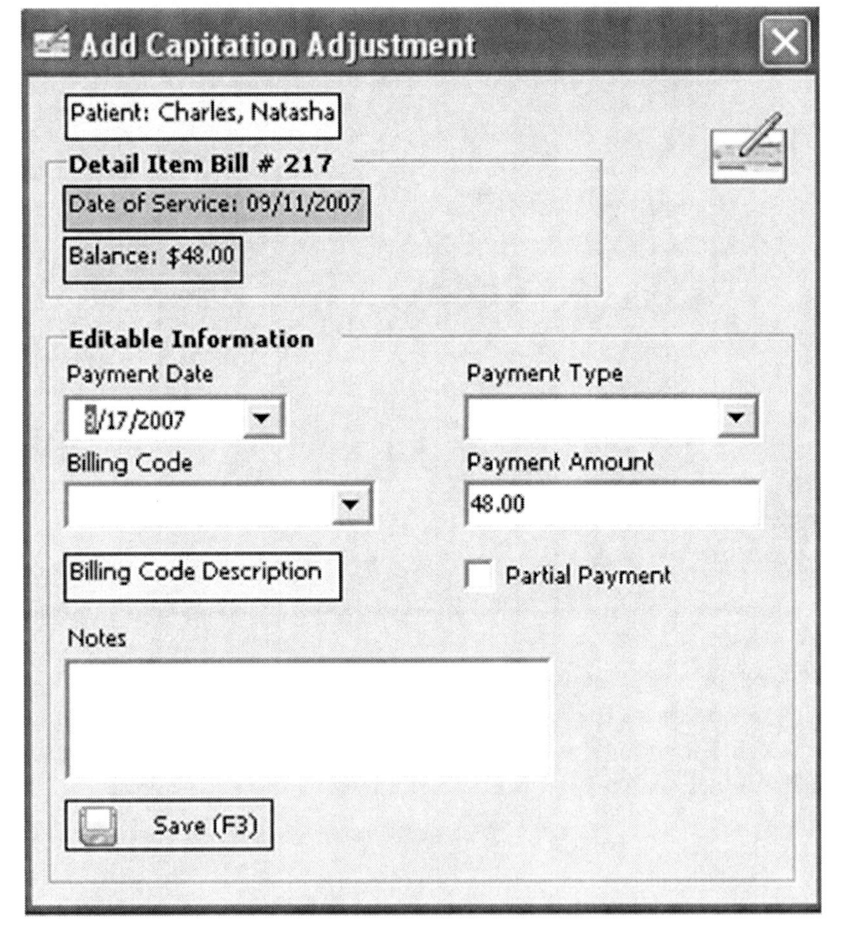

Next, highlight the line item to which you want to apply the capitation payment and click the Add Adjustment button to bring up the Add Capitation Adjustment window, as shown in Figure 7-38.

Unlike insurance and patient payments, with capitation adjustments you accept the entire amount of the charge for the adjustment. In effect, you are zeroing out the entire charge using the capitation payment. Click SAVE. Next, move on to the next capitation patient who has outstanding charges, and add a capitation adjustment for each line item for that patient.

Eventually, after going through every patient who has capitation coverage under the insurance agreement with your provider, you will zero out all outstanding balances for this month. At that point, you will then be able to determine if the capitation payment is either positive or negative – in other words, did the cumulative capitation adjustments you entered *surpass* or *fall under* the amount of the capitation payment? This tells your client if he or she made a profit from the single monthly capitation payment or lost money under the capitation payment.

For example, assume your client receives a check for $3,000 for 50 patients under the capitation plan for the month of May. When the check comes in, you search all patients in the capitation plan who used the provider's services that month and find 18 of them had charges in May. Then, as you go through all their charges, you add a capitation adjustment to each charge in the full amount. When you are done applying the capitation payment, you discover that the cumulative fees for services for these 18 patients amounted to $3,632. This effectively means that the provider incurred a loss of ($632) that month, because the capitation payment of $3,000 was less than the total $3,632 in fee-for-service charges.

Note that by following the procedure explained above, MedOffice helps providers determine whether it is wise for them to join insurance contracts that pay them under capitation. MedOffice also has a report, called the Managed Care Analysis Report, which allows you to show your client a comparison of the two income streams: capitation payments vs. fee-for-service. Of course, over a period of time, some providers make money on capitation contracts with insurers because they collect more in payments than they would have in fees for services. For other providers who don't earn more in capitation payments than they would have in fees for services, they may nevertheless feel less stressed about running their business, knowing that they have steady cash flow each and every month because of their capitation clients.

Step II-9: Prepare and Mail Patient Statements

The next step in operating your full practice management business is to send out patient statements. Most providers send statements each month to all patients who have outstanding balances after all insurance payments and prior payments from the patient have been recorded. Some providers let their patients pay an outstanding balance over time, though more and more providers are beginning to charge patients interest on balances that remain unpaid beyond 30 days following the insurance payment.

The procedure for issuing patient statements in MedOffice is similar to that for processing claims in that the process is done according to individual transactions. You begin with the Process Claims / Statements screen, as shown in Figure 7-39.

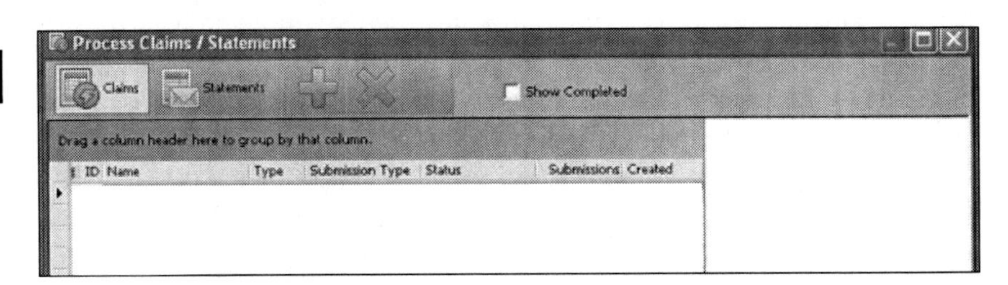

Figure 7-39

Process Statements screen in MedOffice.

Instead of selecting Claims, click on the Statements button in the upper portion of the screen to bring up the Add / Edit Statement group window, as shown in Figure 7-40. Then, in this window, you can define the param-

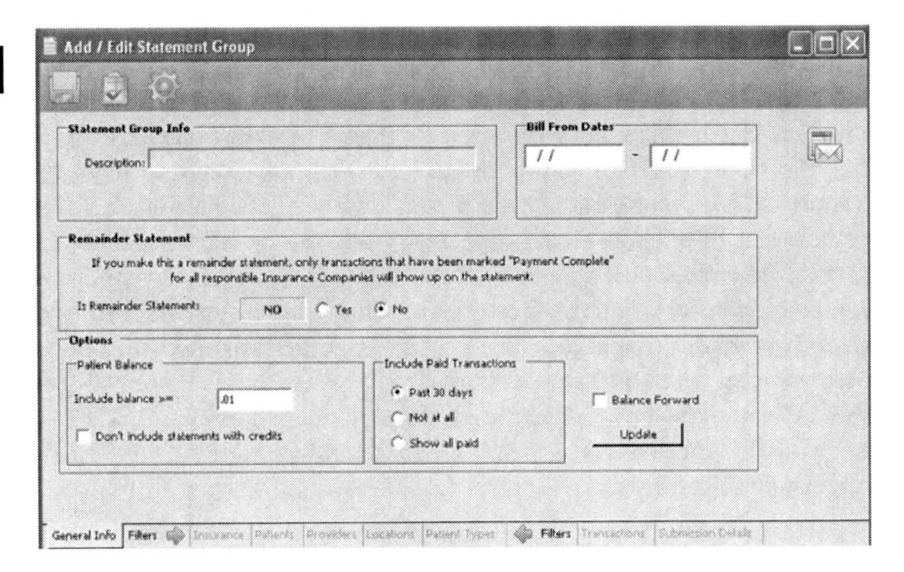

Figure 7-40

Creating a statement group using filters in MedOffice.

eters of the transactions you want to find in the same manner that you add filters to claims when you are batching them. In other words, you first create batches of transactions that will eventually become patient statements.

Once you define and apply filters to identify which transactions you want to find, you begin the process of pulling in those transactions, just as you did with claims. Figure 7-41 shows an example in which MedOffice found 101 matching transactions to a set of filters that were defined for sending patient statements.

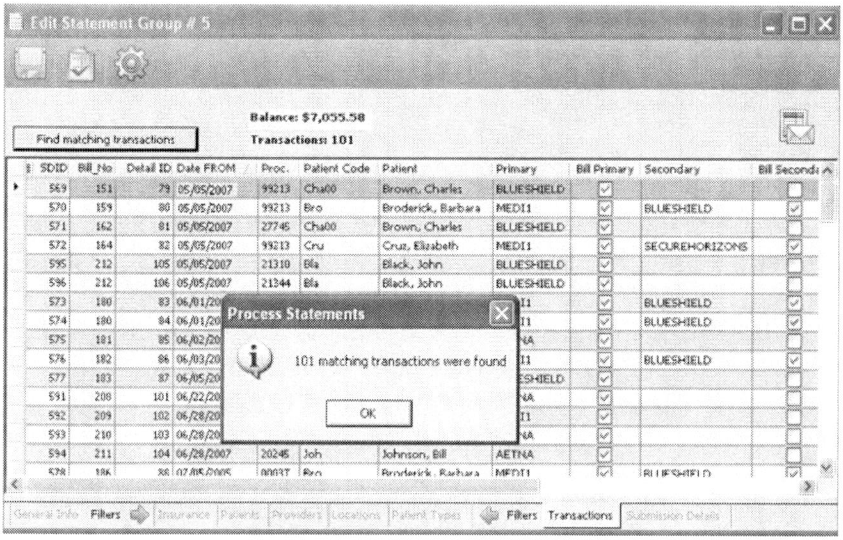

Figure 7-41

Finding transactions for statements in MedOffice

The next step is to pull the transactions together to print patient statements. Figure 7-42 shows how MedOffice offers 14 types of statements. Some statements are basic with or without aging, while other statements break down the amounts due into insurance amounts due vs. patient amounts due.

Note: MedOffice accounts for two types of aging: insurance aging and patient aging. For insurance aging, the aging date begins when you transmit the original claim to the clearinghouse or print the claim, rather than the date of patient service. This helps you keep track of how long it takes to receive payment from the insurer. For patient again, the aging date begins on the date the first statement is sent to the patient. This is because it is unfair to patients to send them a statement saying their charges are overdue by 30 days when they have not yet received a statement from you asking for payment.)

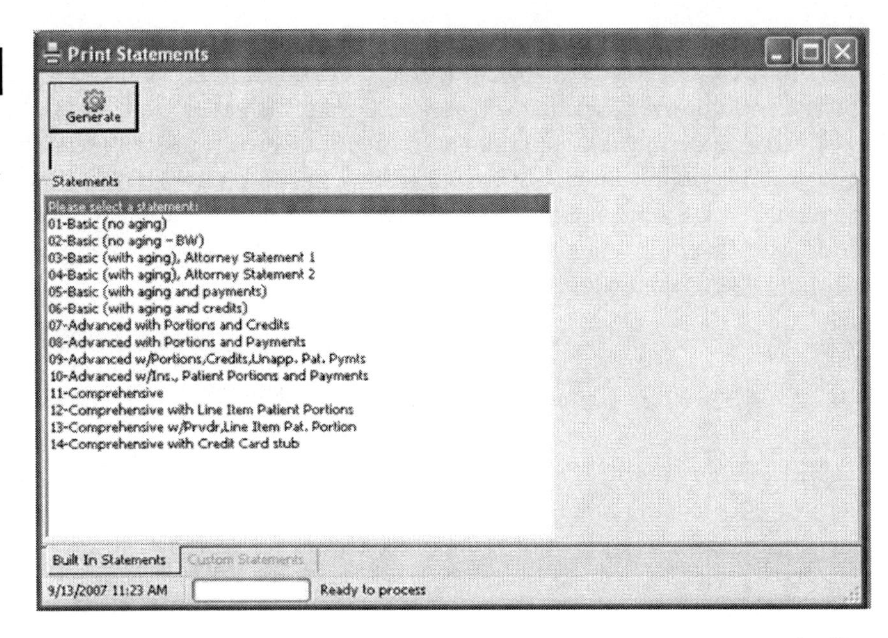

Figure 7-42

Print statements screen in MedOffice, from which you can choose the type of statement you want to send.

Once you select the type of statements you want to print, MedOffice displays them on the screen so you can review them and confirm that you want to print them on paper. Figure 7-43 shows an example of the top portion of a patient statement that shows aging by insurance and by patient.

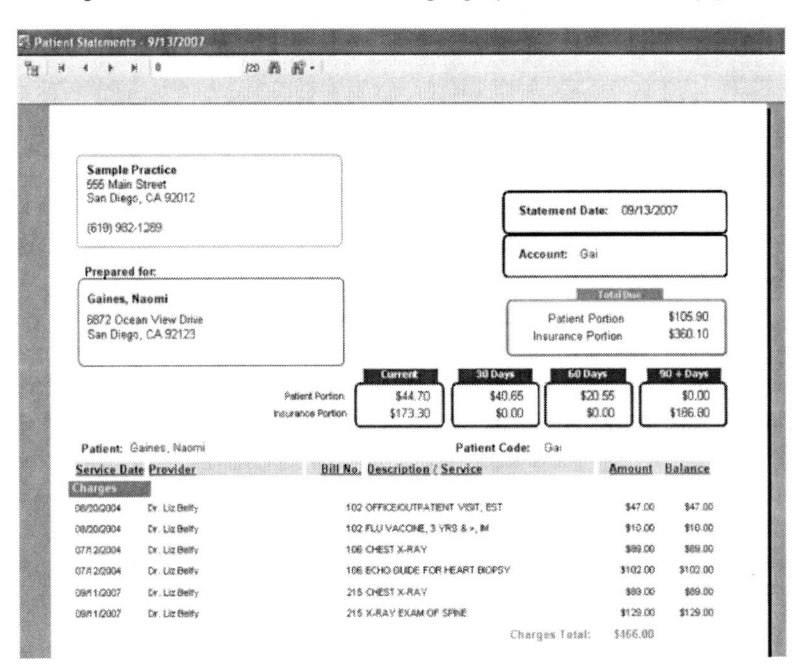

Figure 7-43

Sample screen shot of a patient statement from MedOffice.

Note that one of the features of MedOffice allows you to send patient statements electronically to a clearinghouse where they will be printed, folded, stuffed in envelopes stamped, and mailed for you. The fee for this service is very reasonable considering the work it saves you to print, fold, stuff and stamp hundreds of statements yourself.

Step II-10: Prepare Reports for Your Client

The final task that you must usually do as a full practice management billing agency is provide your client with various reports, usually on a monthly basis, so that the provider can assess numerous factors of his or her medical practice. Depending on your client, you might want to print, fax, or e-mail from half a dozen to a dozen or more reports on various aspects of aging claims, financial, general practice, and practice analysis.

MedOffice offers more than 100 reports, divided into 11 categories as shown in Figure 7-44.

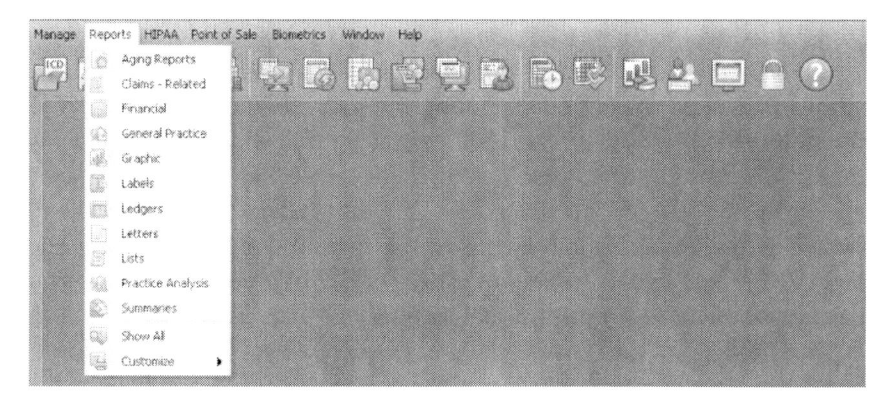

Figure 7-44

Menu listing 11 categories of reports in MedOffice, with over 100 separate reports available under these categories.

For each separate report offered in MedOffice, you can apply various filters to limit the report to certain data, such as a date range, a patient range, a provider range, and so on. Figure 7-45 shows the control panel for one report as an example of the control panel that is used in nearly every one of more than 100 reports you can produce with MedOffice. As you can see, you can apply numerous filters to this report so that it displays only the data your client wants or needs.

Figure 7-45

Control panel for the Insurance Aging report in MedOffice as an example of the control panel in all reports that allows you to filter reports.

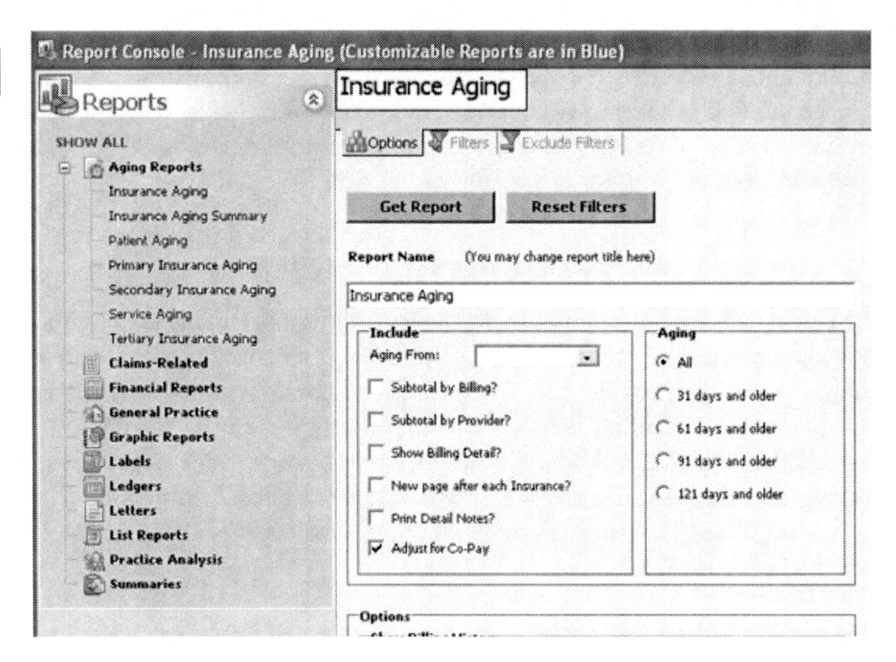

In MedOffice, you can also produce many reports as visual charts or graphs that often make understanding the data easier. For example, you might want to print out a report for your client that shows the most commonly billed procedure codes so your client can see how he or she is generating most of the income that comes into the practice. (This is often very revealing to a doctor, who may not realize that 60% of his or her income comes from just two or three procedure codes.) In graphical reports, you usually have choices to print the reports in many styles of graphics, such as Bar Graph, Pie Chart, Area, or Numeric Axis. Each one serves different functions, though most clients enjoy reading bar graphs or pie charts.

The next two figures show examples of graphic reports you can produce for Charge by Procedure Code. In 7-46, MedOffice prints a bar graph, while in 7-47, MedOffice prints a pie chart – both reports using the same data but showing two different styles of graphic reports.

Filing Appeals for Rejected Claims

Insurers commonly deny or downgrade payments for claims. So, as a full practice management service, you must learn what to do to obtain reimbursement on such claims, especially if you want to keep your client in the future. After all, the more reimbursement you can obtain for your client, the happier he or she will be.

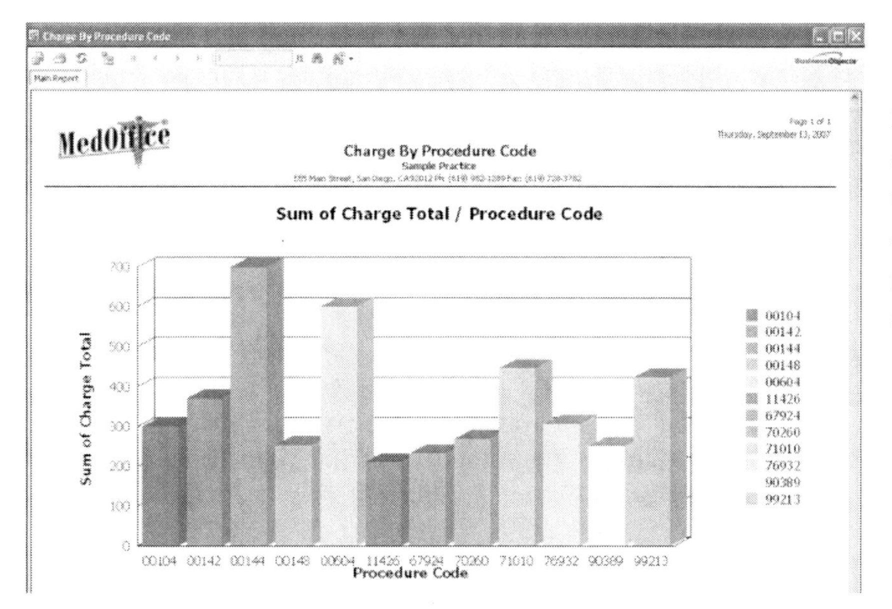

Figure 7-46

Example of the type of bar graph report that MedOffice allows you to prepare for your clients.

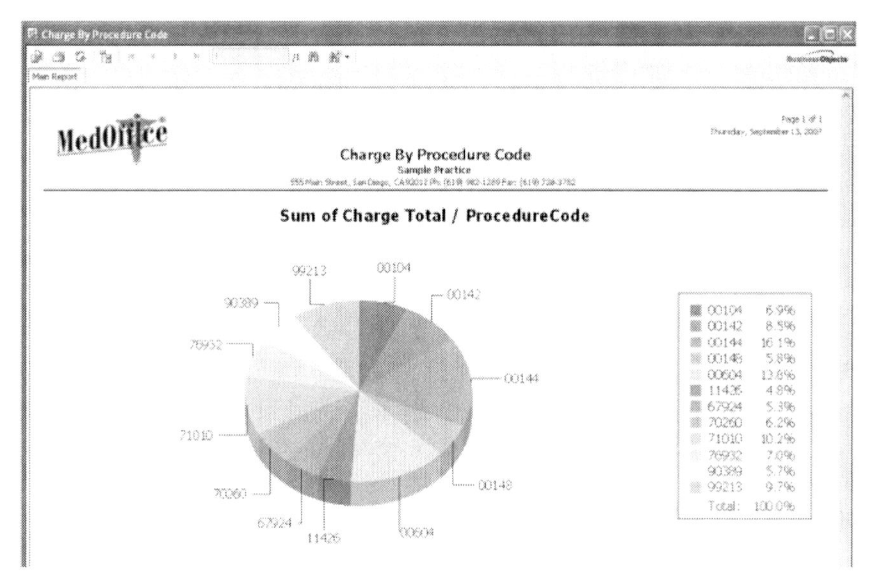

Figure 7-47

Example of the type of pie graph report that MedOffice allows you to prepare for your clients.

Filing appeals depends on the nature of the rejection. If a claim has been outright rejected, the EOB will usually indicate the reason. Some rejections are due to missing information or a lack of supporting documentation, which once rectified, allows you to resubmit the claim. For these types of rejections, it is up to you to track down whatever was missing. Other claims are rejected because the patient had no eligibility for the claim fee.

In these cases, the answer is simply that the patient must pay the entire fee for the service performed. And, of course, some claims are simply not worth resubmitting because their dollar payoff is too low, lower in fact than the time it takes you to reprocess and resubmit them.

Many appeals can be done by simply resubmitting the claim electronically with new information. Others may require you to process the claim and print it on paper to mail along with backup documentation. Insurance companies can become confused when they receive duplicate claims for the same service on the same date, so when you mail paper claims that have already been submitted once, it is useful to mark them "Resubmission" or "Second Filing."

Here are some suggestions for developing a policy about how you will handle rejected claims with or without consulting your client. For each client you have, present this list of guidelines to them and obtain their input and signature:

- You will appeal any denial first by phone or via the Internet if the insurer has a web site that allows this to be done.
- You will send a written appeal for denials over $25 (or some meaningful number for your client).
- You will send two written appeals for denials over $100 (or some other dollar amount).
- You will ask the doctor to get involved for any appeals over $300 (or at whatever dollar figure the doctor prefers).

Summary: Getting Your Business Up and Running

As you can see, this chapter has covered a lot of territory and for good reason – it takes a lot of steps to get your medical billing and practice management company off the ground when you get your first client. Here is a summary list of the steps we've covered.

Phase I: Before Getting Your Client

Step 1 – Set up your office filing system.
Step 2 – Get to know your software.
Step 3 – Research clearinghouses and be ready to select one.

Phase II – Once You Get Your First Client

Step 1 –Create your clearinghouse account and set up your client.
Step 2 – Enter your clients practice data into your software.
Step 3 – Enter your provider's fee schedules.
Step 4 – Enter each patient's data by importing files or as you receive patient demographic forms.
Step 5 – Get the encounter forms and begin keying in claims.
Step 6 – Batch and submit claims.
Step 7 – Print claims or transmit them electronically to clearinghouse.
Step 8 – Process receivables from insurers and patients.
Step 9 – Prepare and mail patient statements.
Step 10 – Prepare reports for your clients.

Along the way, we've demonstrated how you perform these tasks using ClaimTek's state-of-the-art medical practice management software *MedOffice*. By teaching you the steps in this chapter using examples from real software with actual screenshots, we hope you've been able to grasp the complexity of the work that professional medical billers do for clients, while at the same time recognizing that exceptional software such as MedOffice can make a big difference in how quickly you get your business up and running. For this reason, we invite you to download your free demo copy of MedOffice at www.claimtek.com and learn more about this exceptional software product.

In addition, we hope you will also consider the business opportunity that ClaimTek offers you. If your goal is to find and sign your first client quickly, you don't want to risk taking a long time to get his or her claims into a regular billing routine at the clearinghouse, as well as beginning to take over all the accounts receivable functions that this chapter explained. You also don't want to risk performing all these tasks incorrectly, and thus creating mistakes and billing errors. That's why working with ClaimTek might be the solution you need if you're still uncomfortable or hesitant about what to do. ClaimTek will provide hours of training on every one of the steps in this chapter to ensure that, after you sign your first client, all your billing will go smoothly and efficiently.

We're now ready to move on to our final chapter which teaches you about all the additional valuable and income-generating services you can offer your clients. As long as you are doing medical billing and practice management for them, they will appreciate your ability to offer the other services you will read about in Chapter 8.

8

Eight Additional Valuable Services You Can Offer Your Clients (While Making Money Yourself)

Today, to be truly successful as a medical billing and full practice management agency, you need to think out of the box. You can either be like every other agency that does medical billing and offer the usual run-of-the mill practice management functions – or you can be forward thinking and recognize business trends that can turn into excellent add-on businesses for you, while offering services that are very valuable to your clients. You can distinguish your business from every other one by offering more services than your competitors. Having a more comprehensive profile gives you more credibility and a more sophisticated professional image that can impress potential clients.

In this chapter, we are going to review eight ancillary services you can offer that can become substantial add-on revenue streams for you as well as give you a marketing edge up front whenever you speak to doctors. You can select from among these services, or take them all. If you decide to work with ClaimTek, we will make it easy for you to get into these add-on businesses. We supply you with all the marketing materials needed to advertise and publicize your services, and we support you with the backup administration that some of services require. Let's go through each service and teach you what the business is and how you sell it.

Patient Well-Care Management Services

In general, medical professionals want to portray themselves as the most trusted source of healthcare information for their patients. One of the best ways for them to communicate this to their patients is having a proactive outreach service, often called a "well-care service" whereby the physician provides his or her patients with updates on important medical advice and trends in that specialty.

The problem is, most medical practices simply do not have the additional staff, management time, or training necessary to conduct an effective well-care program. But you can offer to take on this task for your clients, for extra fees, of course. As the well-care service provider, you would offer to manage your doctor's outreach program to help them maintain communication with their patients. For example, your service could provide a custom outreach program to each of your doctors, consisting of things like letters or postcards to remind patients of their needs for various services, such as check-ups, testing, immunizations, etc. You might also be able to create a regular monthly e-mail newsletter on behalf of your doctor that updates his or her patients on trends in that specialty. In all these ways, you help your client maintain a positive pro-active relationship with their patients, one that goes beyond just treating them when they are sick and have come in for an office visit.

There is a good reason to go into the well-care service business as well, stemming from government regulations that could impact various doctors. These regulations have to do with managed healthcare systems, because some of them require doctors who are part of the plan to have a well-care program in place for their patients. For this reason, the sooner you begin learning about this field, the better for you. You might even be able to land on top of the trend as it grows, possibly even growing your business to service other medical practice management businesses in this one area.

How do you sell such a program to your doctors? In many ways, the program will sell itself because it provides numerous benefits to doctors:

- It promotes and maintains patient relationships.
- It keeps office staff focused on helping care for current patients.
- It builds the medical practice and increases profits by bringing in patients on a more regular basis than they might come without reminders.
- It complements existing customer care programs that the provider may already offer.
- It pays for itself as patients respond to the program, because the doctor makes money by seeing more patients more frequently.
- It gives the doctor more time to be a doctor by having the program run without the provider having to think about it.

If you work with ClaimTek, we help you get into being able to offer this profitable service by providing you with the training and materials necessary to start your own well-care program to add to your existing medical practice management business. ClaimTek's expertise in this field will give you the foundation you need to start this successful and rewarding business. We'll get you going with the following:

- training
- software functionality used for this service
- professional full-color marketing brochures
- help with pricing your services.

The extra fees you can earn from managing your client's well-care program can range from a few hundred extra dollars per month to thousands if you take on creating newsletters and managing a large-scale mail or e-mail program. ClaimTek can also arrange for you to have professionally written articles in the event that you become involved in a newsletter service for a large medical specialty practice.

Electronic Fund Transfer (EFT)

The next substantial add-on service you can offer is Electronic Fund Transfer, which refers to the process of electronically deducting payments from a patient's bank account (with permission) and transferring the monies into your client's account. The process is also known sometimes as Funds Sweep, Direct Debit, Direct Credit, Direct Deposit, Automatic Checking, Automatic Payment, or ACH Processing.

Why would doctors want EFT? For one simple reason – it usually takes them far too long to get paid by patients, especially when the patient owes a large balance. As you have learned in this book, doctors already often wait weeks to get paid from insurance companies, but even worse is the time they often wait to get paid by patients. Considering that many patients don't believe they should pay their medical bills until after their insurance company has paid, doctors often wait a minimum of 45 to 60 days before some patients pay their first penny.

Furthermore, more and more Americans do not even have health insurance, and when they see a doctor, they agree to pay cash. However, when the time comes to pay, they often ask for a payment plan and end up reimbursing the doctor very slowly and sometimes forgetting to pay.

When you put these two situations together, it's not a surprise that many doctors are more than 90 days behind in their revenue collection compared to their dates of servicing patients. A large number of doctors often carry tens of thousands of dollars on their books, even hundreds of thousands of dollars, and they often know there's a good chance they'll never see some of this money because patients don't end up paying. Having EFT capability allows you, the billing service, to offer doctors a chance to collect on all these outstanding patients' bills.

The way EFT works is that you obtain authorization through a specific bank that ClaimTek has contracted to use their capability for electronic transfers between banks. You sell the EFT service to your doctor-client who asks patients to sign a release form authorizing regular automatic deductions from the patient's checking or savings account. The automatic deductions are pre-authorized only for a specific amount and on a specific day of the month so the patient can budget for the withdrawals. The funds are then electronically withdrawn from the patient's account and deposited into Automated Clearing House (ACH), the financial institution with which ClaimTek arranges this agreement.

Following each patient payment, you notify us by sending the data files to our EFT processing center. They process the data and deposit the money into your doctor client's account on time. They then provide complete and accurate reporting of every transaction. ACH is the electronic network to which 95% of the nation's banks belong - including the Federal Reserve. You earn a small fee ranging from $1.50 to $2 for each transaction you run through the system.

The EFT system provides great benefits for your clients, for the patients, and for you. For doctors, it yields a steady stream of formerly late or uncollected payments. It also allows them to collect monies without harassing or alienating their patients. For patients, it provides them with a secure way to budget paying their bills while avoiding any embarrassment about falling behind on payments. For you, EFT provides an opportunity for an additional revenue stream from the fees you collect on the transactions. In addition, EFT enhances your credibility as a full-service practice management company, given that you now provide a sophisticated electronic service yourself.

You can even sell your EFT capability to other businesses, not just the doctors for which you do practice management. Practically any membership-type business or any business with a monthly billing cycle is a potential client. (i.e., fitness centers, rental companies, tanning centers, security alarm companies, storage companies, pest control, etc.). Let's say you have

10 businesses and you are processing 100 transactions for each business at $1.50 to $2 per transaction as your fee. That adds up to a considerable income. For example, 1000 transactions X $1.50 = $1500 extra income per month for yourself. Now do the calculations for 50 or more businesses.

ClaimTek can help you get set up for this program, so contact us for additional information.

Collection Service

Whether or not you offer EFT, your billing and practice management service can take another step to assure your clients that you will help them get paid on every last dollar patients owe them. As discussed above, some patients never pay their bills and, if they don't agree to an EFT debit (or if you don't offer that service), it's possible that some patients will fail to pay your client for years, effectively shirking the fees. In addition, some insurers also fail to pay claims, dragging the process out for months and months beyond the legal requirements. Most doctors will tell you that between insurers and patients, they probably have thousands of dollars in unpaid fees from the day you take over their practice management.

Since your billing service is not set up as a legal collection agency to deal with unpaid accounts, your client, the doctor, is usually faced with a difficult choice: they can either a) write off the unpaid accounts or b) report the debtors to a hard-core collection agency, which often charges the doctor up to 30 to 50 percent of the uncollected claim fee. Worse though, in addition to the high fee, the doctor will most likely lose the patient as a client because harsh collection measures usually result in the loss of a patient's goodwill.

As the doctor's professional billing service, you can alleviate this scenario completely by selling a valuable service to your clients, the ClaimTek Electronic Collection Service, on which you can make additional profits for your practice management company. This service allows you to pursue and effectively resolve a very high percentage of remaining unpaid claims - at a minimal cost to your doctor clients. ClaimTek's collections plan handles both patients and insurance companies. Here's how it works.

First, ClaimTek offers you a tie-in to a national agency that represents you and allows you to send "demand payment letters" that come from an authorized collection agency. Any time you have an unpaid claim, be it a patient or an insurer, you access a secure web site where you enter information about the unpaid claim. In the case of patients, you key in the patient's name, address, date of discharge or last payment and the amount owed.

For insurance companies, you enter in the dates of service and the amount owed.

As soon as you enter an unpaid claim incident, our collection service sends off a series of demand letters to the debtor, be it a patient or insurance company. We send between three and five demand letters, one at a time, with the letters staggered 7-10 days apart and becoming increasingly firm in demanding payment. The letters advise the debtor to contact you or the doctor's office directly to discuss the account or arrange payment on their account immediately. We also advise them that if they do not respond, the doctor will be forced to use stronger methods to compel their payment. Of course, as soon as your debtors respond with agreements and payments, you can halt the collection efforts. (Note: As payments are received, you should enter them into the system to provide proper balance due information and create detailed collection statistics as they relate to your business). However, if the debtor then does not follow up on the agreed upon payment plan, you can also reactivate the account at the point at which it left off.

The value of this service is that you have access to a national collection agency, which can pursue collections in a legal way on behalf of your clients for very reasonable fees. Our letters are required to include the "Federally Mandated Dispute Clause" that states that all portions of a claim shall be assumed valid unless disputed in writing within 30 days of receiving the notice. This puts the debtor on notice legally, and literally forces the person to either deny the notice or pay the debt within 30 days. If they don't do one of those options, they lose the right to dispute the claim and they may be obligated to pay 100% of the claim if the claim is further disputed in court. Being a national collection agency thus provides you with a very strong paper trail in accordance with your state legislation and regulations regarding collections.

These letters have proven to be very effective with patients who owe payments to doctors. As for insurance companies, the letters can also play a strong role in getting action from a stalling insurer. The reason for this is that virtually all states have legislation in place requiring insurance companies to pay or deny claims within either 30, 45, or 60 days, depending on the state. Given this, our collection service specifically utilizes each state's insurance laws and regulations that force a debtor insurance company to meet whatever state legal requirements govern it. Once they receive these letters, the insurer must take one of four actions to resolve the unpaid claim:

- Pay it – they must pay the claim;
- Deny the claim – but even this solution is useful because it allows the provider to bill a secondary insurance, or sometimes to re-bill the primary insurer with different coding or information, or convert to requiring the patient to pay;
- Indicate that no claim is on file – this solution allows your client to resubmit the claim along with the correspondence from our collection service to achieve maximum efficiency; or
- Suspend action on the claim – this solution may also allow you to resubmit the claim or follow up with the patient.

Any one of these four resolutions on insurance claims helps your doctor, rather than doing nothing and letting an insurer continue to sit on an unpaid claim. The lack of a response is what causes problems for billers, so a collection service applied to insurance companies can truly help terminate the cat and moue game that insurers often play to avoid paying claims. Because of the changes in the mix of payers (HMOs, Managed Care, etc.), our Collections division has designed specific communications for insurance companies that have all the necessary information for them to process the claim. We have the ability to "touch every claim" every 10 days for a low fixed fee, that is impossible for the provider or your billing service to match. We will contact the payer up to five times requesting payment or denial.

The cost of this service is reasonable for your clients to purchase – and you make a profit on it, too. At this time, you can sell this service to your clients for between $11.95 and $14.95 per incident (each incident is three to five letters sent to one debtor), while your cost is only $7.00, so you make between $4.95 and $7.95 per incident, thus generating additional revenue for you. If just one of your doctors has 100 patients for whom you obtain permission to perform this collection service, your client has the potential to collect thousands of dollars in debt for around $1,200, while you can earn at least $500 in profit for yourself without doing much work yourself.

Just as with well-care services and EFT, being able to offer a legal collection service to your clients helps you establish a professional image and adds credibility to your full service practice management agency. This service helps you gain yet another competitive edge over your competition. Generally, doctors, like most professionals, prefer dealing with businesses that can provide comprehensive solutions.

In addition, note also that, like EFT, your ability to offer collection services is not limited to your medical clients. You can easily tap into other business areas as well. Practically any business that extends credit or accepts checks is a potential client to which you can sell this service, including hospitals, retailers, wholesalers, manufacturers, service businesses, and so on.

Remote Backup Services (RBS)

The last thing any business wants to hear is, "My hard drive crashed and I lost all my data!" But this is especially true in medical offices. Imagine if all of a doctor's critical data were lost due to fire, flooding, theft, or even employee sabotage!

If you or your clients think the chances of data loss are small, consider these facts. First, data loss can happen not just from fire or theft or even hard drive failure. It can also happen in any of four ways, as shown in Figure 8-1.

Figure 8-1

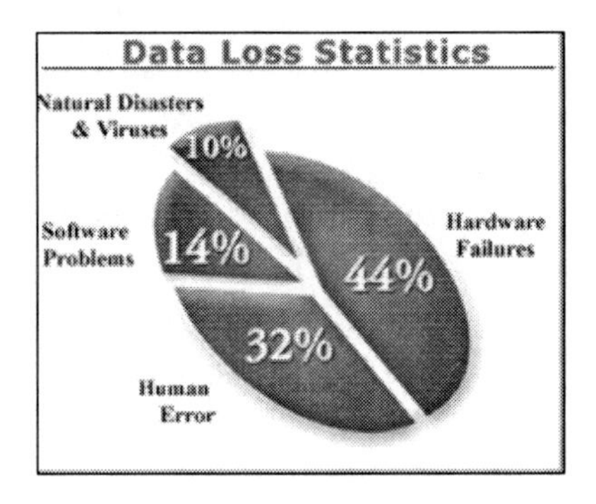

Furthermore, the costs of retrieving data are enormous in terms of time (and lost productivity) as well as costs. While there is no data for medical practices, a recent article in *Inc. Magazine* cited a study by the National Computer Security Association that cites the following statistics:

- It takes 19 days and cost $17,000 to recreate 20 megabytes of lost accounting data;
- 21 days and $19,000 to replace 20 megabytes of sales data;
- 42 days and $98,000 to replace 20 megabytes of engineering data.
- The study also concluded that eventually all computer equipment fails - the failure rate is 100%.

Given the reality of data loss, why not offer as part of your full practice management services what is called "remote backup" capability whereby your clients can store their data at a secure offsite location that has no risk for data loss or failure. ClaimTek makes it easy for you to offer this service, using our Remote Backup System, which provides secure computers for you to use in setting up your clients for regular backups. Your clients do not need to worry about their data, because it remains completely private and can be retrieved quickly and easily 24 hours a day.

The way it works is as follows. ClaimTek's provides you with Remote Backup Service software that you install on your client's computer. This software addresses three important issues to ensure successful offsite backup:

- ***Time:*** Our software compresses your client's data prior to transfer. Roughly 500 MBs of data is compressed to approximately 75 MBs, thus reducing the transfer time to 40 minutes instead of five hours.
- ***Connection Expense:*** Our system leverages your client's existing Internet connection to transfer the compressed backup files. There are no associated long distance charges. You or your clients can backup from anywhere in the world.
- ***Security:*** Our system utilizes multiple layers of access encryption and validation triggers. The security parameters to access your client's backup files are embedded into the binary code on their individual software installation on your PC. This means site security cannot be manipulated or decoded by a third party. Additionally your client can place an 'Unzip' password or PIN number on all the backup files. This means that they cannot be opened by ANYONE except the client who knows the password.

With the ClaimTek RBS software, your client can choose which files to back up and can also determine to perform the backups "attended" or "unattended." They have unlimited backups at any time, and can retrieve their own data 24/7.

The value of this backup service is that it can save your clients a lot of time, worry, and headache. Assume the provider pays an employee to do the backup at approximately $10 per hour and it takes one hour to do that backup. If you multiply this out times five days per week, 52 weeks per year, that ends up at $2,600. However, you can offer this service to your clients for about $20 per month, just $240 per year. Meanwhile, you also make money on the service, because after your costs, your share of the $20 monthly charge is about $12, thus $144 per year profit for each client to whom you sell the service.

And given that you can sell this service to any business or individual that uses computers, you can potentially have dozens and even hundreds of clients. Multiply your $144 profit X 50 clients, and you can see how well this service can pay off: an additional $7000 in profit per year. Imagine even higher numbers to your subscribers like 100 or even 500, and this service can turn into a complete separate business entity for you.

Besides the obvious savings in fees your clients can achieve, what's most important is that, by offering this service, you again prove to your clients that you are truly a full service practice management agency. You demonstrate your concern for their data while offering a solution they may not have considered. This helps you become a one-stop shop for all their practice needs.

Digital Scanning & Archiving of Medical Records

Doctors are swimming in paper records, as are most businesses, and for most offices, paper is simply out of control. The disadvantages of paper records are especially apparent with the demands of today's medical community. The constant filing of paper documents is time consuming and expensive. Finding documents when there are requests for information is frustrating and costly. Re-filing and re-finding whenever there are multiple requests causes the potential for lost records and paper deterioration.

These are all examples of why electronic records are becoming the preferred standard in medical offices. And you can put yourself at the forefront of the move towards digitalization of medical records by offering the ClaimTek Digistore Service. This service enables medical offices to convert their paper medical records to digital media by high speed scanning of documents and transferring the files to secure computers.

When you offer this service to your clients, there are two options you can sell. You can either go to the medical office to scan in their documents for them, or you can teach their staff how to scan their own records in-house. Either way, you can make money through this valuable add-on service to your full practice management agency.

The Digistore service is safe, secure, and flexible. The medical office can retrieve any document within seconds, whether it's a chart or X-ray. Scanning eliminates record loss and also saves space in the medical office. Some medical offices may even be able to convert their former on-site storage space into more profitable uses, such as an extra patient exam room.

In terms of the value of this service to you, you can actually earn excellent fees for either teaching how to scan or by doing the work yourself. This is yet another service for you to consider adding to your medical practice management roster of services.

Electronic Medical Records (EMR)

As the previous service stated, paper medical records are the bane of the medical office. Doctors are drowning in paperwork that costs them thousands of dollars in efficiency and accuracy per year, with time lost to looking for records, filing and refiling them each time a patient comes in, handwriting the notes and duplicating certain aspects of the billing procedure. While the previous service of scanning and archiving of medical records is focused on the past, EMR is focused on the future.

With EMR, doctors use specialized software that allows them to enter their patient records electronically, completely replacing patient paperwork and histories with a digital record. The software stores patient information on a server with complete histories available instantly with a touch or tap of a computer screen, which eliminates typing. Physicians can use their desktop, laptop, or an electronic clipboard-type computer to navigate through their patient charts and record notes, as well as to write prescriptions and coordinate with their medical billing software.

The market for EMR software is hardly scratched. After years of reluctance, EMR is catching on – and catching on fast. Some EMR software providers are experiencing double digit growth each year, selling EMR software to doctors. According to some of the EMR software companies, only about 10 percent of doctors in practices with 10 or less employees currently keep their records electronically. However, as doctors realize that paper records cost them far too much to continue doing and also as legislation such as HIPAA increasingly makes it difficult to run a paper-based practice, doctors will soon begin clamoring for good EMR software that is integrated with the practice management system.

ClaimTek will help you capitalize on this spectacular potential that EMR offers. As we complete this book, we are setting up distributorships with one or more of the leading EMR software companies. When you work with ClaimTek, we will set you up to be a reseller of EMR software that can interface with our MedOffice software. And even if a doctor does not hire you to do their medical billing, you can still make a very lucrative sale of EMR software – possibly on the order of $10,000 – on which you will make a handsome commission.

Needless to say, ClaimTek is also ensuring that you will be reselling one of the most acclaimed EMR programs available. We expect to be working with a leading software company that specializes in small clinics and medical practices, whose program is completely CCHIT Certified, is customizable, and can fulfill the charting and organizing needs of nearly any medical practice.

Software & Hardware Sales, Installation, Training & Support

Computer sales and support is yet another service you might want to provide to clients and potential clients. Most doctors' offices do not have personnel who know much about computer software or hardware. Therefore, if a provider decides not to use your medical billing services, you don't necessarily need to walk away empty handed. Or even if a provider does use you, you may be able to help them with other types of computer sales, installations, or training.

Of course, your ability to offer this service depends on your own knowledge of computers. But if you have the talent, you can make extra cash by keeping your eyes and ears open to many potential needs that medical offices have.

In addition, you can formally sell ClaimTek software, as discussed in Chapter 6. Any doctor's office that insists on doing their own billing is a candidate for you to sell ClaimTek's *MedOffice Medical Practice Management* software. You can earn a profit on the sale, and you can also offer to train the entire medical office on its usage, charging between $50 and $100 per hour, and perhaps as much as $995 per year for support.

If a doctor's office is partially interested in having you do their billing, you can alternatively sell them the MedOffice Remote program, which includes our software called MedOffice Remote, while you do the billing. This program works as follows. The doctor's office has a special copy of MedOffice in their office that allows them to enter patient information, make appointments, and view all the accounting and bookkeeping for receivables. Many doctors want control of these functions, so MedOffice Remote satisfies their need to have access to their own data. However, each day you download from the provider's office all claims that were keyed in and take responsibility for checking them and forwarding them to your clearinghouse for payment.

Meanwhile, the doctor's office also continues to receive payments from insurance companies and patients. They send you the EOBs and you record the receivables just as you would if you were managing the entire billing process. However, on whatever prearranged schedule the provider wants, you upload back to the office computer the updated A/R module so that he or she can review the cash flow and produce any practice management reports desired.

The MedOffice Remote program is a sophisticated solution that helps you stay in the running with providers who want to maintain control over their data. Both you and the provider win. You charge the usual per claim or percentage fee as you would for any other provider, while the provider benefits because the office personnel do not need to become involved in the claims process other than simply keying in claims. Some providers simply feel more secure when they are offered this solution, because they get access to their data so they can review their incoming receivables and take advantage of MedOffice's many practice management reports.

There may be many other opportunities for you to help medical offices install new software or purchase and set up hardware. ClaimTek can train you on some common software found in medical offices as well as offer you wholesale prices on software and show you how to buy hardware wholesale. We can also show you how to bid for accounts and how to price your training and support services. This area can be very lucrative, as today's typical on-site computer trainer can charge between $55 and $125 per hour – depending on your geographical location and area demographics!

Once again, ClaimTek can help you turn your startup medical billing business into a viable operation with comprehensive services!

Advisor on Point of Sale Items

More and more doctors are selling over-the-counter healthcare products as a way to make extra money and add additional credibility to their knowledge of their industry. Hundreds of specialty products are now available that are marketed to doctors to resell to their patients. Some of these products are of great interest to the public, especially herbal and natural care products, but some products are pure schlock and often become an investment nightmare for the doctor, as the inventory sits in their office for months.

As a result, another extra add-on business idea you might consider is becoming a consultant to your clients about what products they might take on that are reputable, sell briskly and consistently, and are respected by patients. To do this, you must read widely about such specialty products and keep your eyes open at other providers you visit for the types of products they sell. If you specialize in certain types of healthcare, you might even become a wholesaler of certain products to resell to your clients, as long as you have enough physicians to whom you can sell your inventory.

As an advisor to your clients, you want to be able to help them add new products and learn how to sell them. For this, you might charge a consulting fee of $50-$75 per hour or more. For example, a lot of physicians make the mistake of adding products and services to sell in their office, but fail to train their staff. Your role, therefore, might be to come in and train the staff on the features and benefits of the product.

In an article in a recent issue of *Physicians' Practice*, it points out that many doctors make the error of not informing their staff and making sure they have the knowledge and time to help sell the product. If the staff does not buy into the product, it will just sit on the shelf. In addition, you can make sure your client is fully enthused about the add-on products. Let him or her know that doctors who do not truly care for what they are selling end up losing interest in it and effectively lose their investment.

The more you know about practice management, the more valuable and professional you will become in the eyes of current and prospective clients.

Epilogue

We are pleased you made it through this book and hope you have learned everything you had hoped to learn. We have truly aimed at providing you with the most comprehensive information about the medical billing profession, and short of sitting with you for several days and training you personally, we think we have delivered about as much as a book can. The only better way to learn about this industry and how to create a successful medical billing and practice management business is to contact us.

Let's summarize what you've learned. You read about the complexities of the American healthcare system, the many forms of commercial and government health insurance and how they work, about coding, the operation of a doctor's office, how to set up a medical billing business in a home office or commercial office space, what equipment to buy, how to market to healthcare providers, how to talk to a doctor during an appointment, how to win a billing and practice management contract, how to price your services using either the "per claim" or percentage approach, how to write a brief business plan, how to actually go through setting up your first client and begin processing medical claims and recording insurance and patient receivables, and finally how to tap into as many as eight ancillary services to sell along with your full practice management service.

You are truly armed with extensive information about this business. You know you can get into it for as little as a $4,500 investment, plus a month of startup training and education, along with a few more months to build your learning curve. You know that you could literally be in business in as little as 30-45 days from today!

So, are you ready to make the move? Does this business excite you and give you a feeling that you would enjoy doing it? Can you see yourself learning about billing, claims, and receivables, working with doctors, and making a livelihood out of operating a full practice management company?

We hope you can, but just to be sure, take a few moments now to read this 15 question survey as you reflect on your next steps. If you decide to work with ClaimTek and buy one of our medical billing business opportunities, we want you to be completely positive and convinced that this is the right business for you. As we've said from the start of this book, ClaimTek is a company that has unparalleled integrity in selling business opportunities to interested individuals. We know you are investing your hard-earned dollars in us, and in return, we want to work with people who will take full advantage of the many benefits we provide in our training so that they can succeed on their own.

Consider the following questions.

1. Did you read this book with sincere interest in starting a new business for yourself or your family?
2. Do you desire to be an entrepreneur, making your own decisions, running your own business, and profiting from your own work?
3. Do you have any prior background or training in general business, sales, accounting, computers, healthcare, nursing, or office management that can help you get started in this business and feel confident about going into medical billing and practice management?
4. Are you a detail-oriented person who can get into keying in claims and recording payments from insurance companies and patients? If you are not a detailed person, could you manage a part-time paid employee to do these tasks for you?
5. Do you enjoy challenges and puzzles such as those you might encounter when tracking down missing claims, missing payments, and unbalanced accounting?
6. Do you like to think you can earn unlimited income from your own hard work, intelligence, and business savvy?
7. Do you enjoy talking to intelligent, educated people such as medical office personnel, doctors, chiropractors, psychotherapists, and other healthcare providers?
8. Are you interested in the American healthcare system and making sure you know a lot about it to help not only your clients but yourself in the future?
9. Would you get pleasure out of making sure that your clients make more money because of your diligent efforts and business

intelligence? Would you get even more pleasure out of this if you, yourself, made more money by helping them make more money?

10. Would you like a job that combines some inside work along with outside work, such as managing a medical practice while sometimes going out to doctor's offices?
11. Would you like to set your own schedule, so that if you cannot work on a day when your child is sick, you can work another day when you have the time?
12. Are you interested in finding a new career that you can begin doing almost immediately at a reasonable cost?
13. Do you have a vision of growing a business and hiring one to three employees who can do most of the labor while you are the brains of the operation?
14. Would you like to be in a business that has many ancillary spin-off activities that can bring in additional profits, where you can sell add-on products and services that increase your potential income?
15. Would you like to work with a superior company that supports you as you begin your new business and does not gouge you with huge fees or demands for royalty payments like most franchise business opportunities do?

If you answered Yes to most of these questions, it is very likely that you should, *at the minimum*, look into medical billing for your next career. A Yes to most of these questions indicates that you have the right preparation and mental attitude to do well in medical billing and practice management.

ClaimTek would be happy to talk with you further and make sure all your questions are answered. Should you decide to purchase one of our programs, we would be delighted to work with you as you train to start your business. As we've said throughout this book, *we want you to succeed*, and we will do everything in our power to help you do just that.

Thank you for reading this book. Please feel free to call us at any time at 800-224-7450. We'll be pleased to hear from you, and be sure to tell us that you've read this book.

Appendix 1: Why Work with ClaimTek?

Before choosing which business entry program is best for you, ask yourself the most important question: Are you serious and determined to succeed? If so, then you can be sure that ClaimTek is the company you need to move you to your goals.

ClaimTek provides you with what no competitor does. We go to great lengths to ensure that you have the most advanced practice management and billing software in the entire industry, superior personal training, and marketing materials that are unique and designed to push you up the ladder of success quickly and effectively. And you receive the finest support from our experienced, professional staff that knows the ins and outs of electronic medical billing and practice management better than anyone else.

Yes, you can buy cheaper business entry programs. But why would you want to sacrifice all the elements you get from ClaimTek that have been designed to bring you success, to get only basic software, poor training, sub-standard marketing and support? If you want to be really successful, we are the company to work with and our program is the one you want.

Comparing Apples to Apples

If you wish to compare ClaimTek with other companies, make sure you truly study the range of items each competitor provides. Many competitors glide over the details of buying their system and fail to give you accurate, in-depth information on the specific tools and features of their components. But you need to make your decision by learning more about the details *before* you invest. After you make your purchase, it's the details that bring the benefits alive.

For example when a company says they give you "an automated marketing system," or that "our marketing experts will help you," make sure you understand specifically what steps and techniques are involved. What are the precise tools you will receive for your marketing campaign? Apply the same questions to their software, training, and support. Learn about the capabilities of their software and the services that you'll be able to offer your clients, and how your services will help you stand out compared to "the guy next door."

So if you are truly interested in this great business and are evaluating ClaimTek against our competitors, we ask you to make a detailed, close-up comparison of our programs. You are about to invest thousands of dollars in your future and we know this is a serious decision for you. We respect entrepreneurs and we want to be sure you are completely and honestly informed about what we offer versus what our competitors offer.

If you have the right tools, you'll be competitive, credible, and convincing in your presentations and will ultimately succeed in your venture. Only ClaimTek offers you the real tools to do this.

Experience, Knowledge and Commitment versus Hype and False Promises

As we told you in the Preface, the medical billing business has been prone to vendors selling the concept of success without backing up their claims with quality professional-level tools to prepare you for a serious business. Frankly, we still find that many companies today that sell medical billing business opportunities continue to hype their offerings in misleading ways intended to make you think their program is as comprehensive and effective as ClaimTek's in setting you up in business and training you to work with doctors. Many of our competitors attempt to make it seem simple to start a medical billing business. But if you look closely at their offerings, you will find they spend more time selling you the image of success in medical billing than in giving you detailed, accurate information and professional tools to start your business. As it is said in marketing, "they sell you the sizzle, not the steak." Don't be fooled by such approaches.

We invite you to visit our web site at www.claimtek.com and click on the button for "Compare ClaimTek." When you visit this page on our web site, you will be able to read an extensive chart that compares many facets of doing business with ClaimTek versus our competitors. In this chart, we show you how to identify hype and false promises that are designed to make you think success is automatic and that their offerings are sufficient to run a professional business. We point out illogical statements our competitors make and show you the types of empty promises you may encounter. This is not to say we are adverse to competition; we are not. However, we have succeeded in our business for more than 15 years by being honest and forthright, and we treat our potential licensees with respect and we give them accurate information. We expect our competitors to do so as well. Since some do not, we feel obliged to point it out to the serious entrepreneurs who are looking to choose the right company to work with.

Imitation is the Best Flattery

Finally, we also want to say that each time ClaimTek develops a new business development item or marketing / sales support item for our licensees, our competitors imitate us. You will find that many of the programs offered sound similar to you, with similar benefits and add-ons. However, while we appreciate the flattery of our competitors following in our footsteps, it is important to know that ClaimTek has been the pioneer in developing leading-edge software, marketing support and business development materials, training, and add-on income programs for our licensees.

We continue to explore new ideas to help our licensees succeed, such as setting you up to sell Electronic Medical Record software, the newest wave in medicine that doctors are required to switch to for their record keeping over the coming years. For the record, ClaimTek is the first medical billing business vendor to accomplish this for our people. We are able to do this because we are a respected software developer that attracted that attention of several EMR firms seeking to work with us.

In sum, we believe we offer our licensees the best programs, which translate into the best opportunities for success in business, a profitable income, and a lasting career.

Appendix 2: About the ClaimTek Programs

Once you have made a decision to work with ClaimTek, the next question is which of our programs to purchase. All of our programs provide our advanced MedOffice software plus extensive training and support. All of our entry programs shine among our competitors. In fact, if you are comparing business opportunity programs, we recommend that you compare our smallest program with any competitor's top-of-the-line program and you'll see that we still offer more than anyone else, even with our least expensive package.

ClaimTek offers three levels of professional entry into a medical billing business.

- **Preferred Program**
- **Principal Program**
- **Essential Program**

Each level includes a version of our advanced MedOffice software, plus a varying degree of training, marketing, and support. Here are details about each program as of the writing of this book. Please check our website at www.claimtek.com for updated information.

SOFTWARE

Our software solutions are the most technologically advanced in the country. They include MedOffice, MD Practice Analysis Wizard, MD Code Reviewer, MD Contact Manager, Electronic Fund Transfer (EFT), On-line Collections, RBS and others. Each software program is designed to perform specific tasks with each one fitting together like a glove on a hand. Our software more than meets the needs of your business. The number and version of these software programs you receive depends on which business program you purchase.

Our MedOffice software can handle all types of medical practices and specialties, and you can run it locally on your PC or access it via the Internet, giving you the ultimate flexibility in the way you conduct your business.

SERVICES

The services you'll be able to offer your potential clients are diverse and comprehensive. You will meet the growing needs of healthcare providers with a wide range of services. Like most busy professionals, doctors prefer to establish stable, long-term business relationships with people and companies that do a great deal for them at a reasonable price. Especially when you select ClaimTek's Preferred program you'll be able to offer great all-inclusive services unmatched by competitors. So, your chances of landing the plum accounts are great. You'll have the competitive advantage right from the start.

MARKETING

The marketing tools we supply you are professional and graphically appealing. They are written by professionals and designed by experts. You'll receive hundreds of colorful pieces of impressive and convincing marketing items, which will reflect your professionalism in every possible way. The number and nature of the marketing pieces differs for each business program.

TRAINING

The training you will get with ClaimTek is the most detailed, personable, and private available anywhere. We'll train you on three important aspects of the business: the software, the marketing, and the billing. And the training is hands-on . . . right from the comfort of your own home and at the time that's convenient for you. The length and type of training you receive varies for each business program you can purchase.

SUPPORT

The excellent ClaimTek support is uniquely designed to meet the needs of your small business. With the Preferred Program especially, you get FREE toll-free support for two years. Special support privileges are available through our Emergency Support Services (ESS). With our other programs, the length of your support varies.